Your
Money
and Life
Your

Your Money *and* Your Life

© 2012

Hamodia Publishing
POB 1306 / Jerusalem, Israel

Feldheim Distributors
POB 43163 / Jerusalem, Israel
208 Airport Executive Park
Nanuet, NY 10954
www.feldheim.com

Questions or comments may be sent to:

Mesila
P.O.B. 57116, Jerusalem 91570, Israel
Tel: +972.2.500.0475 • Fax: +972.2.500.0478
info@mesila.org • www.mesila.org
Reg. Amuta No. 580361236

Parts of this book may require *genizah*. Please do not discard.

Contents

Acknowledgements   5

Introduction   6

One   Attitudes and Outlooks   9

Two   The Bottom Line on Budgeting   27

Three   Making 'Cents' of Spending   61

Four   Debt: The Bleak Business of Borrowing   99

Five   Planning for the Future: Savings and Investments   131

Six   Employment: Making Work Pay   165

Seven   Beginning a Business   225

Eight   Managing a Business   253

Nine   The Blessing of Financial Independence   269

Ten   Peace and (Financial) Harmony   287

Eleven   Our Financial Future: Children and Money   299

Twelve   Integrity at All Costs   327

Appendix I: Mesila's Guide to Financial Stability   343

Appendix II: Budgeting Worksheets   357

About Mesila   366

Acknowledgements

Mesila's *Hamodia* column was the fusion of the efforts of many different people. First, I'd like to thank *Hamodia* and its devoted staff for sharing Mesila's vision of a better financial future for *Klal Yisrael* and for helping us promote that vision by publishing our columns.

The columns were researched and written by Mrs. Malky Heimowitz, Mesila's communications coordinator, in close consultation with me and the other members of Mesila's staff. I wish to thank Mrs. Heimowitz for overseeing all aspects of the column's preparation and for ensuring that this column, like all of Mesila's other written material, meets the standard of quality for which our organization strives in all its endeavors. Mesila's devoted staff and volunteer counselors were always available to share their experiences and insights, which formed the basis of many of the columns in this book, and I thank them for their wholehearted involvement.

Thank you to all the readers who took the time to share their thoughts about the column and present their own dilemmas and questions to us. Your feedback – at times enthusiastic, at times critical – helped us to shape and refine the column. The ongoing dialogue between our staff and our readers enabled us to craft your experiences and ours into an enjoyable and highly relevant read.

I thank all of Mesila's friends and donors for their support and encouragement, which have allowed Mesila to grow into the flourishing organization it is today. Most notable among these supporters is my brother Dovi Margulies, of London, who helped me create Mesila and never tires of promoting the organization in any way he can.

Shmuli Margulies
Mesila Chairman

Introduction

This book presents real-life financial dilemmas. A compilation of Mesila's financial advice columns, which ran in *Hamodia* from November 2006 through November 2009, it shares the real problems of real people and Mesila's responses and advice regarding those situations.

Mesila's unique strategies for helping people achieve financial stability were developed through careful research, consultation with Rabbanim and *Gedolim*, and the input of many professionals, including economists, financial advisers, debt-management counselors, psychologists and others. Since 1998, when we launched our Family Counseling Program, our strategies have been tested and fine-tuned through our work with thousands of families and businesses.

Yet, Mesila's staff members are not economists, financial advisers or debt-management professionals, and the material in this book is very different from the material you will find in other books on financial management. Our goal in writing this, like our goal in all our activities, was to combine *Torah hashkafah*, professional knowledge and the experience we have amassed in our years of working with families and businesses. This book is meant to help people successfully navigate contemporary financial challenges and achieve financial stability.

Every person's path to financial stability is different. People's upbringings, families, station in life, values, economic status and a host of other factors come into play. But the *principles* of how to achieve financial stability are the same for everyone – young and old, male and female, rich and poor. It's the practical application of those principles that differs depending on the circumstances.

In the appendix to this book, Mesila's "Guide to Financial Stability" briefly outlines the primary attitudes, attributes and actions necessary for achieving financial stability. In our *Hamodia* columns, collected here, we translate these principles into practical reality.

Each section addresses a different person, in a different financial situation, with a different financial challenge. Each section speaks to a different reader – and together, the chapters talk to practically every reader. Regardless of how much or how little one relates to the dilemmas presented, the challenges are essentially universal, because the ultimate goals of gaining financial control, avoiding debt, raising financially responsible children and more are topics that resonate across the board.

By presenting over sixty different viewpoints in the chapters of this book, we have attempted to make *your* voice heard, to express *your* personal challenge. In essence, we have tried to write *your* book on how to achieve financial stability.

This book is meant to be a springboard for further thought and discussion. We welcome your questions and comments, and we'd love to hear about your challenges and any other challenges we may not have covered in this book. We also want this book to be read by as many people as possible, so please pass it on to your relatives, friends and neighbors!

Mesila's vision is to become a worldwide movement synonymous with the Torah path – *mesila* – to financial stability. Through our counseling and educational programs, which now operate in Israel, the United States, Canada and England, we are witnessing the realization of our vision, one family and one community at a time. This book is yet another step toward making that happen, *b'ezras Hashem*.

Mesila

August 2012/Av 5772

Note: Throughout the book, readers' questions appear in *italics* and Mesila's responses, which follow, appear in regular type.

1

Attitudes and Outlooks

"It is obvious that [for]
something that is the
nature of the world...
it is a mitzvah to prepare
in advance so that he will
not become dependent
on others."

(Harav Shmuel Halevi Wosner,
Shevet Halevi 4:1)

In this chapter:

❯ On Bitachon | 11

❯ Bitachon and Budgeting | 14

❯ Money, Happiness and Bunny Rabbits | 17

❯ Attitudes Toward Money | 23

On Bitachon ❯

Bitachon is the most important and most effective tool for achieving financial stability, as *bitachon* is a direct vehicle for blessing and *parnassah*. Hashem promises to provide for those who trust in Him, as David Hamelech says in *Tehillim*, "Cast upon Hashem your burden, and He will sustain you," (55:23), and "One who trusts in Hashem, kindness surrounds him" (32:10).

Bitachon differs fundamentally from the rest of our advice on financial stability. So much of what we advise is related to *hishtadlus*, which is Mesila's primary focus. But there is no use telling people how to do their *hishtadlus* correctly if they do not have *bitachon*.

Doing *hishtadlus* without having *bitachon* is like trying to drive a car without fuel. You can go through all the motions of driving, but the car won't run. If the other improvements or efforts that lead to financial stability are the car's engine, steering wheel, accelerator, tires, brakes and gears, then *bitachon* is the fuel. Fuel alone cannot drive the car, but it is the invisible force that propels all the car's internal mechanisms.

Similarly, any *hishtadlus* we do has to be fueled by *bitachon*, in order to merit the Heavenly blessing that will propel our efforts to success. And just as a car needs frequent refueling, people also need continual *chizuk* in *bitachon*.

As important as *bitachon* is, however, *bitachon* alone is not enough. We are also required to put in our effort, our *hishtadlus* – and we are required to take our *hishtadlus* seriously. There are certain extraordinarily righteous individuals who are exempt from the requirement of *hishtadlus* – people of the ilk of Rabi Chanina ben Dosa and Rabi Shimon bar Yochai – but those individuals are the rare exceptions. The rest of us are obligated to do our *hishtadlus*, and if we don't, we risk forfeiting our *parnassah* – not as a natural outcome, but as a penalty.

Why do we need to put in *hishtadlus*, if we believe Hashem is the One providing *parnassah*? Because from the time Adam Harishon sinned, Hashem programmed the world to operate according to a set of principles called nature. And He desires that we follow those principles and go through the motions of obtaining our *parnassah* through natural means.

Since Hashem requires us to do our *hishtadlus*, we cannot use *bitachon* as an excuse for neglecting our financial obligations. It is ludicrous to think Hashem will provide us with *parnassah* if we do not follow Hashem's prescription for *parnassah* – namely, "By the sweat of your brow will you eat bread."

Bitachon without *hishtadlus* is problematic, but *hishtadlus* without *bitachon* is downright dangerous. That is because any form of *hishtadlus* involves trust in *something* – be it a job, a business, an investment or a unique talent – and "when a person trusts in something other than Hashem, Hashem removes His providence from that person and leaves him in the hands of that in which he trusted" (*Chovos Halevavos, Shaar Habitachon*). In other words, if a person relies on his boss, his customers or Wall Street to bring him *parnassah*, he will be subject to the whims and vicissitudes of those forces – a frightening prospect indeed.

Hishtadlus can only succeed when it is accompanied by a clear recognition of where *parnassah* comes from. To achieve a harmonious balance between *bitachon* and *hishtadlus*, we need to act as though our *hishtadlus* is what brings us *parnassah*, while knowing that is all just an act.

People who have *bitachon* never have any reason to be fearful or anxious about their finances, for they have the peace of mind that comes with knowing that Hashem will see to all of their needs.

As we watch economic earthquakes rocking the bastions of financial security – banks, investment companies and even govern-ments – we cannot help but be reminded that our sense of security has to come from a different Source entirely. Times of financial crisis should prompt us to strengthen our *bitachon* and reevaluate what it is that we rely on for our *parnassah*. At the same time, we *daven* that Hashem bless us with the fortitude and the resources to weather the current crisis, and that He spare us from further uncertainty and hardship.

On Rosh Hashanah, our livelihood for the year was determined. Now we need to put in enough *hishtadlus* to ensure that we do not block the channels of *parnassah*, all the while basking in the security of Hashem's loving care.

Bitachon and Budgeting ❯

I think that kollel families receive a certain amount of siyatta diShmaya that helps make ends meet, in a near-miraculous manner. If they were to begin to keep close track of their income and expenditures, they would realize that their finances just do not add up, and the husband might feel pressured to leave kollel.

Therefore, I don't think it's advisable for bnei Torah to adopt Mesila's budgeting practices nor to become Mesila clients. Instead, they should have bitachon that Hashem will provide for them and not look too closely at their finances.

In Rabbeinu Bachyai's classic work, *Chovos Halevavos* (*Shaar Habitachon*, Introduction), he states clearly that a *baal bitachon* — someone who relies on Hashem — will be provided for at all times.

The requirement to have *bitachon* and believe that Hashem is the quintessential Provider applies to all Jews — working families and *kollel* families alike. It could therefore be argued that for believing Jews, budgeting is a totally unwarranted activity. After all, if a person believes that Hashem will provide for him, why should he have to think about how much he is earning or spending?

The flaw in this argument is that intellectual beliefs and spoken declarations of faith do not a *baal bitachon* make. Rather, the litmus test of a *baal bitachon* is his lifestyle.

True *baalei bitachon* live on an elevated spiritual plane in which material aspirations and physical desires have no place. They are satisfied with whatever Hashem has given them, even if it is the absolute minimum. Regardless of their physical circumstances, they have no fear or worries. They do not need, desire or enjoy material luxuries. Their luxury is living according to Torah ideals while relying on Hashem to provide for them.

These *baalei bitachon* can be secure in the knowledge that they will always have what they need and never be lacking. For them, budgeting is unnecessary.

The Torah does not prohibit people from having more than the absolute minimum. However, people who wish to live with more than the minimum — whether or not the husband is in *kollel* — have an obligation to make sure they can afford to pay for what they want or feel they need.

People today are bombarded with advertisements, special offers and a dizzying array of available products and services. At the same time, banks and credit card companies offer them instant access to money that is not theirs. How is anyone to withstand these material enticements if not by making careful calculations of their income and expenditures and being aware of just how much they are able to spend?

Some *bnei Torah* and their families are truly *baalei bitachon*. They are capable of withstanding all material enticement and subsisting on the minimum. Other *bnei Torah* do not possess as great a degree of *bitachon* and are unable to live on a subsistence level.

Bnei Torah and their family members whose lifestyles reflect less than absolute *bitachon* are required to carefully scrutinize their finances to ensure that they do not spend more than they have.

A person who borrows and does not repay is called a *rasha,* an evil person (see *Tehillim* 37:21) — not a *baal bitachon. Bitachon* cannot be used as an excuse for overspending or lack of financial responsibility. If there is a possibility that a person might fall into debt, he is obligated to budget and do whatever else it takes to make sure he does not incur the label "*rasha.*"

Mesila's assistance involves helping families develop an awareness of exactly how much they earn and how much they spend. Of the hundreds of Mesila clients who have achieved financial stability, many have been *kollel* families. There have been numerous instances in which *bnei Torah* switched to better-paying *kollelim* or took on side tutoring jobs after becoming Mesila clients. This way, they were able to enhance their ability to provide for their families without weakening the quality of their learning.

We do not know of a single case, however, in which a man left *kollel* as a result of measuring his expenditures against his income. In fact, many of our clients have reported that their Torah study improved dramatically after they adopted careful budgeting practices.

It is unquestionably true that *bnei Torah* merit a special *siyatta diShmaya* that enables them to devote their energies to undiluted Torah learning. For individuals who are on high levels of *bitachon,* as evidenced by their modest lifestyles and their contentedness with those lifestyles, the *siyatta diShmaya* they receive obviates the need for living with a budget.

But for the vast majority of *bnei Torah,* budgeting is not only appropriate, it is a requirement. And when people do what is required of them, their *siyatta diShmaya* is not diminished, but increased.

The above section was prepared by Mesila in consultation with its Rabbinical Board.

Money, Happiness and Bunny Rabbits ❯

For many years, my husband earned a six-figure salary working for a prestigious financial institution. His company was hit hard by the crisis and had to downsize drastically. My husband, who was a senior employee, was offered the choice of being laid off and receiving a mediocre severance package, or continuing to work for the company at a greatly reduced salary. The prospect of unemployment was not one that we were prepared to face, so we chose the latter option.

My husband's salary is still sufficient to live on, but it is not nearly enough to support the type of lifestyle our family is accustomed to. It looks as though we will have to sell our second car, cancel our planned family vacation to Switzerland and eliminate the children's art and music lessons.

I have also become much more careful about spending. I never used to look at prices when I went shopping — I just bought whatever I needed. Now, shopping is torture for me, because I have to think twice before I buy anything.

Cutting down our expenses has been a bitter pill to swallow. I suppose I should be grateful that we can still pay our bills, but I find myself focusing much more on the things that are now lacking in my life. How can I cope with this situation — and help my children cope — without feeling deprived and bitter?

Kol hakavod to you and your husband for acknowledging your financial reality and for your readiness to make the necessary modifications to your lifestyle. Many formerly prosperous individuals are too accustomed to their former way of life or too afraid of what other people will think to adjust their lifestyle to their means. Instead, they attempt to maintain their previous standard of living, with disastrous results.

It is never easy for a family to lower its standard of living, and that is why Mesila tries to avoid telling families to reduce their spending. Even when it is clear that spending cuts have to be made, we never tell a family which expenditures to reduce or by how much, because the members of the family are the only ones who can decide which cuts can be made without inflicting severe damage on the atmosphere in the home.

What we do advise families is to refrain from establishing a high standard of living in the first place, because reducing that standard can be very painful, as you can unfortunately testify.

On the bright side, however, there are ways to minimize the pain of spending cuts and to turn the challenge of a reduced standard of living into an opportunity to achieve greater contentment.

To minimize the pain, we suggest that you and your husband — and possibly your children, depending on their ages and the family dynamics — sit down together and evaluate which items in your budget are the best candidates for elimination or reduction.

It's important to realize that the budget items that initially seem to be the most obvious places to cut are not always the best ones, because the absence of these items might be too glaring and painful. For example, if the lack of a second car means that your mobility is drastically curtailed and you feel miserable as a result, perhaps you would be better off keeping the car and feeding your kids scrambled eggs and peanut butter sandwiches for dinner. But if a menu of scrambled eggs and peanut butter sandwiches would lead to a revolt in your house, then by all means, get rid of the car and leave your menu alone.

The point is that even when budget cuts have to be made, they should be made in a way that causes your family the least pain. And what causes your family the least pain will be different than what causes another family the least pain. When deciding what to cut, you should consider only your family's needs, not anyone else's. It doesn't matter what anyone else considers important — what matters is that you retain the elements of your lifestyle that you and your family need in order to function well and maintain a pleasant atmosphere in your home.

After you have decided what budget items to cut and by how much, you can use some creativity to find ways to substitute for what is now missing in your lifestyle. While canceling your trip to Switzerland, for instance, you can still take the family on a low-cost trip to a picturesque vacation area close to home. The destination is not what makes a vacation enjoyable — it is the break in humdrum routine, the family togetherness and the shared memories.

Minimizing the pain and finding creative budgetary alternatives should help reduce the anger and bitterness you feel. Along with that, you have to train yourself and your family to focus on the half of the cup that is full. You may not be able to afford music lessons, but you have food to eat, clothing to wear and a roof over your heads. Your husband is making a decent living. Revel in the joy of living in a way that you can afford to live, of living off money that is yours.

Life does not have to be any less enjoyable on a tighter budget. Have you ever experienced the pleasure of finding an item you want marked down to half-price? Have you ever experienced the pleasure of making a *simchah* yourself, at home, instead of hosting a lavish, but impersonal, catered affair? Have you ever experienced the pleasure of scrimping and saving until you have enough money to buy something you really want? If not, now is your chance to discover these pleasures!

If in the past you enjoyed spending money freely, now you can learn to enjoy getting the most for your money. For many people —

even rich people — getting a bargain is much more pleasurable than buying without looking at the price. Instead of feeling stifled by having to keep an eye on prices, look at it as a challenge — a fun challenge — to get what you need while remaining within your budget. It might take a conscious attitude shift on your part, but it is definitely possible for you to derive satisfaction from becoming an informed, savvy consumer.

It may also be a comfort to you to realize that your life has not really changed all that much. You had spending limitations before your husband's pay cut, and you were happy; you now have different spending limitations, and you can still be happy. The reason your previous spending limitations did not cause you distress was because you were so used to them, you were hardly even aware of them. When you went shopping, you instinctively gravitated toward items that were in your price range, without feeling deprived or bitter. But now that your spending limitations have narrowed, you are very conscious of them, and you are finding them difficult and restrictive. If you accept your new spending limitations, instead of chafing at them, you will find yourself once again gravitating painlessly to items that are in your new price range.

Beyond all the measures you can take to minimize the pain, there is another approach you can use to dispel any vestiges of deprivation and bitterness. This approach can be illustrated with the case of the man who went to a psychologist because he loved bunny rabbits.

"I dream about bunny rabbits all the time," the man confessed. "Wherever I go I look for bunny rabbits."

This man's problem is not so unusual. Most of us do not have a particular affinity for bunny rabbits, but we do feel a pull toward things like fashionable clothing, upscale cars, jewelry, fine dining, home furnishings, leisure travel and recreation. Like bunny rabbits, these things do have a place in the world. But a small place.

To give prominence to any type of material pursuit is to fill our world with bunny rabbits. How sad it is that so many people today are chasing bunny-rabbit happiness! True happiness comes from giving, growing and doing, not from getting, buying or going.

Perhaps Hashem is taking away some of our bunny rabbits during this economic crisis to show us that there is more to life than bunny rabbits. If so, we should not look at these times as a crisis, but as an opportunity to re-evaluate our values, priorities and goals and reshape our lifestyles to match those values, priorities and goals.

If family is our priority, doesn't it make sense to spend less time shopping and on the go and more time at home with the family? Or, if our goal is to learn as much Torah as possible, then shouldn't we avoid the type of leisure activities that serve to distract us from Torah?

The fringe benefit of reshaping our lifestyles to match our true values, priorities and goals is that this usually translates into considerable financial savings — without causing anyone to feel deprived. That's because the things in life that are really important, the things that bring true contentment — *avodas Hashem*, relationships, health, accomplishment — do not have a price tag.

And the happiness that comes from living in a way that is consistent with what we really want out of life is far more genuine than the happiness that comes from having the things we want.

Not being able to afford the type of lifestyle you are accustomed to is unquestionably challenging. But instead of wallowing in the pain and feeling deprived and bitter, you can delight in the deep, lasting contentment and fulfillment that are yours for the taking.

Attitudes Towards Money ❯

Many financial problems stem from flawed attitudes toward money. So much unnecessary anguish comes from misguided reasoning, which can be remedied with a conscious shift in perspective. Adopting correct, Torah-based attitudes will enable you to manage your finances wisely and avoid countless financial difficulties. Here are some examples:

My old attitude toward money:

❯ Why do you have to bring up money again? Enough already!

❯ If only I had enough money…

❯ Money comes and goes. It's not important, and it's not worth paying attention to.

❯ The less I think about money, the happier I'll be.

My new attitude toward money:

❯ Money is part of life. I will deal with it as matter-of-factly as possible without letting it become personal or emotional.

❯ I have enough money. Hashem gives me exactly what I need.

❯ Money is not *the* most important thing, but it is important, and I have to give it the attention it deserves.

❯ I think about and plan my finances, but I do not allow money to become the focus of my life. I control my money; it does not control me.

❯

Old attitude...

> How does it help to have a budget?

> I saved $20 at the supermarket, but then my washing machine broke and cost me $200 to fix. What did I gain?

> If I run into a financial problem, my parents will bail me out.

> Everyone else is buying it. Why can't I?

> No money? No problem! The store has a payment plan.

> How will it help me to calculate my income and expenses? I won't have enough money regardless.

> I only buy what I need. Having a budget won't help me.

New attitude...

> It's a good thing I have a budget. When my washing machine broke, I was able to pay for it with the money I had budgeted for home repairs. I even had some money left over because I saved $20 at the supermarket.

> I'm trying hard to avoid financial problems. I don't want my parents to have to bail me out.

> Just because other people have something doesn't mean I need it, too.

> A payment plan? You mean I'll be paying for this thing for a whole year?

> If I know where my money is coming from and where it is going, I'll make sure not to spend more than I earn. I can also look for ways to earn more or reduce my expenditures.

> Since I started working with a budget, I discovered that I really can manage with less.

> If I wouldn't know exactly what was going on with my finances, I wouldn't be able to sleep at night.

Old attitude...

> If I would know exactly what was going on with my finances, I wouldn't be able to sleep at night.

> A bar mitzvah is a once-in-a-lifetime event for my son. How can I cut corners?

> My spouse runs the finances in our house, and I don't want to have anything to do with it.

> I don't appreciate when people tell me what to do with my money.

> Advertisements and marketing ploys that try to convince me to buy things are so bothersome.

> All this stuff about budgeting is great when the kids are young. When you start making weddings, it's hopeless.

> No matter what we manage to save, it's never going to be enough.

New attitude...

> Children have a lot of once-in-a-lifetime events. It's no reason to let my finances spin out of control.

> I make sure to be aware of our finances so that I can make informed spending decisions.

> Our mutual involvement in running our finances contributes to our *shalom bayis*.

> I make sure to seek advice and guidance when I have to make a financial decision I am unsure about. Accepting input from someone else doesn't mean I'm any less capable.

> Ads don't frustrate me. I know they are meant for people who need those products and can afford them.

> If I develop good budgeting habits when my kids are young, there's hope that I'll manage to stick to a budget when I have to marry them off.

> I can only afford to save a small amount every month, but I make the effort anyway. I do what I can, and I leave the rest up to Hashem.

>

Old attitude...

> ❯ If I run out of cash, I'll just use the credit card.

> ❯ I'm optimistic that my financial situation will improve, and then I'll be able to pay back my debts.

New attitude...

> ❯ I decide which purchases to make in cash and which to put on the credit card. This way there are no nasty surprises on my credit card bill.

> ❯ I believe that whatever happens will be good for me — but in the meantime I make sure to fulfill my financial obligations.

2

The Bottom Line
On Budgeting

"Living with a budget
is emancipating; it
allows you to truly enjoy
everything Hashem gives
you without having to
worry about whether you
can afford it."

("Before You Throw in the
Towel on Budgeting")

In this chapter:

❯ What on Earth Is a Budget? | 29

❯ In Defense of Budgeting | 34

❯ Making Your Budget Work for You | 37

❯ Before You Throw in the Towel on Budgeting | 43

❯ A Tale of Two Incomes – and a Deficit | 49

❯ Learning to Disconnect From the Dollar | 55

What on Earth Is a Budget? ❯

I am not a numbers person, and I just cannot seem to get a handle on my family's finances. My wife and I both work at salaried jobs, and we have a respectable combined income. But with several young children, our money seems to fly out the window, leaving us wondering where exactly our paychecks are disappearing to.

We are always struggling to finish the month, and we never manage to put anything aside in savings, even though we do not live extravagantly. I know that I need to start living with a budget, but frankly, I haven't the faintest idea how.

Mesila's experience has been that most people need to be taught the basics of budgeting. You don't have to be a math whiz or a "numbers person" to budget. All you really need is a pen and paper, a calculator, some time and a little discipline.

A budget is simply a plan for managing your money, based on your estimated income and expenses. Creating and living within a budget will put you in control of your finances and give you the freedom to decide what you want to do with your money.

Here are some straightforward steps for creating a workable budget:

Step 1: Determine your income.

a) Add together your net annual salaries.

b) Now add to that any additional income (money from side jobs, investment earnings, interest, government allowances or other money you receive). *Do not include possible windfalls — such as gifts or year-end bonuses — in your annual income.*

Step 2: Track your expenditures.

a) To track your expenses, you and your wife will need to write down every shekel, dollar or pound you spend. You will need to do this for a minimum of two to three months. During this time, keep all your receipts, or carry little notebooks with you to record expenses as they occur.

Initially, you might find it restrictive to record all your expenses, but after doing it for a few days you will begin to feel empowered. You might also notice where money is going to waste.

b) In addition to recording each purchase, you need to think about all the other places you spend money. Invisible costs like bank and credit card charges, automatic bank account withdrawals, and items you buy with pocket change are often responsible for the discrepancy between what you think you spend and what you are actually left with (or without) at the end of the month.

Step 3: Calculate your expenditures.

a) After you have tracked your expenses, you will need to categorize your expenditures. Fixed monthly expenses include things like mortgage or rent, tuition, property tax payments, insurance (life, health, home, automobile and the like), car payments, child care, savings plans and domestic help. *There should be no guesswork in this category.*

b) Fluctuating monthly expenses are a bit trickier to figure out. Examples are: food, utilities (telephone, cellular phone, electricity, water, gas, etc.), gasoline, household products (toiletries, cleaning products, paper goods, and similar items), medications, bank charges, dry cleaning, and *tzedakah* contributions. After tracking your expenditures for two or three months, you should be able to determine a range for these fluctuating expenses. *Budget using the higher end of the range.*

c) All monthly expenses should be recorded under the month they were incurred, not the date they were paid. For example, if a pipe bursts on January 31, and you pay your plumber with a check dated February 28, record the cost of the repair under January's expenses.

d) Annual and occasional expenses are things like summer camps, children's extracurricular activities, medical and dental bills, clothing, shoes, vacations and outings, *simchos* and parties, home repairs, car maintenance, Yom Tov expenses, furniture and appliances. Estimate these costs to the best of your ability, using previous years' expenditures as a guide.

e) To determine your total annual expenditure, add your fixed and fluctuating monthly expenses and multiply the total by twelve. Then add your annual or occasional expenses to that.

f) Now that you have a fairly accurate estimate of your annual expenditures, pad this figure to allow room for unanticipated expenses. This will give your budget the flexibility to accommodate surprise expenses like parking tickets, lost knapsacks or passport renewals.

g) We recommend that you then divide your annual income and expenditures by twelve so you can work with a monthly budget, which is easier to follow than a yearly budget.

Step 4: Compare your income and expenses.

Once you have determined how much you are actually spending every month and where all the money is going, you can measure your expenditures against your income.

a) If your income exceeds your expenditures, your situation is ideal: You have a surplus, giving you extra money to save or use as you see fit.

b) If your income is less than your expenditures, you are running on a deficit. Governments have the luxury of operating with deficits; you do not. Even a small monthly deficit, when accumulated, can easily spiral into out-of-control debt. You have no choice but to find additional sources of income or think of ways to decrease your expenditures.

c) If your income and expenditures are equal, then your budget is balanced. Although this is an acceptable situation, it means that: (1) You do not have much leeway for unanticipated expenses; (2) you do not have much to put away for the future; and (3), if you incur any additional debts, you will be unable to repay them. We therefore advise you to try to earn a little more or cut back a bit on your expenditures.

When you have at least a small monthly surplus, you can congratulate yourself on having successfully created a workable budget.

Step 5: Follow your budget.

Living within a budget requires discipline, but it should not make you feel deprived. If you have created a realistic budget, you should be able to buy all the things you *need* — but only some of the things you *want*.

Step 6: Review your budget.

a) Now that you have created a workable budget, you and your wife should schedule monthly or bimonthly meetings to assess whether you have stayed within your budget.

b) If necessary, adjust your budget to reflect your family's changing needs.

In Defense of Budgeting ❯

I think it is dangerous to encourage people to live within a strict budget. When people have to record every penny they spend and constantly make sure they are staying within their predetermined budget, it will inevitably increase tension in the home.

Money turns into a major issue that can cause friction between husbands and wives and parents and children.

We disagree. Our experience with hundreds of families has conclusively demonstrated that in homes that run according to a budget, money is less of an issue than in homes where spending limits are only loosely defined.

This should come as no surprise, really. It is axiomatic that structure creates freedom.

For example, in a home where there are no rules or limits, are children happier? In a lawless society, is there less interpersonal conflict? Of course not. Both children and adults crave the security of knowing exactly what is acceptable and what is not.

The need for clear limits applies to money matters just as it applies to all areas of life. In a home where budgetary limitations are not clearly defined, there is more room for disagreement and squabbles over how money is to be spent. When reasonable, predetermined spending limits are in place, however, people can spend money without fear of a backlash from their loved ones — or from the bank.

Yes, there is definitely a measure of discipline and self-control involved in living within a budget. But it is far healthier for spending restrictions to be imposed by an impartial, unemotional budget than by a husband, wife or parent. With a budget in place, there should be no financial power struggles. Instead of husband, wife or parent having to say "no," the budget becomes the authority that decides whether money is to be spent or not.

Consider the following scenario:

One day Mr. Cohen decides he needs a new car. Mrs. Cohen thinks the old one is just fine and that they cannot afford a new one right now. If the Cohens have a budget, the decision of whether to purchase a new car can be made objectively, based on the available budgetary allotment for vehicular and transportation expenses. The issue of "Can we afford it?" should be an easy one to resolve, since the family's financial balance sheet will clearly indicate if money is available for this purpose.

If the Cohens do not have a budget, the decision might, and probably will, be made based on emotion: How badly does Mr. Cohen want the new car? And how insistent will Mrs. Cohen be that the children's tuition or her new *sheitel* come before the new car?

When husband and wife (and possibly children, if they are old enough) decide ahead of time where they want their money to go, they are, in effect, eliminating possible sources of friction down the line. Once a year, or once every few months, when they readjust their budget, they can discuss how they want to spend their money. The rest of the time, money should be a non-issue.

A home is in many ways similar to a small business. At Mesila, we advise businesses to view their finances as a cake. The last, and most important, piece of cake is the profits. Suppliers, employees, landlords, the government and others are all eager to get their hands on the cake before business owners can "eat" the profits. Unless business owners carefully plan for that last piece of cake, the cake will disappear quickly, and they will be left holding an empty tray.

The family finances cake also needs to be apportioned carefully so that it does not disappear. A smart parent knows better than to cut big pieces of cake for a few of the children and leave nothing for the rest — he or she will divide the cake in a way that ensures that there will be enough for everyone. When one child begs for more than her share, the smart parent will be able to say "no" firmly but lovingly, rather than give in shortsightedly and leave another child with only a tiny sliver.

Similarly, the only way to divide the family's income cake fairly and effectively is to do so ahead of time, setting aside money for basic expenses while allocating reasonable amounts for the needs of individual family members and the family as a whole.

The smart parent will also make sure to leave a bit of cake over at the end. In the family budget, these are the "profits," which might go to a savings plan or be used for something special — a family vacation, for instance.

Of course, for a budget to contribute to harmony in the home, it has to be realistic and somewhat flexible. If unbudgeted-for expenses continually arise, or if routine expenses consistently exceed their budgeted allotment, these are indications that the budget is too austere and needs to be reworked.

A good budget is one that generously covers all essentials, leaves some room for non-essentials, makes provisions for unanticipated expenses and incorporates savings in some form.

This type of budget creates financial structure, takes the home's focus off money issues and contributes to an environment in which healthy family relationships can flourish.

Making Your Budget Work for You ❯

I am using Mesila's budget questionnaires, and I have a number of budget-related questions. First of all, when completing the questionnaires, how do you determine whether expenditures belong in the "vital," "beneficial" or "luxury" categories?

Would a taxi ride to the other side of town (which costs a bit more but saves an enormous amount of time) be "vital" or "beneficial," especially when one is on a tight schedule? Does buying take-out food when the mother works full-time constitute a "vital" necessity? Is a much-needed vacation a "luxury"? Also, are there any halachic or fiscal limitations on how much money should be spent on a mitzvah? Where does hiddur mitzvah come into the picture?

Second, if a family is on a tight budget, does that mean they should spend money only on items in the "vital" category, or would that be considered tightfistedness? What if spouses have slightly different ideas of what constitutes a necessity — do you feel that the more "tightfisted" spouse should overlook the other's purchases?

Third, after one has collected data by religiously recording income and expenditures for several months, how does one plan a monthly budget and an annual budget?

Fourth, how does a family stick to a budget when many family members do the shopping? Is there some way for the family members to keep track of where they are vis-à-vis the monthly budget without looking over the other family members' shoulders and micromanaging?

Fifth, would you advise that a family always record their expenditures or would you say that after keeping track of expenditures for several months, the family can stop keeping records?

Lastly, we just bought a house and took out a fixed-rate mortgage, but our savings are depleted and we anticipate incurring house-related expenditures. Should we try to build up our savings to the point where we have a "nest egg" to save for a rainy day before prepaying the mortgage, or should we prepay the mortgage, which will knock many years off the life of the mortgage? (The interest owed on the mortgage is more than what we would earn in any low-risk savings plan.)

I thank you in advance for your guidance and direction!

Thank you for your important questions about planning your budget. Since you grouped your questions into six different sets, we will respond accordingly:

1) Financial management is a subject that has several definite rules. Some of those rules are: spend less than you earn; save a portion of your income for future expenses; and don't borrow money unless you have a plan for repaying it. Beyond the rules, however, there is a lot of room for individuality.

Deciding whether something is "vital" or "beneficial" is a personal choice. For instance, take-out food is a necessity for some families and a luxury for others. We provide the categories of "vital," "beneficial" and "luxury" in our budget questionnaires to help you see where your money is going and establish spending priorities. But only you can judge which items belong in which categories.

2) We cannot say that if you are on a tight budget then all of your expenditures must be in the "vital" category, since "vital" is very subjective. What we can say, however, is that your budget plan should allocate money first to the expenditures in the "vital" category, then to those in the "beneficial" category, and only then to those in the "luxury" category. For instance, if you consider supplemental health insurance "vital" and a new air conditioner "beneficial," you should pay for the insurance first and buy the air conditioner only if there is money left over. But if you consider the air conditioner "vital" and the insurance "beneficial," then the air conditioner should be purchased first.

After you decide which items belong in which category, we recommend that you ask an objective person outside your immediate family to review the items in each category and tell you whether your classifications seem reasonable. This will give you a reality check and allow you to take a step back and reassess your spending standards.

With regard to the amount of money that should be spent on *mitzvos*, the halachah is that a person should not spend more than one-fifth of his assets to fulfill a positive *mitzvah* (such as *tefillin* or *arbaah minim*), but he is required to spend all of his money in order to avoid transgressing a negative *mitzvah* (such as speaking *lashon hara* or eating forbidden foods). In addition, a person should spend up to one-third more on a *mitzvah* item for the sake of *hiddur mitzvah* (such as buying a nicer *esrog*). These *halachos* are discussed in

Shulchan Aruch, Orach Chaim 656:1, but you should consult a Rav for their practical application in specific situations.

You also raise the issue of whether one spouse should overlook the other's expenditures when he or she deems them unnecessary. No two people have identical spending priorities, and the fact that they happen to be married to one another does not mean that each one will necessarily agree with the other's ideas of how money should be spent.

The key is to create an atmosphere of mutual consideration in which each spouse feels that his or her needs and preferences are acknowledged and respected. In such an atmosphere, it is possible for a married couple to plan their budget as a team, deferring to one another and focusing on what we want, instead of quibbling over what I want and what you want.

3) You ask how to plan a budget based on the data collected by tracking income and expenses. The answer is, transfer the data to the monthly and annual budget forms by adding up the data in each income and expense category. Once the data is neatly organized in the monthly and annual budget forms, review each income item and decide whether it can be increased, and review each expense item and decide whether it should be reduced. Then take a fresh set of monthly and annual budget questionnaires and fill in the projected future amounts for each item, based on the data you have collected and any budgetary changes you have decided to implement (i.e., increases in income and reductions in expenditures). Also include one-time earnings or expenses anticipated in the upcoming months and years. The projections you have written in this new set of questionnaires will be your new budget plan.

4) Now let's tackle the question of how to stick to a budget when multiple family members are doing the shopping. This is essentially a *chinuch* question, not a financial question, but we will provide a

few basic guidelines. All the people doing the shopping have to be made aware of the relevant family budgetary policies. If it has been decided, for instance, that all expenditures are to be recorded, then everyone has to record their expenditures. Or if you have decided that each child can spend only a certain amount on clothing each season, you should explain to your children that their purchases should not exceed that amount.

If you find that a certain family member has difficulty sticking to the budget, you can think of creative, nonconfrontational ways to prevent problematic situations from arising, such as by arranging for the family shopping to be done by someone else. When the person who has trouble sticking to the budget needs to go shopping, you can either come along or give that person the exact amount of money needed — in cash.

The question of whether to monitor children's spending depends very much on the ages and personalities of the children. In general, however, you are correct in your assumption that micromanaging is counterproductive and should be avoided, if possible.

5) With regard to recording expenditures, this again is very individual. Some people find it liberating to record all of their financial transactions, since it makes them aware of what is going on with their finances, gives them a sense of control over their money, and helps them plan for the future. Other people, however, feel stifled when they have to record their expenditures.

At times, there is an objective need for a family to record expenditures, such as when trying to create a budget plan. Once the budget plan has been created, it is up to the family to decide whether continuing to record expenditures will be beneficial or detrimental.

6) Finally, about prepaying the mortgage versus building up a nest egg: There are several reasons why prepaying a mortgage might take precedence over establishing a savings plan. One reason is if

the interest rate on the mortgage is higher than the return on your savings (after taking the taxation benefits of the mortgage into account). Another reason to prepay a mortgage is that the savings are guaranteed and risk-free, whereas no savings plan is without risk. One of the biggest risks of a savings plan, by the way, is that you might decide to use it prematurely.

Depending on the type of mortgage you have and the savings options available to you, opting to prepay your mortgage rather than build up a nest egg might make financial sense. But that is only true if the nest egg is intended as a long-term savings plan. Every family needs to have some short-term, rainy-day savings — an emergency fund — even if those savings are earning little or no interest.

If you have no savings and you know you will be incurring significant expenses, it seems clear that your priority should be to build up a nest egg. Consider this: If you were to prepay the mortgage and then have to borrow money to cover your expenses, you might have lost whatever gain you had by prepaying the mortgage.

We are confident that if you manage to put together a nest egg, you will also manage to put something toward prepaying the mortgage. Knowing that every extra amount you put toward your mortgage will cut down the life of the mortgage will motivate you to find ways of prepaying the mortgage even if you are saving up for another purpose simultaneously.

Before You Throw In the Towel on Budgeting ❯

My family would probably be described as typically middle class. Our income is decent, but not great, and our expenses are close at the heels of our income — too close for comfort, probably, but no worse than most other families. Our home is not in danger of foreclosure, so we can't be doing that badly, considering the crisis.

I've been following your column for some time now and I've actually tried implementing much of your advice. I tried sitting down with my wife and building a budget plan, but it was a dismal failure. We decided to record all of our expenditures so we could see where our money was going, but we just could not remember to write everything down. That attempt petered out after a few days.

The first month of our new budget plan, we ended up spending so much more than we had planned and buying so many things that weren't included in the budget that we just gave up. We also tried putting aside money for savings — and this is something we both really wanted to do — but when our washing machine broke suddenly, it wiped out all of our newfound savings and we just couldn't manage to get the savings habit started again.

> *No matter how many times I try to manage my finances the way I would like to, I always find myself falling back into the same old patterns time and again. Before I throw in the towel on budgeting I thought I'd ask you why I'm having such a hard time with this.*

Your question is one that we are sure everyone can relate to on some level. Financial management can be very frustrating. It can be very tempting to let go of the financial steering wheel and allow your finances to coast along on their own. The problem is that the path to financial stability is strewn with hazards, and navigating that path on cruise control can lead you into a tailspin of debt, dependency and unbearable stress.

Financial management today is a complex, bewildering task, one that requires a combination of strategic planning, self-discipline and persistence. For some very disciplined people, financial management comes easily, but for most, it is a difficult and frustrating task. That's why even bright, capable people like you feel they are "not cut out" for budgeting.

Financial management wasn't always as hard as it is today. In the not too distant past, money was something you carried in your wallet or kept under the floorboards. If you wanted to buy something — and there wasn't that much to buy — you took out a few coins or bills and never had to think later about how to pay for it. If you didn't have the money to buy what you wanted, you either did without or scrimped and saved until you did.

Back then, money was something tangible, not a bunch of abstract numbers on a bank statement. Budgeting was a straightforward task: You counted your money and then allocated it for the things you needed the most. You also tried to put something aside for a rainy day, so that you would not have to go hungry if your source of income dried up.

Many people ask us why there is a need for an organization like Mesila nowadays, since "our grandparents managed just fine without Mesila." Indeed, our grandparents did not need Mesila — they had Mesila in their bones, and living without a *cheshbon* was unthinkable to them. They also were not under continuous bombardment by a multibillion-dollar advertising industry hawking the wares of the global marketplace and modern technology, nor were they at the mercy of banks and credit card companies offering "attractive financing options" to pay for all that the twenty-first century has to offer.

Mesila started out over a decade ago as an organization that helped people in Israel who were in debt and could not get their finances under control. But in the process of helping hundreds of families and businesses work toward financial stability, we realized that financial management difficulties transcend geographic and socioeconomic divides. Almost everyone today needs help managing their finances. That was why we shifted our focus to education and prevention, instead of crisis intervention.

The economic crisis we are now experiencing is the result of poor financial management at every level, from corporate bigwigs all the way down to the little guy with the big mortgage. We believe that the answer to this crisis is not dramatic government bailouts, but old-fashioned self-discipline and careful budgeting.

Thankfully, you are still a step ahead of the crisis. But that is much too close for comfort. You are lucky that you had some savings to fall back on when your washing machine broke, but what would happen if your boiler went? We are not trying to be pessimistic, but we think that burying your head in the sand and hoping that things will work out is not optimism but poor planning. You need to be aware of what is going on with your finances, you need to establish financial goals for the future, and you need to create and follow a budget that will help you realize these goals. The other option is financial mayhem, which in the worst-case scenario leads to disaster and in the best-case scenario leads to putting out fires.

What does "putting out fires" mean? It means discovering all of a sudden that your bank account is overdrawn and you have to face all the people to whom you wrote bounced checks. It means paying 20% interest on your credit card balance until you come up with "extra" money (we've never actually heard anyone say they have extra money) to pay it off. It means waking up in the middle of the night and remembering that you don't have the money your daughter needs in the morning to pay for her school trip. And it means living a life of balance transfers and debt juggling, borrowing money from one source to repay a loan from a different source.

If correct financial management is difficult and time-consuming, poor financial management is infinitely more difficult and time-consuming. The difference is that correct financial management requires you to exert yourself and exercise self-discipline ahead of time, while poor financial management allows you to take the path of least resistance and suffer the consequences later. Although this path is ultimately the harsher one, it is the default route and therefore the one more trodden.

Many people tell us that they don't have time to create, follow and review their budget plans on a regular basis. That's a bit like saying you don't have time to look both ways before you cross the street. If you think that analogy is exaggerated, that is because you haven't spent as many hours as we have helping families to extricate themselves from financial crises that could have been avoided.

We don't want you to become one of those families, and that's why we are trying to help you understand that correct financial management is not just a nice bonus; it's a necessity. The investment of time and effort now to create and follow a budget can spare you a tremendous amount of time and frantic effort later to come up with money to pay for sudden (or not-so-sudden) expenses.

Besides preventing financial difficulties in the future, correct financial management has tremendous positive benefits. Having your finances under control will reduce the amount of financial tension in your life, which will in turn make you a more relaxed person and therefore a better husband and father. If your finances are being managed correctly, you will have an easier time concentrating during your *davening* and Torah learning, and you will be free to pursue your livelihood to the best of your ability without feeling like a slave to your *parnassah* worries.

Living with a budget is emancipating, for it allows you to truly enjoy everything Hashem gives you without having to worry about whether you can afford it. Although it may require you to give up certain comforts or conveniences, living with a budget will bring you peace of mind and security, which will make every moment of your life sweeter. Shlomo Hamelech says as much when he tells us, "A dry piece of bread [eaten in] peace is better than a banquet where tension and strife reign" (*Mishlei* 17:1).

Correct financial management compels you to look inward and make decisions based on what you need, what you can afford and what is important to you, instead of looking outward at what the neighbors have and wondering how they can afford it. Focusing on your neighbor's Lexus will never bring you happiness, but focusing on what you really want out of life will. A budget, by forcing you to clearly define your priorities and goals, can help you manage your money in a way that will bring you the maximum satisfaction out of life.

Understanding the benefits of correct financial management is the best way to motivate yourself to muster the self-discipline and persistence to track your expenditures, stick to your budget plan and save for the future. Your wife also has to be convinced of the benefits of correct financial management, since the slightest resistance on her part can torpedo your efforts.

Once both of you are convinced of the benefits, the next step is developing a system of financial management that works for you. You might have to experiment with a few different approaches, but if you persist, we are sure you can find the approach that is right for you.

Here are some practical suggestions for coping with the specific issues you mentioned:

❯ To track you expenditures successfully, keep a small notebook with you at all times. This way you can record expenditures as they happen. Save all your receipts, bills and bank statements.

❯ To ensure that you stick to your budget, schedule specific times when you and your wife can sit down alone to review your budget and make any necessary changes. You and your wife are teammates, not adversaries, and your "budget meetings" should be calm, pleasant discussions. These meetings are the time for you and your wife to communicate any concerns you may have and to look for ways to address those concerns. Decisions made at each of these budget meetings should be written down, since writing down budgetary information contributes to financial control and discipline.

❯ To strengthen your resolve, you can read Mesila's articles and other materials, use our budget questionnaires (see Appendix) or attend a Mesila financial management workshop. (If you wish to organize a workshop series in your community, please contact us and we will try to arrange it.) Being part of the Mesila movement can turn financial management into a rewarding experience, instead of a pain in the neck. It can give you the tools and enthusiasm to take control of your finances in a lasting way.

A Tale of Two Incomes And a Deficit

Our financial situation was always such that we never were able to make ends meet. For the first few years after we got married, my husband learned in kollel. We lived very frugally, but nevertheless got into debt. We were always running to gemachim.

Eventually, my husband got a full-time job with an income that started at about $25,000 a year (this goes back some twenty years). At that time, although the income was adequate to cover our expenses, we got ourselves into serious credit card debt.

I became a dental hygienist several years ago and bring home about $3,000 a month. Our total monthly take-home income is $10,160, plus my husband's year-end bonus of $10,000.

We owe a lot of back taxes, and we have a monthly arrangement to pay these taxes. But we often end up buying food with post-dated checks, and we still occasionally get shut-off notices from the utility companies. Our financial situation has caused my husband major stress and has really affected the atmosphere in our home.

I'm concerned that we may be really mismanaging our money, since, considering our income, we should be managing comfortably. When I list the expenses, though, it looks as though we need several thousand dollars a month more.

Our monthly expenses (not including food, household supplies, clothing, Yom Tov costs, gifts, etc.) are $9,346, itemized below:

Mortgage: $2,250
Property taxes: $700
Gas and electric: $600
Water: $80
Cleaners: $120
Tuition for two children: $1,050
School transportation: $230
Allowance for son learning in Israel: $400
Cleaning help: $320
Pay back on down payment for house: $300
Gemach payments: $925
Income tax (owed from past): $350
Car payments: $516
Car insurance: $300
Gasoline: $350
Homeowners' insurance: $125
Credit card debt (old): $250
Credit card payments: $120 (just interest)
Medicine: $100
Telephone: $100
Cell phones (3): $160

Any help or advice you can offer would be greatly appreciated.

Mesila's response:

We welcome your inquiry, and we will be happy to assist you to the best of our ability. The situation you describe is all too common, particularly in the United States: two parents working hard to earn a respectable combined income, yet struggling to meet their financial obligations.

Mesila's counseling program involves three stages. The first and most basic is helping a family become aware of its exact financial situation. You have done an excellent job coming up with a detailed budget breakdown, and we congratulate you on taking this first step toward financial stability. Because you have provided us with a breakdown of your budget, we can hopefully zero in on the source of the problem and offer some suggestions for solving it.

What seems to be preventing you from achieving financial stability is the fact that about 20% of your income is going toward repayment of old debts — not including your mortgage — so you continually have to borrow money to cover your ongoing living expenses.

The way Mesila recommends that you break this vicious cycle is by separating debt from living expenses, using what we call the "divide-and-conquer approach." Debts and living expenses have to be viewed as two distinct financial obligations and managed as two separate accounts. Your income is meant to cover your living expenses, and your debts have to be paid for from a separate fund.

In the budget breakdown you sent us, debts are lumped together with living expenses and are not itemized. (For instance, when you say "*Gemach* payments," how many *gemachim* are you paying and how much do you owe to each of them?) The first thing you need to do, therefore, is create a separate, itemized list of debts.

Second, you need to ensure that your annual income is covering your annual living expenses. You have done a good job of itemizing a portion of your monthly expenses above, but it is crucial that you add to your list food, household supplies, clothing, Yom Tov expenses, gifts and whatever is included in "etc." so you can determine how much you are really spending. You also need to account for annual and occasional expenses (such as summer camp, or car and home repairs), so your figures reflect the true annual picture of your finances, rather than a narrow monthly slice of the yearly expense pie.

Once you have accurate figures of your annual income and expenses, you will be able to calculate your annual balance by subtracting expenses from income. If the balance is positive, then you have an annual budget surplus, and you can move on to build a long-term debt repayment plan. If your balance is zero, slightly more than zero, or negative, then you will have to work on increasing your income and/or decreasing your expenditures so you can carve out a budget surplus, which will become your debt repayment fund.

Whether your annual balance is positive, negative or zero, you should never use borrowed money to pay for living expenses. Borrowed money includes post-dated checks, installment plans, buying on credit at local stores and even credit cards, if you are carrying over a balance from month to month. It is critical that your living expenses be covered by your income, to ensure that your debts do not continue to mount.

A family that runs an ongoing monthly deficit is headed for financial disaster, so if you find that your income is not covering your living expenses, you will have to implement emergency measures — which may include working overtime, implementing spending cuts or even taking *tzedakah* — to close the gap.

We are hopeful, however, that your living expenses can be covered by your income, considering that you are earning a very respectable net income of $10,160 a month. Assuming that this is the case, once you have calculated your annual budget surplus, you can work on creating a fund for debt repayment. This is done by allocating money for all of your living expenses, and then building a long-term debt repayment plan based on your annual budget surplus, which is the amount you can afford to put toward debt repayment every year.

To illustrate, let's say your annual budget surplus is $10,000. If that is the case, you may decide to repay $833 ($10,000 divided by twelve) every month. Or, you may decide that you prefer to repay $1,000 ten times a year, so you do not have to make debt repayments around Pesach and Sukkos time, when your expenses are higher and your income might be reduced. Either way, your debt will be reduced by $10,000 a year.

If you find that you can afford to channel more money into your debt repayment fund as time goes on, that is wonderful, but you have to be very careful that paying extra does not result in financial hardship. That could lead you to take on more debts or abandon your debt repayment plan because it is too constricting.

In order to create your debt repayment plan, you will probably have to renegotiate the repayment terms of some of the old debts so that your monthly payments can be tailored to an amount that reflects your annual budget surplus. Another option is to consolidate your debt by taking out one large loan to pay off all the old debts.

If you decide to take out a new loan to consolidate your debt, make sure that (a) the monthly payments do not exceed the amount you can afford to repay and (b) the new loan is exactly equal to the amount you owe. (If it is more than you currently owe, your debt will increase; if it is less than you currently owe, you will still be saddled with the burden of repaying multiple debts.)

The advantage of paying back your debts in this manner is that you are able to eliminate your debts as quickly as you can afford to without having to take on any new debts in the interim and without severely compromising your standard of living.

To create a realistic, workable plan, you need to invest time and effort to build it. As time goes on, you will also need to continually reevaluate your financial situation and your debt load and fine-tune the plan based on your changing financial realities.

Because building — and following — such a plan is challenging, we strongly recommend that you either find someone whom you trust to act as your financial counselor, or apply for Mesila's assistance.

The road to financial stability is often long and arduous, but you seem to be organized, disciplined and motivated enough to succeed in the journey.

Learning to Disconnect From the Dollar ❯

> After getting married two years ago, we moved from the United States to Israel so I could continue learning. My wife found a job that paid relatively well by Israeli standards, and between my wife's income and the money our parents send us, we were managing financially — until the dollar collapsed.
>
> My wife is paid according to a dollar rate, which is converted to shekels. With the dollar so low, her wages have gone down significantly. In addition, the money our parents send us is now worth much less, so it is becoming harder and harder to cover our basic living expenses.
>
> And several months ago, our landlord switched our rent from dollars into shekels — using a rate of NIS 4.5 to the dollar! Is that fair? Is there any end to the low dollar in sight? And is there anything I can do to improve the situation?

There are many people in Israel today who are in situations similar to yours. Anyone whose income is dollar-based is finding it much harder to cover his expenses. Before discussing what you can do about it, it is important to understand what has happened.

During the years after the 1973 Yom Kippur War, economic growth in Israel stalled, inflation soared and government expenditures rose significantly. By 1984, inflation had reached an annual rate of close to 450%.

The economic reforms that were implemented at the time were so successful in stabilizing the Israeli economy that they became a model for other countries facing similar economic crises. But the runaway inflation of the early 1980s caused Israelis to lose confidence in their own currency, and since that time, Israel has had a psychological dependency on the dollar.

Now that the shekel has strengthened considerably against the dollar, Israelis are moving away from doing business in dollars. Actually, that makes good financial sense. It is unhealthy for a country to distrust its own currency to the extent that it sets prices and performs transactions in another country's currency.

There is no reason why the shekel should not become the preferred local currency in Israel. The Israeli economy is relatively stable, and has actually outperformed the U.S. economy consistently in recent years. Israel's GDP (gross domestic product) has boasted growth of over 5% in each of the last three years, while the U.S. GDP has grown by only 2%-3% during each of those years.

Of course, the trend toward doing business in shekels makes things difficult for anyone in Israel whose income is dollar-based. Israel's Central Bank has taken steps to curb the rising shekel and protect exports, but it is questionable whether these steps will have a significant impact.

To answer your questions, it would appear that the switch from dollars to shekels is something that people are just going to have to get used to. The dollar has regained some ground against the shekel recently, and it is possible that it will continue to regain ground. But that does not mean that people in Israel will — or should — revert to setting prices according to the dollar.

The Israeli real estate market, which traditionally fixed its rates according to the dollar, has now begun to embrace the shekel, conveniently ignoring current exchange rates and using historic exchange rates of over NIS 4 to the dollar to determine the price of property rentals and sales. Your landlord simply did what many other landlords are doing. Fair or not, it's a free market, and prices go up or down based on the laws of supply and demand.

What can you do to protect yourself against the falling dollar? Mesila generally recommends that, if possible, the currency in which you pay for your expenses should be the currency in which you receive your wages. If your wife can arrange to be paid according to a shekel rate, that would be preferable to being paid according to a dollar rate. With the shekel-to-dollar rate so low, however, she may want to wait and see what happens to the exchange rate before converting her salary to shekels.

Alternatively, she can try to negotiate a higher salary in shekels than she is currently earning. Even if her employer refuses, however, it may still be preferable for her to be paid in shekels at current exchange rates than to have her salary linked to the dollar. That is because earning money in dollars and spending it in shekels exposes you to unnecessary currency risk: If the dollar falls, you have fewer shekels to spend. Since the money you earn is money you are living off — not investment money — you should try to avoid this currency risk, if possible.

Forex, or foreign exchange trade, is very risky. In fact, statistics show that 90% of forex investors lose money. There are methods investors can use to make money by investing in currencies — such as hedging your position by buying an option or a put — but these are not relevant to your situation. Mesila's recommendation to most people is to stay far away from any type of forex trading, and we advise you and others in similar situations to take measures to protect yourself against currency risk.

We do not know if the dollar will continue to recover or will weaken further. No one does. Beware of people who tell you that they know with certainty what is going to happen to the dollar — or to any other currency or investment. They are probably either liars or fools.

Frankly, the question of what will happen to the dollar is irrelevant. You cannot manage your finances based on what might or should happen to the dollar. You need to manage your finances based on what is happening now and take steps to ensure your own financial stability, irrespective of the dollar's possible vicissitudes.

Many people are reluctant to transfer their wages or assets into shekels because they think that it is only a matter of time before the value of the shekel goes back down to what it used to be. This reluctance does not stem from logic, however, but from an emotional attachment to exchange rates of the past. The rule, "What goes up must come down" applies to certain markets that follow cyclical patterns — the real estate market, for instance — but it does not apply to the currency market. Therefore, nostalgic longing for traditional exchange rates should not be a factor in your financial decisions.

Some parents who are supporting their children in Israel have started to send more money, in recognition of the fact that the dollars they send do not go as far as they used to. But many parents in the United States are suffering financially and are not in a position to extend themselves any further. You would be wise to look for ways to reduce your living costs in order to ease the burden on your parents. If you cannot manage without asking your parents for additional help — and you think your parents can afford to help you out a bit more — you might want to ask *daas Torah* whether it is appropriate for you to broach the subject with them.

We encourage people in Israel to disconnect their emotions and their wallets from the dollar. If you are not in a position to move your income into shekels, or if moving to shekels does not alleviate the problem, then you will have to deal with the falling dollar in the same way you would deal with any other financial challenge: Find ways to increase your income or reduce your expenditures.

**For more on budgeting,
see also:**

"Pesach Finances" Chapter 3
"Should Kids Pay Their Own Way?" Chapter 11

3

Making 'Cents' of Spending

"The goal is not to cut
corners, trim the fat or
tighten your belt — the goal
is to optimize your spending
and build a brand-new
spending budget tailored to
your family's needs."

("Taking the Pain Out of
Belt-Tightening")

In this chapter:

❯ Taking the Pain Out of Belt-Tightening | 63

❯ Keeping a Lid on the Grocery Bill | 69

❯ How Much Should I Spend on Food? | 76

❯ Pesach Finances | 79

❯ Can 'Wedding' and 'Financial Stability' Be a Shidduch? | 83

❯ Am I a 'Shopaholic'? | 91

Taking the Pain Out of Belt-Tightening ❯

I am choking financially, and I hope you can help me. I own a store in a large Jewish community, and my revenues have taken a nosedive as a result of the economic crisis.

During the good times, the store provided enough for my family to live on, but not much more. Now, however, it is not possible for us to live off what the store brings in. I am hoping that business will pick up soon, but in the meantime, my family has had to make dramatic cuts in our standard of living.

There does not seem to be anything left in our budget to cut, but even so, we are not making ends meet, and we are falling into debt. Do you have any advice as to how we can squeeze our budget further?

In general, the way to cope with any type of financial difficulty is to look for ways to increase income and decrease expenditures. From your description of your situation, it appears that the steps you have taken to deal with these difficult financial times have been primarily focused on decreasing your family's expenditures.

Have you taken any steps to increase your income at the same time, whether by trying to boost the sales in your store or by finding other avenues of income? Have you and your wife brainstormed about ways to supplement the family's income during this recession?

First, increase income.

The Mesila approach is to focus first on increasing income, then on decreasing expenditures, because increasing income has several advantages over decreasing expenditures.

First, increasing income is a positive, constructive step, while decreasing expenditures is a negative, restrictive step. As such, a family can more easily muster — and maintain — enthusiasm and motivation for increasing its income than for decreasing its expenditures. Second, encouraging people to increase their income involves no implied criticism of their lifestyle, while encouraging them to decrease their expenditures suggests that they are overspending or spending incorrectly. Third, the potential to increase income is unlimited — at least theoretically — while the potential to decrease expenditures is limited.

We would advise you to make sure that in your efforts to balance your budget, you are investing at least as much effort in increasing your income as in decreasing your expenditures. It is true that in today's economy, increasing income can be very difficult. But that is all the more reason to put effort into it.

Decreasing expenditures does have one important benefit over increasing income, however: It provides immediate, clearly defined budgetary relief, while increasing income takes time and is not always predictable. Along with working to increase income, therefore, it is definitely important for you to look for ways to decrease your expenditures.

Drastic cuts are a problem.

It is important to note that the goal is not to drastically reduce expenditures — even if you and your family are willing to do so — because that will squeeze you into a very tight budget. Mesila has found that such drastic cuts rarely last. Instead, they create pressure and tension in the home and can cause you to despair and give up on balancing your budget.

Even minor spending cuts can result in tension between spouses and between parents and children. When people have to get used to living with less than they are accustomed to, it hurts, especially in the beginning. For that reason, we urge anyone who is trying to reduce spending to do it in a way that will cause the least pain to the family.

The approach that we recommend turns reducing expenditures into a positive exercise, rather than a negative one. In this approach, the goal is not to cut corners, trim the fat or tighten your belt — the goal is to optimize your spending and build a brand-new spending budget tailored to your family's needs.

Instead of focusing on your past spending habits and seeing what you can cut, you will erase all your spending history from your mind and come up with creative ways to meet your needs cost-effectively.

The way you have been spending money until now is definitely not the only way to meet your family's needs. It is probably possible for you to meet those needs just as well — or better! — while spending less money. In fact, even if you would not have an urgent need to decrease your expenditures, it would be a good idea to periodically rethink your spending patterns and determine how you can get the most value for your money.

Build your new spending plan.

When you sit down to make a new spending plan, keep your mind open to all possibilities. Do not accept anything you have done until now as a given. What you have done in the past, and what your friends, relatives and neighbors are doing, is only marginally relevant during this exercise.

Your new spending plan should itemize all of your family's needs — from housing to dental work to keeping the children occupied during summer vacation. But it can involve major changes to the way you are meeting those needs. To illustrate: The housing market is down right now, so you may be able to renegotiate your rent or mortgage payments, or even move to a different house, at a considerable savings.

Your dentist might be an old friend whom you have been going to for years, but other dentists may do work that is equally good — at better prices. And you might not have to spend thousands of dollars to make summer vacation an enjoyable time for the whole family.

When building this new spending plan, do some research about the different options available to you, and don't be afraid to think out of the box. In addition, do not hesitate to switch any type of service provider, whether it's your phone company, your bank or your insurance agent.

Plug the leaks.

Although you are erasing your old spending habits and building a spending plan from scratch, it is still important to examine your past and present spending patterns. These old spending patterns should not serve as a guide for building your new spending plan; they are important mainly for their research value.

Reviewing your spending will give you valuable information as to what your family's needs are and will alert you to the many areas of your budget that you should reassess. It will also help you see where money is leaking out unnecessarily.

You and your wife should track your expenditures for a period of two to three months. After that, prepare an itemized list, broken down into categories, in which you will tally how much you are spending on every item of your budget, from vitamins to haircuts to credit card fees. Then you will be able to evaluate which of these expenses can be eliminated or reduced. This exercise can save you a great deal of money, much of it painless.

Think before you spend.

You will likely find that just the act of recording your expenditures results in significant savings. Having to write down what you are spending prods you to think before you spend, and thinking is one of the greatest money-saving tools available.

So much of our spending happens thoughtlessly — we buy a snack on the road when we could easily have taken one from the house, we pay late fees on bills that we simply forgot about, or we run to the hardware store to buy a tool when we have the identical tool sitting on a shelf in a storage room. By training ourselves to think before reaching into our wallets, we can bring ourselves significant budgetary relief.

Focus on big-ticket items.

When cutting expenses, people often focus on budgetary items that are relatively trivial ("No more candy! No more art lessons! Shut the lights!"), while overlooking the big-ticket items that comprise the lion's share of their budget. Things like rent or mortgage payments, insurance premiums, and car payments are huge expenses, and it is in these areas that spending cuts can provide the greatest financial relief.

At the same time, however, it is important to remember that every drop adds up, and every little bit you save is significant. Your budget contains hundreds of small items, and when added together, these small items amount to a considerable percentage of your spending.

Another important aspect of streamlining your budget is ensuring that you are receiving all discounts, tax breaks and government benefits you are entitled to. As a small-business owner, you may be eligible for certain types of assistance, and we recommend that you speak to a competent accountant about this.

What works for you?

The challenge of decreasing expenditures is to streamline your budget without compromising the family's physical and emotional well-being. This challenge is highly individual, for one family might feel deprived living without something that another family is perfectly satisfied doing without. For instance, one family might have no problem buying generic or store-brand products — from detergent to breakfast cereal to clothing — while another family might find it very difficult to abandon the brand names it is accustomed to.

Which family is right? It's not a question of right and wrong. It's a question of what works.

If you are willing to think creatively and reprogram your family's spending habits, you may be pleasantly surprised to find that your budget can go a lot further than you thought.

Keeping a Lid on the Grocery Bill

I am unsure whether it is preferable to do my shopping at a large supermarket or at the local grocery. Obviously, the supermarket has lower prices, but I find that I end up buying much larger quantities, which tend to get used up very quickly. When I buy at the local grocery, where prices are higher, I buy small amounts at a time, exactly what I need.

How do I keep my food bill to a minimum — by shopping at the supermarket or at the corner grocery?

Grocery shopping is a recurring, unavoidable expense and one that represents a hefty portion of your monthly budget.

The good news is that unlike fixed expenses — such as insurance, tuition or rent/mortgage — the grocery part of your budget is a relatively easy place to save money.

Where should you do your shopping? The answer to that question is highly individual and depends on many factors. We will try to guide you through the various considerations to take into account when making your decision.

Accessibility: How far is the large supermarket compared to the corner grocery? What method of transportation do you use to get there?

Price difference: How much more expensive is the local grocery? When you factor in costs such as transportation, parking, delivery, time lost from work, babysitting and so on, how much are you actually saving by going to the supermarket?

Products: Are the items you are likely to buy at the corner grocery imported or gourmet and, therefore, more costly? Do you tend to make impulsive purchases when confronted with the lure of specialty foods often found at a local store? Alternatively, does the supermarket, which is large, well-lit and attractive, influence you to buy things you didn't intend to?

Time: Which takes more time — frequent trips to the corner grocery, where you may not be able to buy everything you need (e.g., fruit and vegetables) or less-frequent trips to the supermarket, where you can get everything at once?

The shopper: Who does most of the shopping in the family? Is it the breadwinner, whose time could be put to better use? Is it a busy mother who has to take children along with her or pay a babysitter? Is it a child, teenager or adult who has plenty of time to run errands?

Customer service: If you have a problem with a product, will you be more likely to go back to the supermarket or the corner grocery? Some supermarkets have no-hassle return policies, while others are bureaucratic; some grocery store owners are pleasant and accommodating, while others are difficult to deal with. Where will you get better service?

Storage: How much storage space do you have? If you live in a small apartment, you may not be able to stock up on groceries, so the trip to the supermarket might not be saving you much. On the other hand, if you have an extra freezer and lots of storage space, buying in bulk might be a good idea.

You have to divide your shopping between the supermarket and the local grocery in a way that works for you. Strive for a balance that matches your lifestyle and is as convenient and affordable as possible.

To help achieve this balance, you might want to keep two separate shopping lists — one for the local grocery and one for the supermarket.

If you live close to the grocery and far from the supermarket, your grocery list might contain perishable items such as bread, dairy products and eggs, while the supermarket list might contain non-perishables such as canned, packaged and frozen foods, cleaning products, toiletries and the like.

Alternatively, if you prefer to make one shopping trip to the supermarket at the beginning of the week and a trip to the grocery at the end of the week, your supermarket list might contain your weekly basics while your grocery list might contain your pre-Shabbos needs.

In general, the best approach is to try each method for a month. Record your purchases and then evaluate where you spent more. Ultimately, regardless of the option that works best for you, being disciplined about your purchases is the key to keeping your grocery bill under control.

Although not a strictly financial consideration, another important point you may want to consider is to whom you are giving your business.

While it might come out cheaper to shop at a large supermarket owned by a huge corporation, local groceries are often owned by *frum* Jews struggling to earn a living, and giving them *parnassah* is actually a fulfillment of the *mitzvah* of *Vehechezakta Bo*. In certain instances it might be permissible to deduct the difference from *maaser* money; consult with your Rav for guidance.

If you wish to keep your grocery bill to a minimum, it is not only important to think about where to shop, but also how to shop.

Your shopping goal is to get what you need at the lowest price. But stores have a different goal: To get you to buy as much as possible. They do this by convincing you that you need more things, more expensive things and more of each thing.

This awareness will empower you to detect some of the marketing ploys being utilized to get you to buy things you weren't planning to purchase and don't really need.

The moment you walk into the store, you are greeted by an array of tantalizing freshly baked goods, sale displays (look carefully — are they actually on sale?) and "seasonal" items that might not even be in season (think of the menorahs that appear on the shelves right after Sukkos).

Flyers touting sales and special offers beg to be picked up, inducing you to look through pages of "deals" you never needed or wanted, but may now start to consider.

If you walk straight ahead when you enter the store, chances are that you will not find what you came for. Store owners know that your natural inclination is to walk straight down the middle of the store, so that is where they put all the things you don't need.

As you walk down those center aisles, you will likely discover a need for all the nonessentials begging to be removed from the shelf. Your basics — bread, milk, meat and other staples — are located along the outside walls, and that is where you should head immediately.

When taking items off the shelf, pay attention to where you are taking them from. Stores place the most expensive products at eye level. Take a few seconds to scan the prices of products found near the floor or on the top shelf, and you could save yourself some money.

Children's items, on the other hand, are placed at their eye level, so they can quickly spot the candies, toys and sweet cereals that make you sigh ... and then buy. (If possible, try to shop without the kids. You can save a lot of money — and aggravation — that way.)

While you shop, your senses are being used against you. Stores motivate your buying impulses by manipulating your hearing, sight and smell. Did you notice that a recorded voice in the supermarket is telling you what this week's specials are ("only 79 cents a pound, while supplies last")? Or that the music the store is playing is carefully selected to slow you down, making you dawdle before all those luscious arrays of foods?

Attractively designed displays beckon, while the sight and aroma of fresh food entices your subconscious.

Sales and special offers are another thing that require caution. Low prices induce people to buy more than they need — but if you don't need it, it's not a bargain. And if you really only need one of a particular item, it is not cheaper to buy half a dozen.

Even worse than sales are non-sales. Supermarkets pile items at the end of the aisles, creating the impression that these items are on special — which is not always the case. Be wary of items that are advertised as bargains when purchased in larger quantities, such as packages of crackers that are "on sale, 4 for $9.99," but are regularly priced at $2.50 each.

Many impulse purchases take place during the time you spend in line at the checkout. Stores know that, and that's why they place all sorts of interesting and potentially useful items at arms' length while you wait. Once you've finished your shopping, resist the urge to add things to your shopping cart. There is nothing wrong with a half-full shopping cart.

We all have a psychological defense mechanism that leads us to convince ourselves that those added impulse purchases were really important and necessary. The extra magazine, the batteries, the candy bars — sure, they're nice to have, but they add up to a hefty amount that could likely be put to better use in other areas of your budget — savings, for instance.

There is nothing wrong with buying magazines, batteries or candy bars — but if they weren't on your shopping list, chances are you will manage without them.

Keep your storage capabilities in mind. Every added item that you bring into your house needs a place. The less you buy, the less clutter you will have. And the less you buy, the less of a chance that you will have to throw things out because they got stale or spoiled.

Also, the more food you have in your house, the more people will eat. It's a fact — the more you have, the more you use, even when it may not be necessary.

Stores today are designed to make you look at a lot of products and do a lot of impulse buying. And these tactics are surprisingly successful — statistics show that impulse shopping accounts for an astounding 40% of all supermarket purchases.

The best way to protect yourself from the onslaught of marketing tactics you face any time you go shopping is to prepare a list beforehand — preferably with the required quantities of each item — and stick to it.

It is also a good idea to set aside a certain amount of money for your shopping trip, and resolve not to go beyond that amount (even if it means putting a few things back when the cashier tallies your bill).

Try not to do your shopping when you're hungry or tired or when the store is busy. Each of these factors impedes your ability to think through your purchases clearly. You'll end up buying a lot of things you weren't planning to buy and spending more than you would have otherwise.

Of course, you are only human, and it is understandable that you will occasionally buy on impulse or that you will notice an important item that you forgot to write on your shopping list — perhaps even in someone else's cart while you wait on line.

The above pointers are not inviolable rules — they are only suggestions to help you achieve control over your grocery bill. As in many financial matters, awareness, planning and discipline are the keys to becoming a savvy shopper.

How Much Should I Spend on Food? ❯

I have been keeping track of my budget regularly with Excel since I got married. I am concerned, however, that I may be spending too much money on food.

We are a family of six (four kids), and I don't know how to gauge whether my monthly food expenses are appropriate for my family size. Is there a maximum percentage of my income that should go toward food?

We commend you for your conscientiousness in keeping track of your budget. Having an awareness of where your money is going is the first step in achieving financial stability, and recording your expenditures is an excellent way to reach that awareness.

Being conscientious has a flip side, though: There is the risk that you will become overly preoccupied with the amount you are spending.

You write that you are concerned that you may be spending too much money on food, but you do not write why this is a concern to you. Is it because you are short on money and you need to cut down your expenditures in order to pay your bills? Or is it because the amount of money you are spending on food just seems too high?

As you are probably aware, food prices around the world have skyrocketed recently, with flour, rice, corn, eggs, dairy, chicken, meat — and, it seems, almost everything else — costing a lot more than they used to.

Rising food prices are linked to climate change, market speculation and the developing economies of China and India. They are also linked to the high price of oil, which translates into higher shipping and transportation costs and leads to diversion of farmland to the production of biofuel. But whatever the reasons are, food price hikes are something we all have to learn to live with.

If you are not experiencing any financial difficulty, the fact that your food bill seems high is not necessarily a cause for concern.

Spending choices are highly personal. Some families prefer to spend more on food, some prefer to spend more on vacations, and some prefer to spend more on domestic help. If you are managing to cover all of your expenses and put aside money for the future, it is okay to spend a bit more in some areas of your budget.

Contrary to what many people think, Mesila does not advocate reducing expenditures unless there is a good reason to do so. If you are experiencing financial difficulty, if you are unable to put aside money for the future, or if your standard of living is significantly higher than is acceptable in your community — those would be good reasons to reduce your expenditures. But we would not recommend that you reduce a particular expenditure only because it seems high.

The same way Mesila discourages people from spending more than they can afford, we also discourage people from reducing their expenditures without good reason. Reducing expenditures is even more likely to cause stress and friction in the family, if it is unwarranted.

Your conscientiousness in budgeting should not lead to tightfistedness. Such an atmosphere in the home is extremely unhealthy, and it is actually a sign of financial instability. (Mesila defines financial instability as what happens when finances become a source of anxiety, difficulty or strife.)

Having said all this, we will now suggest a practical strategy for determining whether your monthly food expenses are appropriate for your family size.

Our suggestion is that you take an informal survey of several families that are the same size as yours, whose children are around the same ages as yours, who live in the same area as you, and have a standard of living similar to yours. Ask each of them how much they spend on food. If they spend more or about the same amount as you do, then you can be fairly confident that you are spending a reasonable amount.

If most of the families you survey spend significantly less on food than you do, you can then begin to consider cutting down your food expenditures. At that point, feel free to consult with us again and we will be happy to offer guidance on how to reduce your expenditures in the most effective and least damaging way. (If there is a different reason why you feel it is important to reduce your expenditures, we will be equally happy to assist you.)

Feeding a family of six is not a cheap proposition. But it is an expense that you should be grateful to have. Look at it as a blessing, not a burden. If you are managing well financially, we would advise you not to think too much about your food expenses.

Pesach Finances ❯

Ordinarily, my income is sufficient to cover my family's needs. But when Pesach approaches, we experience a severe financial crunch. The money just seems to fly out the window. There's extra cleaning help, babysitting or entertainment during all the days the children are off from school. And we eat out on the days before the chag. Then there are the costs of matzah, wine, meat and other Pesach products. And, of course, let's not forget clothing and shoes for the whole family.

On top of all that, I lose a great deal of time from work during Nisan, so my income is much lower during that month. I cannot help but dread this time of year, since I know that I will end up with an overdrawn bank account and a credit card bill that will take me months to repay.

There are numerous organizations that distribute money, matzah and even clothing and shoes before Pesach. Some offer their assistance to anyone, not only to "charity cases." I am strongly considering approaching these organizations for assistance this year, but I wanted to hear Mesila's view on the matter.

When making Pesach, it is critical to maintain a clear perspective of what this time of year is all about. Pesach is a time of the collective rebirth of the Jewish people. It is a time of spiritual rejuvenation and renewal for every individual as well.

If we view Pesach as a burden — financial or otherwise — then this season of freedom turns into the season of bondage. It's true that Pesach involves a great deal of work and expense, but there are things we can do to prevent ourselves from becoming overwhelmed.

You say you dread the Pesach season. Do you dread paying income tax? If you are an employee, your income tax is probably deducted from your monthly paycheck, without your ever having to take the money out of your pocket. So when tax season rolls around, you should have nothing to fear.

If you approach Pesach expenses in the same way, you will not need to dread Pesach.

You know when Pesach is coming. You know that your income is less during Nisan and that your expenses are high. Don't just sit back passively and "dread" the terrible financial crunch. Be proactive!

Make a yearly budget that includes your Pesach expenses, the same way it includes your tuition and medical insurance. Then put money aside every month for Nisan. This way, when Nisan rolls around, you will not have to panic. You may be able to make Pesach without going into debt.

Some pre-Pesach expenses are avoidable. By keeping a record from year to year of the actual quantities you use during Pesach, you can ensure that you do not buy too much very expensive *shemurah matzah* or get stuck with boxes of macaroons that no one will touch after the *chag*. By preparing a comprehensive shopping list for the supermarket, you can save yourself the time and expense of multiple trips to the corner grocery.

And by taking inventory of everything in your freezer and pantry several weeks before Pesach, you can plan meals that will use up many items you might otherwise have to burn on Erev Pesach. This also reduces the need for expensive meals out.

One of the keys to keeping Yom Tov costs to a minimum is ensuring that everyone in the family maintains their peace of mind. When people are frazzled, they tend to make impulse purchases and spend much more money than they would if they were not under stress.

If, despite your best efforts, you still cannot cover your Pesach expenditures, then you have two options:

The first, and much preferred, option is to simply scale back your Yom Tov. Making a more modest Yom Tov does not require you or your family to have a miserable Pesach. It does, however, require you to do without some of the things you maybe would have liked to have.

If you are working with limited means, you should discuss with your Rav exactly how to fulfill the *mitzvah* of *simchas Yom Tov*. Then, together with your wife and perhaps your children, you should create a Pesach budget and establish a list of priorities. What is more important to your wife — extra cleaning help or a new dress? Would the children prefer to get *afikoman* presents or go on a family Chol Hamoed outing? And so on.

The second option is to accept the assistance of the tzedakah organizations you mentioned. Before you decide to do this, you have to ask yourself, and your Rav, if you qualify to be receiving *tzedakah*. And make no mistake about it — any distribution of money, food or clothing is *tzedakah*. Even if the distributors claim that they are offering their assistance to anyone, they are saying this to protect the dignity of their recipients.

When deciding whether to approach organizations for assistance, take into account that there is a limited amount of assistance available, and if you accept such assistance, another needy person may be denied it.

That does not mean that you should not take the help, if you need it. All it means is that the decision to accept charity funds is not one that should be taken lightly. Note, however, that it is better to accept *tzedakah* than to borrow money that you have no way of repaying.

Encouraging people who could be self-sufficient and manage on their own to accept contributions and rely on others is not true *chessed*. Mesila's goal is to give people the tools to support themselves without having to resort to charity or loans. This way, they can release themselves from the vicious cycle of poverty and debt and achieve financial stability.

May we all be *zocheh* to enjoy Pesach — and the Yamim Tovim — in the true spirit of freedom.

Can 'Wedding' and 'Financial Stability' Be a Shidduch? ❯

Our oldest daughter just became a kallah, baruch Hashem, and we are now starting to prepare for the wedding. We have some money saved up, but it is not nearly enough to cover all the wedding expenses, and we are now looking into different options for borrowing money — mortgage, home-equity line of credit, gemach loans, etc.

Never having made a wedding before, we have no idea what things should cost, and we have no idea how much money we will need. Can you give us some pointers for handling the financial aspects of the wedding?

Mazal tov on your *simchah*! The period of a child's engagement is usually a whirlwind of emotions, things to take care of and huge expenses; many people — even responsible budgeters — feel that they totally lose financial control by the time they walk their child to the *chuppah*.

Because the costs associated with making a wedding are so high, and because it is so easy for expenses to spiral out of control, correct financial management is critical at this time. Otherwise, people can end up with a mountain of debt that takes years, or even a lifetime, to climb.

Your daughter's wedding is a monumental event, but it is only the beginning of her new life. With Hashem's help, there will be many more happy times in her life — and perhaps challenging ones, as well — and you need to keep yourselves healthy and financially stable so you will be able to share these times with her. It is wise, therefore, to plan your wedding budget in a way that will not leave you with insurmountable debts — or, *chas veshalom*, a heart attack.

In order to keep the wedding finances under control, you need to go in with a budget plan — preferably a written plan — that reflects the total amount you will be spending as well as the approximate amount you wish to spend on each aspect of the wedding. No plan is perfect, and unexpected expenses will always come up, but if you have a plan you have a chance of remaining in the driver's seat instead of being dragged along for a joyride of spontaneous purchases.

Consult with experienced, responsible people.

The costs of making a wedding vary greatly depending on factors such as the community you live in, your standard of living and your overall financial situation.

Since at this point you have no idea how much things should cost, we recommend that you consult with people who have made weddings before, are financially responsible, and whose standard of living and income bracket are similar to yours. These people should be able to give you an idea of what the total cost of making a wedding is and what each aspect of the wedding will cost.

Ideally, it would be advisable to work with a professional consultant who can help you build your wedding budget and advise you on how to get the most value for the money. The cost of making a wedding is about the same as the cost of opening a small business, and just as there are business consultants whose job is to help save business owners money and headaches, people should have the option of hiring wedding consultants to help them save money and headaches when marrying off their children.

In the meantime, however, we will offer some pointers for maintaining your financial stability — and sanity — through the engagement period and beyond.

Get a list.

Many people who have married off children have compiled comprehensive lists of all that needs to be bought and paid for, and we are sure you can find people in your social stratum who would be willing to share this information with you.

Getting lists — along with approximate price ranges — from people who are experienced and objective will give you an idea of what you can reasonably expect the various aspects of the wedding to cost.

Settle on a budgetary figure.

Once you have done your research and calculated how much things should cost, you should decide on a figure that realistically reflects both the approximate cost of making a wedding and the amount you can afford to spend.

If you see that the costs of planning the type of wedding you wish to make far exceed the amount of money you have, you will either have to find ways to keep costs down, or borrow money in order to increase the amount you can spend on the wedding. When borrowing money, however, keep in mind that it is dangerous — and possibly halachically forbidden — to borrow money if you don't know how you will pay it back. Tempting as it may be to borrow more than you can afford to repay, it is important that you do not jeopardize your financial stability or overextend yourself to the point where you cannot afford to marry off your other children.

Itemize your spending budget.

After settling on an overall budgetary figure, you should decide how much you wish to spend on each item on your list. Allocate money for each of these items.

There are four major categories of wedding-related expenses:

1. The wedding itself. This includes the hall, caterer, music, photography, flowers, guest accommodations, transportation and similar expenses.

2. Gifts and clothing. These are the jewelry, *chassan/kallah* gifts, wedding gown, *sheitels*, clothing for the entire family and the like.

3. Other events. The *vort*, *aufruf* and *sheva brachos* (including guest accommodations and transportation) will also entail expenditure.

4. Setting up a home. Furniture, appliances, kitchen equipment, linens and other household goods will need to be purchased.

A possible fifth category, relevant mostly to people in Israel, is the purchase of a house or apartment. Financial support for the couple is not included in the wedding budget because it is an ongoing expense, not a one-time expense. If you are going to be helping the couple financially after the wedding, you need to take that into account when building your wedding budget.

Break your overall budget into these four (or five) major categories by allocating amounts for each one. Then, break each category down further by writing down how much you plan to spend on each item within that category.

Be flexible.

Not all your projections will be 100% accurate — you may spend more on some items and less on others — but going shopping with a ballpark figure of how much you plan to spend will help you stay within range of your budget. It will also help focus you on the type of merchandise you want, and it will protect you from salespeople who try to convince you to spend more than you can afford to.

For instance, if you go shopping with your daughter for dishes knowing that you need two sets of dishes and you plan to spend up to $300, you will know right away that the sets that start at $500 are out of your price range. This way, you will not leave the store wondering how the saleslady sweet-talked you into walking out with a whole extra set of serving pieces that you never planned to buy.

If you do go over your budget, do not become disheartened. Adjustments to your budget can and should be made when necessary. These are not a sign of failure. Even if you end up spending more than you planned, it is far better to know you are going over budget than to abandon your budget altogether and completely lose track of what you are spending.

Don't make budgetary adjustments under stress.

You cannot expect all your spending projections to be accurate. It is inevitable that you will have to make adjustments. But these adjustments should not be made on the spur of the moment or when you are under stress.

"Under stress" can mean when you are in a store and have limited time and privacy. It can mean at the last minute, when you simply must pick up a certain item and the price becomes almost irrelevant. It can mean when you are feeling tired, emotionally drained or in a bad mood. And it can even mean when you are excited or on a high.

In stressful or exciting situations, people tend to make poor decisions, without thinking them through, and they neglect to use their budget as a rudder for their spending. Instead, they think or say things like, "A wedding is a once-in-a-lifetime-experience," or "My child deserves only the best," or, "Some things are more important than money." These statements may be true, but they are generally not a good excuse for spending more than you planned.

Manage your time wisely.

The time between the engagement and the wedding is limited, and there is a tremendous amount to do. Along with planning your wedding budget, therefore, you also need to plan how you will budget your time in a way that will allow you to accomplish everything that needs to be done, while keeping stress to a minimum.

Money and time are often inversely proportional: the less time you have, the more money you spend. If you have the time, you can do your research, comparison shop, negotiate better prices and get the most value for your money. But if you don't have the time, you will find yourself spending more money and getting less value in return.

It's important to keep in mind that not everything has to be purchased before the wedding. It's okay if the *kallah* does not have her mixer or all her linens by the wedding day. In fact, she might even enjoy and appreciate these things more if she gets them after the wedding, when she actually has a use for them or knows better what she wants. Prioritizing what needs to be done now and what can be done later will reduce stress and help you use your time more efficiently.

Divide and conquer.

It is critical that your wedding budget be completely separate from your ongoing living expenses. The money set aside for the wedding expenses has to be kept apart from the money you use for your grocery shopping and utility payments — whether in a separate bank account, a separate envelope or on a separate credit card — so that you know how much money is being used for each.

If the two accounts are mixed, and you pay for the *chassan's* watch from the same account you use to buy gas for your car, you will likely lose track of how much you are spending, and you will very possibly end up spending far more than you wanted to. On the other hand, if you are careful to pay for all wedding-related expenses with money designated for that purpose, you will able to monitor your spending and ensure that money does not fly out the window uncontrollably.

This is an important application of the Mesila "divide-and-conquer" approach.

You can't have everything — so choose what's important.

Making a wedding involves maintaining a delicate balance between the *kallah*, the *chassan*, the *mechutanim*, social norms and what you can afford.

You want your daughter to have the best of everything, and you want to do your utmost to ensure the future happiness of the young couple. At the same time, you want to please — and impress — the *mechutanim*, and you want to marry off your daughter respectably, in a way that conforms to the standards of your community and the community to which the *chassan's* family belongs.

The problem is that all this has to be done within the constraints of your budget, and it is often not possible to meet all these criteria without overextending yourselves financially. It is important, therefore, to acknowledge — and to explain to your daughter — that you will not be able to have everything, and that you and she will have to choose how to use the money you have at your disposal in the way that will be the most beneficial.

If the *kallah* understands this, then instead of making demands — or even polite requests — and becoming upset when she does not get the things her friends have, she will be able to decide what really matters to her and make her choices accordingly.

During the frenzy of the wedding preparations, it is easy to lose sight of priorities. Keep in mind, however, that expenses that seem extremely important when planning the wedding often seem trivial the day after the wedding. How many people remember whether the flowers at the wedding were fresh or artificial? And does it really make a difference whether the gowns were borrowed or bought?

Focusing on the overall picture, rather than becoming fixated on details, will help you to direct your money in a way that reflects your real priorities. For instance, you may decide that it is worth going with a simpler wedding menu and investing more in the couple's furniture and appliances, since the wedding lasts only one night, and furniture and appliances should last many years. Or you may decide that you would rather put more money toward the couple's financial support, or toward a house, than toward gifts or *sheva brachos*.

A wedding budget is not supposed to force you into a straitjacket — it is supposed to serve as a spending guide that lends financial structure to your wedding preparations. Yes, it takes effort and self-discipline to build and stick to a wedding budget, but if you do, you will be rewarded with the peace of mind that will make your wedding a true *simchah* in every respect.

Am I a 'Shopaholic'? ❯

Shopping has been my favorite pastime ever since I've been a teenager. I love to buy things — groceries, clothing, household items, you name it.

I often find myself heading out to a store in the evenings when I have nothing else to do. I've noticed a pattern in which I'll go into a store on the spur of the moment and buy a few things, only to go back to that store a few days later to return some items, at which point I'll inevitably find something else to purchase.

My family and friends comment about my spending habits, calling me a "shopaholic" and telling me that I spend too much. How do I know if I really have a spending problem? And if I do have a spending problem, how can I overcome it?

Not knowing the details of your lifestyle and spending habits, we cannot tell you whether you have a spending problem. But we can tell you that your willingness to confront the issue is a very good first step in overcoming your spending problem, if indeed you have one.

When does spending become a problem? Any type of behavior or characteristic taken to an extreme is problematic, and spending is no different. The Rambam teaches us that the middle road is the golden path, and the ability to strike a balance between the two extremes in every *middah* is the hallmark of healthy behavior.

Spending problems come in two varieties — stinginess and extravagance, representing the two polar extremes of the spending spectrum. Our goal is to find a middle road that allows us to spend enough to meet our needs and obligations, but not so much that we squander money needlessly.

The terms "stinginess" and "extravagance" are quite subjective, because the size of a person's budget is a major factor in determining whether the person spends too much or too little. But how much money a person has is by no means the only factor in determining whether he or she has a spending problem. Spending problems are as a much a behavioral issue as a financial issue. There are poor people who are miserly, and there are rich people who are miserly. There are poor people who overspend, and there are rich people who overspend.

The sign of a stinginess problem is when a person has difficulty spending money on items that he and his family clearly require — not because he doesn't have the money, but because he cannot bring himself to spend it. This creates an atmosphere of deprivation and penny-pinching in the home, which is often accompanied by a fixation with money and prices.

When does overspending become a problem? For every person, the line between healthy spending and overspending will be drawn in a different place, but we can identify four general parameters that can help you to determine whether you are overspending:

1. You spend more than you can afford.

There are three ways to assess whether you are spending more than you can afford:

a) If you consistently spend more than you earn, and you either accumulate debt or eat away at your savings as a result.

b) If your income is reasonable but you are nevertheless unable to put aside any money for the future.

c) If you spend money on luxury or nonessential items and you are then unable to pay for basic or essential items.

2. You spend money to fill an emotional void.

While shopping can be a pleasurable experience and can provide some measure of stress relief, it should not be used consistently as an outlet for negative feelings such as sadness, inadequacy, boredom, guilt, fear, anger or nervousness.

Spending money is not a healthy response to negative feelings, because the act of swiping a credit card and walking away with a shopping bag does nothing to dispel the source of those feelings. Any feeling of emotional relief that shopping provides is therefore short-lived and superficial.

3. You buy things you do not need and never use.

If your closet is full of items that still have price tags, if you often wonder what possessed you to buy a particular item that you have no use for, or if you frequently make excuses for — or worse, lie about — your purchases and how much they cost, then it is likely that your spending is problematic.

4. Your spending is adversely affecting other areas of your life.

Even if you and your family are not suffering financially because of your spending habits, your spending might be harmful to you or to your loved ones in other ways.

Do you have frequent arguments with family members about your spending habits? Are your children being neglected because you are out shopping too much? Has your marriage been reduced to a collection of shared things, instead of shared goals and shared communication? Does your life revolve around material acquisition, to the point that you are desensitized to the pleasures of spirituality and meaningful relationships?

Severe Overspending

In extreme cases, people can actually develop an addiction to shopping — known scientifically as oniomania, or colloquially as "shopaholism" — if they get used to spending money in order to squelch negative feelings. These people might buy ten items when they really need only one, or they might pay outrageous amounts of money for things they have little or no use for.

Shopping addicts experience a rush of endorphins when they spend money, which gives them a brief but exhilarating escape from life's painful realities. As soon as that feeling of euphoria subsides, they begin to crave the pleasurable sensation they associate with shopping and feel an uncontrollable urge to spend money again.

Between spending episodes, shopping addicts are typically plagued by anxiety, shame and guilt, and think about money excessively. This cycle is typical of addictive behavior, and professional intervention is usually required to break the cycle.

Overcoming the Problem

If your spending has reached out-of-control proportions, to the point where it can be classified as compulsive or addictive, then you will need to seek professional help. But if you still have some measure of control over your spending, we will offer several suggestions for reining it in to a point where it is no longer problematic.

❯ Don't carry your wallet with you when you don't need it. If you don't have money or a credit card with you, then you will have to come back later if you want to buy an item that you see. This is a good way to test whether you really need or want the item, and can help to reduce impulse purchases.

❯ Get rid of your credit cards. When used properly, credit cards can be a very convenient and useful tool. But if you have a tendency to overspend, you should avoid credit cards completely. Credit cards make it dangerously easy to spend money, since they eliminate the pain you experience when you have to part with your money. The pain of parting with money is actually a healthy pain; it ensures that the item you are spending money on justifies the pain involved.

❯ Shop when you are not sad, stressed, excited or in a rush. People tend to spend more, and buy things they don't need, when they are feeling down or when they are under pressure. People who are very happy, excited, or on an emotional high also tend to spend more. And the less time people have, the more money they tend to spend.

❯ Avoid temptation. Stay away from the stores you tend to spend money in. If you have a particular friend who spends a lot, don't go shopping with her.

❯ Develop constructive emotional outlets. There are many constructive ways to relieve negative feelings, but spending money is not one of them. If you are feeling down, talk to a friend, pick up a *Tehillim* or go for a walk. Don't instinctively head for the mall. Keep in mind that "retail therapy" is therapeutic for retailers, not for customers.

❯ Find alternative recreational activities. You don't have to buy anything in order to have a good time. Instead of associating shopping with leisure and relaxation, condition yourself to see shopping primarily as a functional and task-oriented activity, and plan leisure activities that do not involve any purchases.

❯ Learn to express love and gratitude in non-tangible ways. People who enjoy buying things often ascribe disproportionate value or importance to tangible objects and resort to gift-giving in order to express love and gratitude. But emotions like these are best expressed in words, whether spoken or written. Tangible gifts should be reserved for special occasions; otherwise, they lose their value in the eye of the recipient. Even when you do decide to buy a gift, remember that a gift is only as meaningful as the sentiment underlying it. The amount of money you spend on a gift does not determine its value.

❯ Build a budget that includes an allowance for discretionary spending. If you tend to overspend, then it is doubly important for you to have a clearly defined budget that governs the amount you spend on variable expenditures such as food, clothing, gifts and household items. But in order for you to succeed in sticking to your budget, it is also important that you give yourself some breathing room and allocate some money toward nonessential or impulse purchases. This way, you will not feel stifled by your budget and you will not be tempted to abandon it any time you succumb to the temptation to buy something that is not absolutely necessary. To make sure that you remain accountable to your budget, you should build it together with your spouse or a close friend or relative, and review it together with that person on a regular basis.

4

Debt: The Bleak Business of Borrowing

"A debtor is a servant
to the creditor."

(Mishlei 22:7)

In this chapter:

❯ How to Get Out of Debt | 101

❯ Loans: Not Always a Favor | 104

❯ Son in Debt | 107

❯ Paid Late, Again | 111

❯ The Tuition Conundrum | 115

❯ Climbing a Mountain of Credit Card Debt | 122

How to Get Out of Debt ❯

My wife and I are generally responsible people. We have a pretty good idea of how much we earn and how much we spend. We live within our means, and we are careful not to go into debt.

A number of years ago, however, we decided to give our kitchen a face-lift. We put aside $3,000 to cover the job, which was supposed to be purely cosmetic. The problem was that soon after the work began, we discovered that the kitchen plumbing was in terrible condition and needed to be replaced. Once we had to redo the pipes, most of the old kitchen had to go.

We tried to keep the expense down, but the job ended up costing $14,000. I had no choice but to borrow $11,000 from a friend to cover this unexpected expense.

That loan has been haunting us ever since. Whenever we come up with extra money, we put it toward the loan, but despite all our efforts, we still owe most of the original amount. In the four years since the kitchen renovation, we have never borrowed money, but we just cannot seem to pay down this debt.

Needless to say, I cannot look my friend in the eye anymore. What should we do?

First of all, we commend you for being careful about not going further into debt. Many people who find themselves in a small amount of debt, which they cannot pay back, continue to fall further and further into debt. You have successfully avoided that trap — and that is a remarkable achievement.

You say you have a "pretty good idea" of how much you earn and how much you spend. Were it not for the fact that you owe money, that would be fine, as long as you can make ends meet and pay all your bills.

But as soon you go the slightest amount into the red, approximations are not good enough anymore. If you owe money — regardless of how much you owe — you need to be working with an exact budget.

The first step toward climbing out of debt is coming to an awareness of exactly how much you are earning, exactly what your household expenses amount to and exactly how much money you can set aside every month to repay your debt. Mesila has questionnaires that can help you obtain an accurate picture of your financial situation.

The amount you have left — be it $50 or $500 — to pay down your debt every month is unimportant. What is important is that you know how much you can afford to pay back and that you are working within an orderly, predictable budget.

If you find you have nothing left at the end of the month, you have no choice but to find an additional source of income that will go directly toward covering your debt. This may mean that you and/or your wife take on additional work, or it could mean cutting down on some of your household expenditures and putting aside the extra money toward the loan repayments.

Once you know how much you can realistically afford to pay back every month, calculate how many monthly payments it will take to pay back the remaining debt. You will then have a workable repayment schedule to present to your friend.

If you feel uncomfortable approaching your friend, have a third party do this on your behalf. Hopefully your friend will agree to the repayment schedule. Then all you need to do is stick to it.

Another, less desirable option is to borrow money from a different source to repay the first loan. This should be done only if two conditions are met: (1) You can negotiate repayment that you can afford. And (2): The amount of the loan is equal to the amount you have to pay back. It can't be less, because then you will have to contend with two loans instead of one. It can't be more, because then the extra money will disappear, leaving you in worse debt than before.

Getting out of debt is not easy, especially when it requires you to take on more work or scrimp on things that you consider necessities. But there is no alternative. Living with debt robs people of their peace of mind, destroys their *shalom bayis* and leaves them unable to focus on their *davening* and learning.

We are optimistic that you will be able to pay back this debt within a reasonable amount of time and continue living debt-free. The fact that you are aware of the problem and are actively seeking a solution means you have already taken the first step toward financial stability.

Loans:
Not Always a Favor ❯

A while ago, my brother and sister-in-law started to have financial difficulties. When my brother approached me for a loan, I gladly lent him some money to tide him over. Since then, however, he has approached other family members and gemachim for loans as well, and I see that he is falling further and further into debt.

I don't care if he never pays me back, but I am concerned that he does not realize how dangerous his situation is.

My sister-in-law is terribly alarmed. My brother, on the other hand, does not seem very perturbed. When the electric company and the water company sent notices on the same day that they were going to cut off service, my sister-in-law begged me to convince my brother that taking out another loan was not the answer. I tried to discuss the situation with him, but I got nowhere. Can Mesila help him?

In general, a person who does not want help cannot be helped. Mesila does not offer instant solutions or magic formulas. Instead, we guide people through the often-lengthy process of achieving financial stability. Clients have to be active, willing participants. Mesila therefore cannot help your brother if he does not want help.

We do, however, have some suggestions as to how you and your sister-in-law can help your brother *to want help*. The approach we suggest is "*Smol dochah, yemin mekareves*" — on the one hand, making your brother feel the pinch more acutely, while on the other hand making help available to him.

The first thing you could do is ask a Rav whether you are halachically permitted to discourage people from lending your brother money. If the answer is yes, you should then discreetly approach the family members and *gemachim* who are lending your brother money and tell them that they would be doing him a greater favor by not giving him any more loans. You can also tell anyone who could potentially sign as your brother's guarantor not to do so.

At the same time, you might want to encourage your sister-in-law to adopt an indifferent attitude to the family's finances. Rather than becoming distressed by the bills that need to be paid, she should act as though she is completely unaffected by it.

This advice might sound odd, but it is probably the only way your sister-in-law can get her husband to become more concerned about the situation. As long as she is alarmed, your brother sees no need to be worried. If she turns the tables around and adopts his laissez-faire approach, he will very likely start to feel the pressure.

It will undoubtedly be difficult for your sister-in-law to sit by idly while financial disaster looms. She should know, however, that her indifference can accomplish a lot more than any amount of nagging.

If you and your sister-in-law are successful, your brother will no longer have easy access to money that is not his, and his financial predicament will start weighing more heavily on him.

Once this happens, you can implement the "*yemin mekareves*" aspect of the plan. Arrange for an objective individual whom your brother trusts — not yourself or your sister-in-law — to mention to him that he may be a candidate for Mesila's assistance. At this point, he might just be receptive to the idea. If he, of his own accord, decides to apply to Mesila, there is a very good chance that we might be able to help him.

We Jews are naturally *rachmanim* and *gomlei chassadim* — compassionate and benevolent — and we have an innate desire to help people who are suffering. When people ask us for financial assistance, we automatically reach for our wallets to give or lend them money. While this desire to help is a wonderful thing, it is important that the desire be channeled in a way that is truly helpful.

In certain cases, lending people money can do more harm than good. Repeatedly lending a person money creates a pattern of dependency that reduces the person's motivation to get out of debt and live within his means.

Financial limitations create motivation. If a person feels limited to spending only what he has, he will be motivated to earn money so that he will have what to spend.

But if a person gets used to borrowing money, his sense of financial limitation broadens to include all the money he can potentially borrow. This gives rise to the dangerous illusion that "no matter how much I spend, my brother/ father/friend/etc. will be there to bail me out." As a caring brother, your goal should be to help your brother increase his motivation and accountability so he does not fall further into the trap of debt and dependency.

We encourage all of our readers to consult with *daas Torah* to determine how, when and to whom they should be lending money.

Son in Debt ❯

I have been supporting my married son in kollel for the four years since his wedding.

Shortly after his wedding, my son became involved in commodities trading, and he convinced many of his friends — mostly kollel yungeleit — to invest with him or lend him money to invest. I warned him numerous times against dabbling in what I felt were dangerous investments, and I cautioned him over and over again not to be careless with other people's money. I also told him that I would not bail him out if he got into trouble.

But he knew better, and my words fell on deaf ears.

At the end, the investment was a failure, and my son was left with (he claims) about $150,000 in debts to his friends and various gemachim. The real figure, I suspect, is closer to $250,000. Now he has approached me for help in paying back his creditors.

I, baruch Hashem, own a very successful business, and I can afford to pay back all his debts. But how do I make sure that my son does not get involved in foolish investments again in the future?

The *Gemara* advocates a "*smol dochah, yemin mekareves,* left hand distances, right hand draws near" approach when dealing with children (*Sotah* 47a). Although your son is an adult, we believe that the *smol dochah, yemin mekareves* approach is the appropriate one in your situation as well.

You really have no way of ensuring that your son will not dabble in risky investments again in the future. There is, however, a good way to encourage him to repeat his mistakes in the future. That is by rescuing him now.

The fact that you were emotionally involved beforehand, cautioning your son multiple times against investing irresponsibly, gave him the subconscious message that you will be there to catch him if need be. This is true even though you warned him that you would not bail him out if he got into trouble.

If you reinforce that message now by extricating your son from the mess he got himself into, you will essentially have created a firm safety net that will give him the security of knowing that whatever happens, Papa is there to save him. Rescuing your son financially at this point will position him to repeat his mistakes in the future, possibly with even more disastrous results.

At Mesila, we have been involved in many cases where well-intentioned people tried to save a friend or relative from financial disaster by giving them money, but their intervention ultimately made the situation worse.

True, at this point you are able to cover your son's debts. In the future, however, there is no telling how much financial trouble he might get himself — and others — into. You do not know if you will be able to afford to bail him out in the future, and you therefore cannot afford to set such a precedent now.

To protect yourself, your son and other hapless potential investors, you would be wise to allow your son to suffer the consequences of his own actions, which will force him to learn from his mistakes rather than repeat them. The best way to help people learn responsibility is by giving them the freedom to make their own choices and allowing them to experience the ramifications of those choices.

Forcing him to answer to his creditors is the best way to reduce the likelihood of a similar scenario recurring again in the future.

Of course, as a father, you do not want to see your son suffer, especially because you have the ability to alleviate his suffering. We also understand that your son will not look kindly on this course of action; neither will his friends, who may be shocked at your refusal to cover his losses. Moreover, if this fiasco has become public knowledge, you stand to experience a public backlash for your refusal to repay your son's creditors.

Despite all of this potential embarrassment and discomfort, if you have your son's best interests in mind, you will not intervene at this point.

What we have just described is the *smol dochah* aspect of how you should deal with your son.

As for the *yemin mekareves* aspect, the best way to help your son is to help him find a good financial counselor — possibly a Mesila volunteer — who can work out a plan with him to pay back his debts slowly and independently.

Now is probably not the time to wean your son off your financial support. But to repay his debts, he needs to begin earning money himself so that he will gain an understanding of just how difficult it is to generate income. This will hopefully give him more respect for other people's hard-earned money (including yours).

The financial counselor should be the one to meet with your son's creditors and present the repayment plan. (If the counselor is a

Mesila volunteer, we will make it clear that Mesila's assistance was conditional upon your non-involvement, which will lessen your discomfort.) In our experience, we have found that creditors generally prefer not to take dramatic steps against their debtors and are willing to cooperate if approached correctly.

Eventually, after your son has been sticking faithfully to the plan for a year or two and has paid back a significant portion of the debts, you can reconsider helping him repay the debts — but only under very specific conditions and with the proviso that he still needs to be working with a financial counselor.

In no way should your help be presented as an escape route by which your son can dodge his financial obligations.

Not knowing all the details of your situation, we cannot tell you unequivocally that the course of action we described is correct under your circumstances. Every situation is different, and we recommend that you discuss yours with *daas Torah* and find out whether our recommendations are appropriate for you. We also ask that others do not apply this particular advice to their own circumstances without first seeking individualized financial and Rabbinic guidance.

In general, however, it is important for people to realize that not every financial issue can be resolved with money. Sometimes, giving or lending money to people in need — even if they are close family members — can have disastrous or counterproductive results.

Clearly, it is a tremendous *mitzvah* to help a fellow Jew out of financial difficulty. But before getting involved in a messy financial situation, it is highly advisable to seek professional guidance from Mesila or a similar source.

Paid Late, Again ❭

> I work as a part-time secretary in a small school, and my husband is a rebbi. We have a modest combined income, but we're careful to live within our means. As long as our salaries are paid on time, we manage to finish the month respectably. Unfortunately, though, both the school where I work and the cheder where my husband teaches often pay us late.
>
> Every time a paycheck is delayed, we have to start buying on credit and borrowing money to cover our expenses. When we finally do get paid, we pay all our debts immediately, to ensure that we do not remain in debt. But this is no way to live. Is there any way we can put an end to this cycle?

In general, people who borrow money regularly to cover basic living expenses eventually end up owing more money than they can possibly repay. Debt is like a silent trap that ensnares its victims with a small cash shortfall — and eventually lands them in a vicious cycle of poverty, debt and dependency.

The fact that you and your husband are able to borrow money for living expenses regularly and yet avoid chronic debt indicates that you possess remarkable budgeting abilities and unusual self-discipline.

Nevertheless, it is highly inadvisable to borrow money for living expenses on a continual basis. Once you have gotten used to living off borrowed money — albeit through no fault of your own — you are at high risk for falling into chronic debt.

There are various safeguards you can implement that will help you maintain your financial stability. These steps can spare you the unpleasantness of constantly worrying about whether your next paycheck will arrive on time.

1. Create your own gemach.

This safeguard is the ideal solution to your predicament. It involves creating a fund from which you and your husband can draw "salaries" in the event that your paychecks are delayed. Optimally, the size of this fund should reflect the maximum length of time you and your husband can conceivably go without getting paid.

Try to come up with a worst-case scenario. Let's say, for example, that the longest you ever waited for a paycheck was three months and the longest your husband ever waited was one month. That means your fund should, if possible, be large enough to cover your paycheck for at least three months plus your husband's for at least a month.

How do you go about actually creating this fund? Unless you have some investments you can liquidate quickly, the fund will not materialize overnight. You will have to build it slowly, penny by penny.

While building the fund, try to save every bit you can by reducing your expenditures to the barest minimum. Every time you receive some unexpected cash, put it aside for the fund. You can even ask your Rav if you can use *maaser* money for this purpose.

You do not have to wait until your fund reaches its optimal size to begin enjoying it. As soon as your fund has any amount of money in it, you can start using it to pay your salary, or at least part of your salary, whenever a paycheck is delayed.

However, make sure that you use the fund only for its intended purpose — tiding you over until you receive your paycheck — and that you replenish it as soon as you are paid. Also, never withdraw more than the amount of your salary during any given month.

You should treat every penny you withdraw from the fund as a loan that becomes due the minute you receive your next paycheck. Consider the fund your own personal *gemach* — a peace-of-mind *gemach*, if you will.

If you are unable to put aside enough money to establish this fund, there is another option.

2. Borrow wisely.

Rather than buying on credit or borrowing small sums from several different sources, borrow one lump sum without interest from a *gemach*, family member or friend. It is always preferable to owe a relatively large, but stable, amount of money to one person, than to continually accrue numerous small, volatile debts that are difficult to keep track of.

The amount you borrow should be equivalent to the amount of the delayed paycheck. This way, you can use your paycheck as a form of collateral. You can also repay the loan as soon as you receive your paycheck, since you will have exactly the amount of money necessary to repay the loan.

3. Find a "loan supervisor."

Because borrowing is a dangerously habit-forming practice, we suggest that you find yourself a "loan supervisor." This person could be a sibling, friend, *rebbi* or Mesila counselor, and his or her role is to help ensure that you repay your loans on time and do not slip into chronic debt.

Using other people's money is a serious matter. That's why we believe loans should be subject to supervision. The level of supervision depends on the strength of your self-discipline, but it is always preferable that the supervisor be the one who actually arranges and repays the loan on your behalf.

By implementing the above safeguards, you and your husband should be able to avoid much of the unpleasantness that late paychecks entail.

Of course, these safeguards do not address the root of the problem: the fact that you are often paid late. You need not accept this as a given.

It may be time to consider other employment options, and when you do, count the late-payment issue as a drawback of your current job. You may decide that you would be better off working at jobs that pay less but pay on time.

The Tuition Conundrum ❯

I worked as a rebbi in a yeshivah with a small-class environment for weaker boys. It had trouble meeting its budget. When I was hired, I was told that there was money for the first two years. I was paid on time for the first seven months. But for the next three months I wasn't paid at all. I returned the next year and was told we would start a new cheshbon and leave the old debt for later. Again, I was paid for six months, and that was it. The yeshivah now owes me over $20,000.

The administrator's answer to my many requests is that his responsibility right now is to keep the yeshivah running, and that one day Hashem will help. It is very unpleasant to take such an individual to a din Torah since his motivations are really l'shem Shamayim, and it is also doubtful that a beis din can enforce collection. I am carrying this debt on my credit cards at high percentages, and I really do need the money.

I know many mechanchim in similar situations, and I would appreciate any advice you can offer.

Before we discuss your individual circumstances, we would like to address the point you raise about many *mechanchim* being in situations similar to yours.

It is a disgrace that so many of *Klal Yisrael's chinuch* institutions are unable to pay their employees on time or at all. Isn't it a shame that our *rebbe'im* and teachers cannot concentrate properly on educating our children because they have to cope with financial stress and uncertainty?

True, there are some people who really cannot afford to pay full tuition. But there are many others who would be able to afford their children's tuition if they wanted to. These are the people who can afford vacations, new cars, home renovations, domestic help and designer clothing — but not tuition. It's all a matter of priorities.

Harav Avraham Yehoshua Heschel, the Kopyczynitzer Rebbe, *zy"a,* fled Europe shortly before the outbreak of World War II. The day after he arrived in the United States, he brought his two sons to *cheder* and began discussing tuition with the principal. The principal was quick to assure him that he would receive a discount. But the Rebbe, who was penniless at the time, insisted on paying the full amount.

How could the Rebbe promise to pay in full if he had no money, no property and no source of income? The answer is that to him, tuition was a priority. And when something is a priority, you find a way to pay for it.

Chazal tell us that every person is allotted his annual income at the beginning of the year (*Beitzah* 16a). The only expenses that do not go into that allotment are Shabbos, Yom Tov and *sechar limmud* expenditures.

All through the generations, Jews have exhibited extraordinary *mesirus nefesh* to pay *sechar limmud.* If people nowadays would realize that their *sechar limmud* expenses come with a reimbursement guarantee, perhaps they would be more eager to fulfill their tuition obligations.

In many schools, parents who request scholarships are asked to fill out income and expense reports for review by the school's tuition or scholarship committee. Members of these committees have told Mesila that they routinely review scholarship applications from people who earn respectable incomes and maintain a high standard of living yet beg poverty when it comes to paying tuition.

Obviously, there will always be some individuals who need and are entitled to scholarships. But if fewer people would receive scholarships, tuition costs could be reduced significantly, which would in turn enable more people to pay full tuition.

If yeshivos and schools would not have to supply so many scholarships, they could concentrate less on fundraising and more on enhancing their operations. So many *mosdos* are financially mismanaged because their administrators are too busy raising funds to think about implementing cost-cutting measures. Think of the gargantuan efforts that go into coordinating costly annual dinners, parlor meetings, teas and Chinese auctions. Wouldn't it be nice if these efforts could be redirected into the *chinuch* of our children?

If the pressure of fundraising would be alleviated, administrators could focus on running their *mosdos* efficiently, like businesses. This would also help bring down tuition costs.

All this being said, administrators of yeshivos and schools are directly responsible for meeting their payrolls, regardless of whether parents are paying tuition. If fundraising is necessary, then it has to be done.

Yeshivos and schools that cater to weaker students or students with special needs have no choice but to set up an effective fundraising apparatus, since it is not realistic to expect tuition payments to cover the enormous costs associated with the high staff-to-student ratio typical of these institutions.

For an administrator to tell a staff member, "Hashem will help," is nothing but a copout, a classic example of using misplaced *bitachon* as an excuse for shirking responsibility. Considering the many obstacles to successful *chinuch* today, it is obvious that *chinuch* institutions need a great deal of *siyatta diShmaya*. Scrupulous observance of the *mitzvos* of paying workers on time — *Devarim* 24:15 and *Vayikra* 19:13 — is surely an excellent way for *chinuch* institutions to merit this much-needed *siyatta diShmaya*.

Meanwhile, *mechanchim* who find themselves in this situation have to ensure that they maintain control over their finances.

The profession you have chosen, *chinuch*, is a noble profession indeed. Your work is *avodas hakodesh*, and you are cementing the future of *Klal Yisrael* by molding the minds and hearts of the young generation.

As a *rebbi*, you are one of the *matzdikei harrabim* (*Bava Basra* 8b). And as such, you are promised a lofty place in *Olam Haba*.

While the field of *chinuch* is an exceptionally rewarding one, the rewards tend to be mainly in the next world. In this world, *mechanchim* do not receive the respect, admiration and compensation they deserve — and they are often compensated late.

So, even as you reap your eternal rewards, you have to contend with the hazards of the profession.

Every profession has its risks: A construction worker risks being injured on a job site; a computer programmer risks being rendered obsolete by a new technology; and a doctor risks being sued for malpractice. Those who enter the field of *chinuch* risk not being paid on time, especially if the work is at a non-mainstream yeshivah.

When a person takes a job as a *mechanech* — or any other job, for that matter — he has to do whatever he can to minimize the risks involved. If you know that the yeshivah you work for has trouble meeting its budget, then you have to prepare yourself for the possibility that you will not be paid on time. This requires you to set aside enough money to cover your salary for several months.

It would also be a good idea for you to talk frankly with the administrator and ask him for a commitment to pay your monthly salary, or at least a portion of it, within a certain amount of time after it is due. You can be sympathetic to his situation, but you can also make clear that you need some form of guarantee that you will have food to put on the table and that your salary will not be delayed indefinitely.

As for the money you are owed, you should not be embarrassed to continually pester the administrator, the board of directors and anyone else who wields power in the yeshivah. They have an obligation to pay you, but if they are not fulfilling their obligation, then it becomes your responsibility to see to it that you are paid. Demanding wages is not demeaning; withholding wages is.

Should you take the yeshivah's administrator to a *din Torah*? That is not a financial question, but a *hashkafah* question that should be discussed with someone who represents *daas Torah*. Whether or not you go to *beis din*, you should check with a Rav to determine what forms of pressure you are halachically permitted to impose on the administrator and the yeshivah.

With regard to the $20,000 you now owe to credit card companies, we recommend that you move the debt off your credit cards immediately. Credit card debt bears exorbitant interest, and people who carry debt on their credit cards all too often find themselves sliding further and further down the slippery slope of debt.

Besides their high interest rates, credit cards also make it easy to borrow money — so easy, in fact, that people often do not even realize that they have borrowed money at all.

The hassle and discomfort involved in approaching people to borrow money are actually a good thing, because they act as a safeguard against accumulating further debts. That is why we would prefer to see you asking outright for a loan rather than continuing to carry debt on your credit cards. Borrow from a *gemach*, from friends or relatives, or even the bank — just get rid of your credit card debt.

In general, Mesila recommends that people use cash or debit cards rather than credit cards. Credit cards perpetuate the illusion that you can spend money you don't have; instead of feeling the pinch as soon as you buy something, you postpone the agony to a time when the sweet taste of your new purchase is gone.

Once the debt is off your credit cards, you are under somewhat less pressure to pay it back. You can then sit down and think about your employment options. Can you find a position at a different yeshivah that has a more stable payment history? Can you supplement your income by taking on a side job?

At Mesila, we discourage people from leaving their jobs unless they have a dependable, alternative source of income. Every job has its pros and cons, and you never know if you will be happier, overall, somewhere else. If you do decide to stay at your job, however, you will have to plan your budget to accommodate the vicissitudes of your salary. (Incidentally, make sure that paying your children's tuition is a priority budget item.)

When you choose a profession, you have to know that you are able to live within the means that the vocation provides. In the case of the *chinuch* profession, that might mean that you have to live within a very modest budget — especially if your paycheck is not reliable. And whoever's fault that might be, at the end of the day, you alone are responsible for feeding your family, and you alone are responsible for repaying the debts you have incurred.

We are not downplaying the severity of your predicament. You are facing a difficult *nisayon* with no easy solutions. Nevertheless, we are confident that if the *Ribbono shel Olam* put you into this situation, He has also given you the tools to cope with it.

May you merit the *siyatta diShmaya* to extricate yourself from your financial difficulties, and may you see continued *hatzlachah* in your work cultivating *yiddishe neshamos*.

Climbing a Mountain of Credit Card Debt ❱

I know Mesila is against using credit cards, but I have found that it is difficult for me to keep the right amounts of cash on hand, and I often resort to paying with plastic. As a result, I've built up a bit of a balance on my credit card — or cards, I should say — and I'm wondering if you have any advice on how I can pay it off.

Mesila is not, in principle, opposed to credit cards, nor do we consider cash the preferred payment method in all situations. One of Mesila's guiding principles is to promote financial management principles and attitudes that are universally relevant, while avoiding specific tips and suggestions. So rather than issuing a blanket statement regarding whether or not you should be using credit cards, we will share several general guidelines that should help you decide for yourself.

Credit cards can be a very useful and convenient tool, when used correctly. The trouble is that many people misuse their credit cards by charging more than they can afford each month. Credit card companies actually rely on people misusing their cards; in fact, interest charged on outstanding balances represents the primary source of revenue for credit card companies. In 2007, people in the United States who carried a monthly balance paid $18.1 billion in penalty fees. With annual earnings of about $30 billion, the credit card industry is among the most profitable in the United States.

There are many advantages to using credit cards. You never run of out money. You are generally insured against theft, and you can easily cancel the card if you lose it. In contrast, cash that is lost or stolen is usually gone forever. You can use your credit card to pay for purchases by telephone or online, rather than mailing a check or paying by cash in person. Most credit cards can be used anywhere in the world, regardless of the local currency, and you can order cards for all your family members. Depending on the card-issuer's policy, purchases made using the card may be protected against theft, loss or accidental damage that occurs within a certain period of time.

Credit card statements make it relatively straightforward to track your purchases on a monthly basis and keep a record of how your money is being spent. Cash, on the other hand, has no paper trail, and it is difficult to remember exactly where the money in your wallet went.

We will point out that all of these advantages are available through bank or debit cards as well, although purchase protection may not be offered on certain debit cards. The big difference, however, is that these cards draw on money that is already in your bank account, rather than creating a de facto debt that has to be paid at the end of the billing cycle. The only feature credit cards offer that debit cards do not usually have is the possibility of earning rewards, in the form of airline miles, cash-back offers or other perks.

So much for the advantages of using credit cards. Now let's talk about the drawbacks. The first drawback is that credit cards make it deceptively easy to spend money, whether or not you have it. The act of swiping a credit card is not nearly as painful as taking actual money out of your wallet, and the psychological deterrent to parting with your money is therefore lessened considerably when paying with a credit card.

Studies show that people spend about 30% more when paying by credit card than when paying with cash. We think it is fair to assume that the extra 30% is money that could have been put to better use.

The other major drawback to credit cards is that they are a form of loan. When you take a loan, you borrow money and commit to repaying it at a later date. When you use a credit card, you also borrow money — but without realizing it. Mesila's philosophy is that a loan in which you realize that you are borrowing money is preferable to a loan in which you do not realize you are borrowing money, simply because you are less likely to borrow, and more likely to repay, when the decision to take the loan was a conscious one.

Credit card debt is one of the worst forms of debt, for two reasons. One, it usually carries very high interest rates. Two, there is no repayment deadline for the debt. As long as you keep making minimum payments, credit card companies are quite happy to keep tacking interest onto your balance and let your debt swell to ever-greater proportions.

Unpleasant as it may be to have creditors breathing down your back, it is a far healthier situation when a debt is collected at the end of its term than when a debt is allowed to balloon endlessly.

Not only do credit cards charge high interest, but there is very little limit as to how much they can raise your rate. Credit card companies are legally allowed to monitor your credit report, and should you make a late payment on a loan, a different credit card, or a utility bill, your interest rates can be increased dramatically, even if you have never missed a payment on that particular card. There are a number of other reasons you may see your rates spike. These include bouncing a check, exceeding your credit limit, having too much debt or credit, getting a new credit card and applying for an auto loan or mortgage.

Because credit card debt is so dangerous, our advice is that the only people who should use credit cards are those who:

(a) can rein in their spending despite the painless convenience of plastic and

(b) pay their balance in full every month consistently. People who swipe their cards without giving it the same thought they would when spending cash are better off spending cash, unless they are paying for something that they cannot possibly be spending more for by using a credit card (dental work, for instance, or a utility bill). And people who carry over a balance on their credit cards, even occasionally, should probably avoid using credit cards completely.

If you are able to use a credit card correctly, there are a couple of things we recommend:

Choose the right card.

Make sure your card provides a grace period of at least twenty days from the date of purchase until payment is due. Without a grace period, you'll be charged interest before you even get your bill.

There are cards that offer airline miles, cash back on purchases and points for rewards programs, and if you are using a credit card, you might as well get something in return. However, if there is an annual fee associated with your rewards card, make sure the benefits outweigh the cost.

Don't have too many cards.

Keeping track of even one credit card can be quite a challenge. When keeping track of two or more cards, mistakes (such as missed payments or forgetting to cancel the card before annual fees kick in) are more likely to go by unnoticed. Unless you have a very good reason for keeping a second or third credit card, get rid of it.

But what if you have already fallen into credit card debt? Here are some suggestions for climbing out of the morass.

Ask for clemency.

If you missed only one payment, you can call your credit card company and ask them to waive interest and late fees. Credit card companies will waive these fees on occasion, if you generally pay on time.

Stop using your credit cards.

If you're already behind on your monthly payments, don't aggravate the situation by accumulating more credit card debt. Although this may seem obvious, it is actually the opposite of how people generally work. The tendency is that once people owe money, they lose a major psychological deterrent toward borrowing, and they let their debt slowly inflate. ("What's the difference if I owe $600 or $900?" "If I already owe $60,000, another $5,000 won't make any difference.") Cut your losses now, and don't allow yourself to charge even one additional item.

Take out a loan to pay off your credit card debt.

Almost any type of loan is preferable to credit card debt because interest rates are generally much lower and there is a specific repayment timeframe. With a loan, you can work out repayment terms that reflect your ability to repay, which helps you discipline yourself to put aside a fixed sum every month for debt repayment. With credit card debt, there is no such discipline, since there is no obligation to repay anything more than the minimum payment.

Do a balance transfer to another card.

While you will pay a fee, transferring your outstanding balance to a card with a lower interest rate will decrease the amount you carry from month to month. By doing a balance transfer instead of allowing interest fees to build up, you give yourself some breathing room to pay off your debt. But beware — this is a very stopgap measure. You can't keep doing balance transfers for very long since there are only so many transfers credit card companies will allow you to do. Besides, multiple balance transfers will cause your finances to become chaotic.

Find a card with a low interest rate.

Some credit cards offer relatively low interest rates. Shopping around for a better rate than the one you currently have can save you hundreds or even thousands of dollars a month (that is, if your credit rating is good enough for you to be eligible for these offers). Look out, however, for introductory offers that end after several months or exclusions that limit the low rate to new purchases only.

Negotiate a better interest rate.

You might have to spend a long time on the phone with your credit card company, but it's worth it to get your interest rate reduced by even a few points. If possible, ask your company to match another company's offer. If your company is unwilling to cooperate, you can mention that you may be forced to declare personal bankruptcy, if that is really an option. This gets the companies scared, because they are the ones who stand to lose from a bankruptcy.

Never, ever miss a minimum payment.

Missing minimum payments is a big no-no. This can severely damage your credit rating. Having a good credit rating is important because many types of creditors, besides credit card companies — including utilities, hospitals, landlords, insurance companies and banks — can report delinquent payments to credit bureaus, as well as access your credit history.

Since credit card companies are among those monitoring and contributing to customers' credit reports, a late or missed payment on one charge account could cause your rates and fees to increase on a completely separate account — even your car insurance premiums.

Pay off credit card balances from smallest to largest.

The smallest debts are the easiest to pay off. Clearing them out of the way helps you make the fastest progress toward getting your finances in order. The fewer debts you have to pay back, the easier it will be to see the light at the end of the tunnel, and the more motivated you will be to tackle the larger, scarier debts.

Make micro-payments.

In addition to the minimum payments, send in whatever small amounts you can to gradually pay off your balance.

Get professional debt-counseling assistance.

Climbing a mountain of credit card debt can be a very tough task to tackle alone. If there is a Mesila branch in your community, we encourage you to apply for our family counseling program. If there is no Mesila branch in your community, seek the guidance of a qualified debt counselor.

**For more on debt,
see also:**

"A Tale of Two Incomes" Chapter 2
"Tackling Financial Problems – as a Team" Chapter 10

5

Planning for the Future: Savings and Investments

"Saving is not something
you do when you have
extra money.
There is no such thing as
'extra' money."

("Saving: The Long and Short of It")

In this chapter:

❯ Savings: The Short and Long of It | 133

❯ Kollel and Planning Ahead | 141

❯ Exploring Your Investment Options | 145

❯ The Myth of Guaranteed Returns | 150

❯ Compensation | 154

❯ Making Millions on Dinars | 158

❯ Red Flags Ahead | 161

Savings: The Long and Short of it ❯

I earn a respectable income, and I am able to support my family adequately, baruch Hashem. We live relatively simply, and I don't think we waste money on unnecessary purchases.

The problem is that we can't seem to put anything aside for the future. Aside from our mortgage, we are not in debt, but we have no savings to speak of and we never have any extra money to put away for savings.

This worries me tremendously. I know I should be saving up for retirement and other future needs, but frankly, saving money just seems like an impossible goal. Do you have any ideas for me?

The first step toward successfully saving for the future is appreciating the value and importance of savings. Since you clearly do understand the need for savings, we think a bit of guidance is all you need to begin.

The Maharsha states in *Chiddushei Aggados* that a person should put aside money for his old age (*Niddah* 65b). In his *Responsa Shevet Halevi*, Rav Shmuel Wosner writes, "It is obvious that [for] something that is the nature of the world, such as old age or marrying off children ... it is a *mitzvah* to prepare in advance so that he will not become dependent on others" (4:1).

Clearly, then, it is incumbent upon every Jewish family to plan for their financial future.

How to Start Saving

Like you, many people tell Mesila that they are barely managing financially — or not managing at all — and so cannot even begin to think about saving. But saving is not something you do when you have extra money. There is no such thing as "extra" money; no matter how much money a person has, there are always demands made on that money.

Saving is simply a habit. It is a habit that comes naturally for some people and has to be learned by others.

How does one get into the habit of saving? Here are some pointers:

❯ *Start small.* Put aside your pocket change at the end of the day, put aside $10 a week, or put aside 5% of your monthly paycheck — just save something. *Prutah liprutah mitztarefes* — if you save consistently, the amounts will eventually add up.

More importantly, saving small amounts regularly will get you into the habit of saving in a way that is almost painless.

❯ *Save now.* You will always have good reasons not to save. Don't let these good reasons stop you from putting away at least something. (A caveat to this pointer: If you are carrying high-interest debt — credit card debt, for instance — your priority should be debt repayment and not savings. A balance on your credit card might cost you 18% interest — and that's a lot more than you'll earn on most savings plans or investments.)

❯ *Save your windfalls.* Any time unexpected money comes your way — in the form of product rebates, tax refunds, gifts or similar —

immediately put at least a portion of it toward savings.

❯ *Make savings automatic.* You can set up a savings plan that will withdraw a certain amount of money from your bank account every month, or you can arrange for a portion of your paycheck to go directly toward savings. This way, you barely feel the pinch.

❯ *Pay yourself first.* The first expense that comes off your paycheck should be your savings. Too many people say they will save what is left at the end of the month. Those are the people who never manage to save anything.

❯ *Make it a team effort.* Both husband and wife — and possibly children as well, depending on their ages — need to be actively involved in the savings habit in order for it to work.

❯ *Watch where the money goes.* People who keep track of where their money goes end up spending less and saving more. Knowing how you are spending your money gives you more control over your expenditures and helps you make better spending decisions. This leaves you with more money to save. It also gives you the freedom to decide how to use your money, rather than allowing spending pressures to dictate where your money goes.

Once you have decided to start saving, the next step is to decide what to do with your savings. There are two important categories of savings: short-term and long-term. Each of these requires a different strategy.

Short-Term Savings

This is the money you'll need for emergencies and for foreseeable large expenses.

Everyone needs some short-term savings. If you don't have any short-term savings, even minor financial setbacks can have disastrous results. A burst pipe, or even something as predictable as summer camp, can land you in debt or force you to sell or forfeit some of your assets. You would not want to lose your house or your car because you are temporarily unable to make the payments.

Short-term savings can earn enough interest to keep up with inflation, but it will never yield the high returns associated with higher-risk investments. When choosing a home for your short-term savings, your primary considerations should be accessibility, liquidity and safety of principal.

You need to keep your short-term savings in a place that is accessible enough to dip into in a time of real need, yet it should not be accessible enough that you can use it any time you run out of cash. We recommend that you put your short-term savings in a separate bank account, in a trustworthy *gemach* or in very low-risk investments, such as money-market accounts, money-market funds, certificates of deposit, high-interest savings accounts (available at certain banks and financial institutions) or Treasury bonds.

Each of these options has its pros and cons, but all of them are relatively safe, relatively liquid (easy to convert to cash), and earn relatively low interest.

Your should not put your short-term savings in higher-risk investments such as stocks, commodities or real estate.

How much money should you keep in short-term savings? That depends on your situation and your family's needs. Financial professionals usually recommend setting aside at least three months' worth of living expenses to tide you over in the event of an emergency or temporary unemployment or disability.

Aside from this emergency fund, you should also save for expenses looming on the horizon: your annual car insurance bill, the sputtering refrigerator that will need to be replaced soon, your son's bar mitzvah and so on. These expenses are all predictable, and you have two choices of how to pay for them: save up money and earn inter-est, or borrow the money and pay interest (at a much higher rate).

Long-Term Savings

Long-term savings is the money you'll need for times of consider-able financial strain, such as marrying off children and old age.

When choosing a home for your long-term savings, remember that inflation reduces the value of your money by about 3% a year. By keeping your long-term savings under your mattress, you actually lose money. It is therefore important to put your money in a place where it will earn respectable returns.

That is why the term "investing" is used much more with regard to long-term savings than with regard to short-term savings.

With long-term savings, you have the opportunity to let your investments earn compound interest (interest on interest), which effortlessly multiplies your investment. But compound interest needs time to work its magic.

To illustrate: If you save $2,000 a year for forty years (a total savings of $80,000) and earn interest of 8% annually, you will have $559,562 by the time you are finished. If you save $2,000 a year for thirty years (a total savings of $60,000) at the same interest rate of 8%, you will end up with $244,692 — less than half. (For comparison's sake, saving the same amount at an interest rate of 5% would give you $253,680 after forty years and $139,522 after thirty years.)

Here's another example. Let's say you want to save about $50,000 for your son's wedding. If your son is a newborn, you need to save $100 a month at 8% for eighteen years (a total savings of $21,600) to have that amount. If your son is thirteen, you will need to save $430 a month for seven years at 8% (a total savings of $36,120) to have that same $50,000 by the time he will turn twenty.

People in their twenties don't usually think much about marrying off their children or about their retirement, but if they would, they would reap the rewards later. When you are young, you can invest relatively little and wind up with far more money than someone older who saves much more.

The simplest way to start saving for retirement is to sign up for your employer's pension plan, known as a 401(k) in the United States. If this is not an option, you should speak to a financial adviser about starting your own tax-deferred savings plan (known as an IRA in the United States).

People in Israel should note that pensions have been made mandatory for most workers; speak to your employer. If you are self-employed, talk to an insurance agent who specializes in pension planning.

Putting money into stocks and stock funds — a terrible idea for short-term savings — is actually a very good idea for long-term savings. The stock market is notorious for its volatility, but over the past eighty years it has yielded an average return of about 10% — higher than any other type of investment.

Another advantage of the stock market is that you have the option of investing even minimal amounts. Even if you cannot afford to put away a lot of money, you can still enjoy the long-term benefits of stock market investments.

Higher returns like those associated with the stock market usually involve higher risks. When you are investing for the long term, however, you are able to accept more risk. Since time is on your side, you have the ability to ride out the ups and downs of the economy without being affected every time the market takes a hit.

When investing in the stock market, we strongly discourage active investing or day trading. The approach we advocate is "buy and hold," in which you allow your portfolio to grow over time without selling or exchanging specific investments.

To minimize your risks, it is important to maintain a diversified investment portfolio. This is in keeping with *Chazal's* advice to keep a third of your assets in real estate, a third in merchandise and a third liquid (*Bava Metzia* 42b). (The "third liquid" was discussed in the short-term savings section.)

Diversification ensures that your financial future is not dependent on the performance of any one investment. Mutual funds (including index funds and retirement funds) are a common type of diversified investment, although not all mutual funds are created equal.

A good investment portfolio contains a mixture of stocks, bonds and real estate investments. The exact mixture should be determined based on your level of risk tolerance, which depends on factors such as your present financial situation, your future financial goals, and the age and number of your dependents. We recommend that you work with a licensed financial adviser to decide what types of investments are appropriate for you.

As you approach the time when you are going to need to withdraw money from long-term savings, financial experts recommend that you shift some of your holdings into bonds, which are considered less profitable but also less volatile than stocks.

In this way, you are protected if the stock market suddenly crashes just before you need to dip into your savings.

In comparison to stocks and bonds, certain real estate and business investments require a much larger initial outlay and a far more sophisticated investment strategy. Novice investors should steer clear of these types of investments, which necessitate professional evaluation, extensive research, a thorough understanding of the market, and a high level of risk tolerance.

Once you have started a long-term savings plan, stick with it. There will always be new investment possibilities on the horizon that sound more exciting and promise higher returns, but in the end, the simple, steady and boring usually outperforms the new, exciting and lucrative.

It's never too late — or too early — to start saving for the future. The key is to determine what your savings goals are, and to start — today!

Kollel and Planning Ahead ❯

I have been sitting and learning for several years (since my wedding), and my wife is the breadwinner in the family. We have two children, ages 1 and 3, and we live very modestly. Baruch Hashem we have enough to live on for now, and we prefer not to think too much about the future. We have bitachon that we will continue to manage financially, just as we have until now.

Recently, however, we learned of a very promising investment possibility that offers returns of about 10%. We consulted with two independent financial experts who are familiar with this particular investment. Both were of the opinion that the investment is a sound one and carries relatively low risk.

We own our house, and we are considering taking out a home-equity loan so we can put some money into this investment. Our house is located in a very desirable neighborhood, and if the investment doesn't work out, we would be willing to sell our house and buy an equivalent property in a much cheaper area.

I know that Mesila is against risk, so I was wondering if you would oppose this course of action.

We at Mesila are not, in principle, opposed to risk. Without risk, you cannot earn money, and it is therefore important for every person to take certain risks.

Entering the workforce involves risk (you might not be successful in your job, your employer might not pay you on time); opening a business involves risk (customers might not pay you, competitors might run you into the ground); and investing money involves risk (the investment might fail, you might need the money sooner than it is available). For every person, there is an appropriate level of risk, and we actually encourage people to take the risks that are right for them.

There are two types of risk Mesila is against:

1.   *Risk you cannot afford.* When taking any sort of risk, you have to be able to accept the possible adverse consequences. That means that you have to figure out what the worst-case scenario is and decide whether you are willing to live with the possible consequences. If not, you should not be taking the risk.

2.   *Risk you do not understand.* Even if you can afford the risk and are willing to live with the worst-case scenario, it is foolish to take a risk that you cannot think through and evaluate.

When you understand and accept the risk involved in a certain endeavor, you can take steps to minimize the risk and diminish the amount of disappointment and frustration you will likely experience if things do not work out. On the other hand, if you take a risk that you do not understand, you have no way of protecting yourself financially or emotionally.

You are correct in your assumption that Mesila would usually not advise a low-income *kollel* family to borrow against their home to invest. On the chance that the investment fails, the family would probably be unable to repay the loan and would lose their home. This is a risk most *kollel* families cannot afford.

Your situation is different, however. You can afford the risk of the investment you describe because the worst-case scenario — selling your home and moving to a cheaper neighborhood — is one you are able to accept and live with. And it appears that you understand the risks of the particular investment you are considering, since you have behaved with due diligence by consulting with professionals.

We therefore believe that in your specific circumstances, it would be acceptable to take out a home-equity loan and put the money into the investment you are considering. This type of risk is calculated, not irresponsible, and it is the type of risk we approve of.

Obviously, borrowing money to invest is only justified if the investment offers you a significantly higher rate of return than the home-equity loan you are taking.

Before investing, we urge you to make sure that everything is done legally and above board, with written documentation of all transactions. As long as you take the necessary precautions, we are not in any way opposed to your proceeding with the investment.

Actually, what we are opposed to is the laissez-faire attitude you seem to have adopted toward your financial future. Has a Rav or Rebbe advised you against planning ahead financially?

Mesila believes that unless you have received explicit guidance from *daas Torah* not to plan ahead financially, you should be thinking about and planning your financial future.

"If you fail to plan, you plan to fail," the saying goes. Lack of financial planning means decisions are made by default, rather than proactively. And running your finances by default almost inevitably results in a constant struggle to make ends meet, inability to save and tension in the home.

Many people make the mistake of assuming that planning their financial future reflects a lack of *bitachon*. As we have noted elsewhere, *bitachon* and correct financial management are not mutually exclusive. *Bitachon* does not mean burying your head in the sand, and it is not an excuse for neglecting your obligation to ensure that you remain financially independent.

Financial independence is indisputably a Torah value. Every time we recite *Birkas Hamazon*, we ask, "Do not make us in need of the gifts of human beings or their loans." The *Gemara* also cautions against becoming financially dependent on people (*Shabbos* 118a). And in his *sefer Shevet Halevi*, Harav Shmuel Halevi Wosner, writes, "It is obvious that [for] something that is the nature of the world ... it is a mitzvah to prepare in advance so that he will not become dependent on others" (4:1).

Every person needs to take steps to avoid having to borrow or take money from others — and that requires financial planning.

Right now, your income is sufficient to cover your needs, you own your home, you have a promising investment at your fingertips — and you are able to devote your day to Torah study. Your lot is truly enviable, and you are in an excellent position to plan your financial future.

We strongly recommend that you discuss your situation with *daas Torah* and receive clear guidelines on how to do this.

Exploring Your Investment Options ❯

I recently acquired a substantial sum of money, and I would like to invest it in the most worthwhile manner. These are the options I am considering, along with some of the pros and cons:

1) Putting the money in a bank, where it will earn very little interest.

2) Buying a residential property to rent out. The return we would get from rent is probably relatively low, and there is always the possibility of falling in with a bad tenant.

3) Buying a business or purchasing office space to rent out. The possible returns are quite high, but it would involve opening a registered business or corporation.

4) Investing the money in the stock market, where there is potential for huge profits — and huge losses.

I am in kollel and my wife works, so we do not have much time to be busy with whatever investment we choose. Given our circumstances, which do you think is the best option for us?

We commend you for the responsible way in which you are approaching this. Often people who come by a large amount of money squander it by investing hastily — without proper planning, without seeking advice and without fully understanding the risks of the investments they choose.

You seem to have a good grasp of the potential returns and risks of each of the four investments you mention. Apparently, you have done your research in investigating your investment options. We would like to know, however, how you settled upon these four options, and why you ruled out the many other investment opportunities that exist.

Mesila strongly recommends that anyone looking to invest money should first consult with a qualified financial adviser. An adviser can assess your personal financial situation and determine your risk tolerance. When recommending investments, a good financial adviser will take into consideration such factors as age, family status, total assets and short- and long-term financial goals. He or she will also alert you to the possible tax implications of various investments.

Without a comprehensive picture of your individual circumstances, it is impossible for anyone to recommend a specific investment. What we can do, however, is evaluate each of the options you have presented to give you a clearer picture of how to proceed.

Bank Investments

The insignificant risks associated with bank investments make these the safest investments available. Because the risks are so low, the returns are also very low, occasionally lower than the rate of inflation. Bank investments are suitable for people with no risk tolerance or for people who require immediate liquidity.

Residential Real Estate

There are two types of potential earnings from residential real estate investments: regular income in the form of rent and capital gains in the form of rising property value.

The returns from a residential lease are highly variable, mostly depending on the location and desirability of the property. As you noted, however, residential leases generally offer a relatively low investment return, especially considering that landlords absorb many hidden costs — maintenance, repairs, property tax and depreciation, to name a few. Property management also involves time and headaches — unless you hire a property manager, which further eats away at your rental income.

The other way people make money from residential real estate investments is by buying and holding onto a property until it increases in value. They then sell it at a profit. This type of investment has the potential for significant capital gains, but it also carries the risk of potential losses if the market value of the property drops.

Currently, property values are very high in many parts of the world. Although the real estate market has recently dropped in some places, it has not weakened to the point where bargains are readily available.

Commercial Investments

Under this option, you include buying a business and purchasing office space to rent out. These are actually two distinct options, so we will address them separately.

As a rule, business and *kollel* are mutually exclusive endeavors. Buying a business usually entails becoming involved in management and operations. Unless you are willing to devote a large portion of your time and energies to tending to your business, we would not advise you to go this route. *Chazal* say that one of the best ways to lose your money is to hire workers and leave them unsupervised (*Bava Metzia* 29b, *Chullin* 84b).

In contrast, buying commercial property for lease does not necessarily involve a significant time commitment. If you have the potential of high returns on such an investment, we see no reason why you should not consider this possibility. The fact that it would involve opening a registered business or corporation should not pose a problem; all it means is that you need to hire a good accountant who can guide you through the process.

If you are concerned about having to pay corporate taxes, you should discuss that with an accountant as well. Fear of paying taxes should not be a deterrent to pursing a *parnassah*. Generally, you will not have to pay a lot of taxes unless you have a lot of income — especially if you have children and are eligible for child tax-credits.

Remember: Having to pay taxes is a good sign. It means that you are earning money.

The Stock Market

You write that the stock market has potential for huge profits and huge losses. That is certainly true. Good investors, however, usually do not accrue huge profits or huge losses. They avoid the temptation of day trading and speculation. Instead, they build a diversified portfolio and watch their money grow over time.

While the stock market fluctuates wildly in the short term, it has historically risen consistently in the long term. Time and patience are therefore the keys to successful stock market investing.

As the saying goes, "Bulls make money, bears make money, but pigs get slaughtered." Stock market investors who try to make a lot of money in a short time often find themselves licking the wounds inflicted by their own greed.

At Mesila, we favor index funds over other varieties of stocks. Index funds are linked to stock market indices (such as the S&P or the Nasdaq), and their performance usually mirrors that of their respective indices. Index funds generally yield positive results over time, while funds that attempt to outperform the index frequently end up lagging behind it.

Stocks are an integral part of every well-balanced investment portfolio. What percentage of your portfolio they should occupy depends on your overall financial picture. This is best determined by a financial adviser.

The Myth of Guaranteed Returns ❯

When I got married about a year ago, my parents and in-laws put together a nice sum of money for us to live on for several years, and they suggested that I invest it. I found out about a very promising real estate project that offered 18% interest and had wealthy, reliable backers offering their personal guarantee.

I invested the money into that project, and for the first few months after I invested, I was able to pay my rent with the interest. Then a problem arose with the project, and for the past three months, I have not received any interest payments. I have requested that my capital be returned, but a few weeks have passed and I have not received any money back.

I recently heard about another real estate project that pays only 16% interest, but will give me a lien on the property as a guarantee. When I get my capital back, I hope to invest in this project.

In the meantime, I need money to pay my rent. Would it be advisable for me to borrow money to invest in this second project, in view of the fact that I have a solid guarantee to

> *borrow against? One other question — at what point would it be appropriate for me to approach the guarantors of the first project?*

Your situation is reminiscent of *Chazal's* saying, *"Mi she'achal shum, yachzor veyochal shum,* If someone ate garlic [and is suffering from bad breath], should he go and eat more garlic?" (*Shabbos* 31b).

You were burned once with a real estate investment that sounded, and was, too good to be true. Even if you had more of your own money to invest, why would you take a chance of getting burned again?

As a rule, you should be wary of any investment that offers returns higher than those paid by the bank. (Government bonds are the notable exception; they pay more than the bank, but are generally considered a safe investment.)

Phrases like "guaranteed returns" and "no risk" so often dupe novice investors into naively believing that they can invest their money and, voila, their financial worries will be over. At Mesila, we see the devastating results of this naiveté time and time again.

Although we do not know the details of either of the projects you describe, we can safely assume that any investments promising such high returns are too risky. This assumption is based on the premise that anyone looking for investment capital would prefer to borrow at bank lending rates than at 16-18%.

If a real estate project is offering returns of 16% on your money, you can be sure that no bank was willing to sink money into the project. Is your tolerance for risk, or risk appetite, greater than the bank's? Considering the fact that you do not have money to pay your rent, we think not.

In our opinion, it would be unconscionable for anyone to borrow money to invest in an enterprise as risky as the projects you have described. The lien you have been offered on the second property does not guarantee anything; if the property were enough of a loan guarantee, the bank would have been very willing to take it as collateral, and there would have been no need for private investors like yourself.

Do not let the offer of the lien blind you into risking more capital, especially if the money is borrowed. If you lose the capital — and with such high risk, there is a good chance that you will lose the capital — how will you repay the loan?

The money you invested in the first project is not money you can count on, and definitely not money you can borrow against. While we certainly hope you will get your money back, you should be prepared for the possibility that it may take years of wrangling and legal action before you see a penny of it.

In answer to your second question, we recommend that you approach the guarantors of the first project immediately, before they are inundated with demands from other creditors. The fact that these guarantors were once wealthy and reliable is no assurance that they will be able to bear the financial backlash of a failed real estate proposition.

You should therefore make sure that you are one of the first in line to receive any money that might be forthcoming.

Risking capital for the promise of high returns is not only unwise from an investment standpoint; it's problematic from a Torah perspective as well.

Yaakov Avinu went back across the Yabok River to retrieve some small jugs, the *Midrash* tells us, because *tzaddikim* value their money. The *sefer Be'er Yosef* explains that the reason *tzaddikim* value their money is not because they ascribe importance to material acquisition; rather, it is because they understand that everything they own is a gift from Hashem. And if Hashem gives a person something, he has an obligation to take care of it and use it properly.

When people put money into risky investments, it shows a certain disregard for the *hashgachah pratis* that decreed that the money should be theirs.

In your case, the capital you invested, and now wish to reinvest, is the hard-earned money given to you by your loving parents and in-laws. *Hakaras hatov* would dictate that you should be exceedingly careful not to squander this money.

When you do get back your capital, we urge you to seek the advice of a licensed financial adviser before you invest it again.

Compensation ❯

We recently sold our home and purchased a much smaller one. We invested the money we needed for renovations with a reputable investment company and were promised that the money would be transferred into our account within four days of our giving instructions for the transfer.

The first time we needed part of that money, the money was transferred to our account two days after we gave notice. This last time, however, we gave notice on Monday and were told that the money would be transferred by Thursday at the latest. However, the woman handling this at the investment company was sick, and the money was not transferred.

Meanwhile, we gave out many checks to our workers. Now the checks will bounce or we will have to pay interest to the bank on them. Can we demand compensation for the money we lost? And how do we make sure such a thing does not happen again?

To give you a definitive answer, we require more information. We will, however, outline some of the basic principles governing investments and business transactions, in the hope that these principles will help you determine the appropriate course of action.

You say the investment company "promised" to transfer money within four days. How was this promise made? Over the telephone? By mail? By e-mail?

Business commitments are not made orally (except in certain industries where a handshake is considered a commitment). The rule is, unless you have written documentation of a business commitment, there is no commitment.

You also say that you gave "notice" when you wanted the money transferred. What kind of notice did you give? Do you have any way of showing exactly when you gave notice and to whom you gave notice? Is there a record of your request?

Any time you submit a request, lodge a complaint or engage in any significant business correspondence, you should make sure there is documentation of the correspondence. Always ask for written confirmation — by mail, fax or, at least, e-mail.

In addition, when you speak to a company representative, make sure to record the full name of the person you dealt with. This makes it easier to follow up, since many companies record or otherwise monitor the conversations of their customer service agents.

You are concerned about the costs of the bounced checks or interest charges that you will incur, but we at Mesila are more concerned about the professionalism of the investment company you describe. What makes you so sure this company is reputable? To us, it sounds highly suspect that a reputable company should be unable to transfer money due to the illness of one employee. We are talking about an investment company, not a convenience store.

We are also surprised that an investment company would promise to return your investment within four days. Did you have to pay a penalty for withdrawing your money on such a short notice? If you did, you are probably in a good position to demand compensation.

But if you did not pay a penalty, you have to wonder how an investment company can commit to liquidating your money in a matter of days. This is not the standard practice of investment companies.

Generally, the only investments that can be liquidated in such a short period are money market-type investments. These investments yield minimal returns, due to the minimal risk involved, and are therefore not very lucrative.

If, indeed, the investment company is a reputable one, then all the terms of the investment should have been recorded in the literature you received at the time you initially made the investment. If that is the case, you need only to refer back to that literature to confirm that there was an agreement to transfer money within four days and that a breach of contract has occurred.

Since we do not have all of the necessary information, we cannot give you a definitive answer as to whether you are entitled to compensation. If the financial loss you suffered is significant, we advise you to consult a lawyer to determine whether you have grounds for a lawsuit. Most likely, however, the amount of money in question is not large enough to warrant the ordeal and expense of a lawsuit.

The time for you to think about compensation, however, is after you get your money back. Right now, focus on doing whatever you can to make sure that the money ends up back in your checking account. You can consider legal action later.

In the meantime, you can try to contact your workers and ask them to hold the checks until the funds are transferred. You might feel uncomfortable doing this, but it is certainly preferable to having the checks bounce or incurring interest charges on an overdrawn account.

If you wish to avoid similar situations in the future, you would be wise to insist on receiving written documentation of any agreements you make. Verbal promises are easy to forget or deny, and either side can later claim that a misunderstanding took place.

It is also a good policy never to write a check on funds you don't have. Just because you are expecting a bank transfer, you cannot assume that the money will be there; bank transfers are occasionally delayed by legal or bank holidays, or by technical issues, such as a disparity between the name on your bank account and the name on the bank transfer.

If you are relying on a bank transfer to cover post-dated checks, check your account balance and transactions regularly to ensure that the money arrives when it is supposed to, and make sure you have a contingency plan in case it does not.

With regard to the money you have invested, you would be wise to consult with a qualified financial adviser to determine if this investment is the optimal one for you.

Making Millions On Dinars ❯

A fellow yungerman recently showed me an article describing an exciting new investment opportunity: Iraqi dinars.

The article said that until 1982, the Iraqi dinar was worth about $3. Today, 1 million Iraqi dinars can be bought for only $700. The value of the dinar is sure to rise when the conflict in Iraq is resolved. My friends tell me that if I invest a few thousand dollars in Iraqi dinars now, I'll come out with millions when the dinar goes up.

I have some money put aside that I'd like to invest. I know several avreichim who have already invested in dinars. Do you think this is a worthwhile venture?

Mesila's mission, and the objective of this book, is to convey responsible, Torah-based attitudes toward finances. We will therefore attempt to expose the fallacies inherent in get-rich-quick schemes — and the Iraqi dinar craze in particular.

We will not go into whether it is appropriate for a *ben Torah* to busy himself with investment opportunities. It's true that for someone learning in *kollel*, investing might seem like the ideal way to earn *parnassah* without ever having to leave the *beis medrash*. All you have to do is put your money into a surefire investment, and you're set.

Well, it doesn't quite work that way.

From the time Adam Harishon was told "by the sweat of your brow shall you eat bread," earning a livelihood has been a struggle for mankind. There are no exemptions from this curse, and promises of easy money are always — always — misleading.

Investing, by definition, means risking capital for the sake of an anticipated future gain, or return. As a rule, returns are directly proportional to risk — the greater the risk, the higher the potential return. But the converse is also true: the higher the potential return, the greater the risk.

If someone promises you returns of millions on an investment of thousands, you can be sure of two things: The risk is far too high to justify the investment. And the person is either very naive or a con artist.

Get-rich-quick schemes lure people with the promise of high returns and no risk. But wise investors know that any investment that cannot go down cannot go up either. Never believe anyone who tells you that an investment is sure to go up. If it is *sure* to go up, there would be no risk. And without risk, there can be no significant returns.

Currency speculation is a particularly risky form of investment. It is difficult to predict the movements of any currency, even established ones. Given the volatility of the Iraqi economy, we would not place much confidence in the prospects of its fledgling currency.

What makes you and your friends sure the dinar will increase in worth? How do you know it will not decrease to even less than its current value? And why are you so confident that the conflict in Iraq will be successfully resolved?

Even if Iraqi dinars were worth investing in at some point, you can be sure that by the time you heard about the prospect in your *kollel*, the market price for dinars would have already corrected itself to reflect the latest speculative excitement and the resulting demand.

"Buy the rumor, sell the news" is an old principle of investing. Basically, it means that you should only put your money into an investment before it makes the headlines. Once everyone else has already heard about it and bought in, it's too late. The new Iraqi dinar has been around since 2003, and it has long ceased to be the hot rumor; it is not even news anymore.

Furthermore, there is no real market for Iraqi dinars nowadays. It is therefore unlikely that you would be able to sell your dinars at a profit; you might not even be able to liquidate them at all. And because dinars are not a very commonly traded currency, you will have to pay high commissions and exchange fees when purchasing them. This basically guarantees you a loss from the moment you get your hands on any dinars.

Putting your money into Iraqi dinars, or any other "can't lose" proposition, is not investing. It's gambling. As such, it cannot even be considered part of your requisite *hishtadlus* for *parnassah*. Common sense would dictate that you keep your money far away from anything remotely related to Iraq and spare yourself the pain of watching your money disappear.

You would do your friends a service to caution them against buying Iraqi dinars and explain to them that there is no such thing as easy money.

Having dealt with many clients who lost everything in the process of getting rich quick, Mesila strongly discourages people from investing their money without the help of an investment professional. For investment advice, we suggest that you contact a licensed financial adviser.

Red Flags Ahead ❯

A friend of mine, whom I'll call Eliezer, recently approached me at the yeshivah where I learn. He had an exciting business opportunity for me.

Eliezer owns a business that imports a line of products from France to Israel. He purchases the merchandise from an offshore distributor, who purchases it from the French manufacturer at prices lower than European clients pay. The offshore distributor has an agreement with the manufacturer not to sell the products to European clients, but this agreement is not binding on the distributor's clients, such as Eliezer.

Recently, Eliezer began reselling the products directly to European clients, turning a profit for himself while offering his clients a price lower than the manufacturer will give them. Eliezer says that his distributor is aware of what he is doing and is not opposed to it. Eliezer urgently needs capital to finance the purchase of large quantities of merchandise, and asked me to help him find investors who could provide this capital. He says that each $100,000 of capital should generate profits of $6,000 a month, which will then be split between him, me and the investors.

I know Eliezer well, and he is an ehrliche, reliable person and a capable businessman. I would like to look into this opportunity further and help him find investors, but before I do that I'd like to hear Mesila's opinion.

You are wise to seek an objective outside opinion before you get involved in an investment opportunity, even — or perhaps especially — an opportunity that is as exciting as the one you describe.

Excitement and self-discipline are mutually exclusive, to a large extent. Excitement compels you to do what your emotions dictate, while self-discipline compels you to do what logic dictates — which is often the opposite of what your emotions dictate. For instance, emotion will tell you that you absolutely need to buy something right now; logic will tell you that you don't really need the item or that you can wait to buy it. Emotion will tell you to jump on an attractive investment opportunity; logic will tell you to look out for the warning signs.

Is excitement a bad thing? Not at all. Excitement causes people to focus on the potential benefits of an opportunity and helps them overcome the fears and misgivings that would otherwise prevent them from capitalizing on opportunities. Without excitement, people would not be motivated to take on challenges or assume the risks that are necessary for any type of achievement.

The problem with excitement is that it is a form of emotional bribery. The Torah says that a bribe blinds the eyes of the wise (*Devarim* 16:19), and this is also true of emotional bribery. Excitement causes people to lose their objectivity and makes even the wisest people color-blind to obvious red flags.

Do you see the red flags in this opportunity? We see several.

First and foremost, the prospect of high returns. A monthly return of $6,000 on an investment of $100,000 equals a return of 6% per month, or 72% per annum. A rate of return that high is automatically suspect, because things that seem too good to be true usually are. If Eliezer anticipates such high returns, the risks involved must be very high as well.

That brings us to red flag No. 2, which is the inherent risk of the opportunity in question. Eliezer is undercutting the manufacturer of his products, and it is only a matter of time before the manufacturer catches on to what he is doing and puts an end to it. Even if what Eliezer is doing is legal — and we are not convinced of that — his European competitors may still be able to sue him for ruining their contracts.

Warning sign No.3 is that Eliezer is a friend of yours. When entering a business partnership with a friend, people do things they would never think of doing when entering a partnership with a stranger. They don't investigate, they don't ask for recommendations, they don't formalize the terms of the partnership, and they don't insist on signing legally binding agreements — all because they trust their friend implicitly or because they feel uncomfortable insisting on formalities.

However, if you value your friendship, it behooves you to act with due diligence here, the same way you would if the opportunity would have been presented to you by a stranger. We are not accusing Eliezer of lying, *chas veshalom*, but we are telling you that people's interests often subconsciously narrow or distort their view of a particular situation and cause them to misrepresent the facts slightly, knowingly or unknowingly. We therefore urge you not to take everything Eliezer tells you at face value.

Finally, red flag No. 4 is that this opportunity came to you in yeshivah. A yeshivah is a place for Torah learning, not for business deals or investment opportunities. Good businessmen and seasoned investors do not need yeshivah students to recruit capital for them. Solid investment opportunities are usually snapped up long before they reach the doors of a yeshivah. The types of business deals and investment opportunities that make it through the doors of yeshivos are often the types that are suited to gullible people only.

We would advise you not to bother looking into this opportunity further, since there are far too many red flags waving. The only reason a person should ever look into a business or investment opportunity is to fulfill his obligation of *hishtadlus* and make it appear that the *parnassah* the *Ribbono shel Olam* is giving him is coming about through natural means. If an investment has very little chance of succeeding, it is possible that pursuing it cannot even be considered a fulfillment of the obligation of *hishtadlus*.

We are not saying that there is no money to be made in the opportunity Eliezer is offering you — all we are saying is that it does not sound like a stable investment. Mesila believes that there are no "good" and "bad" investments — there are only stable and unstable ones. Stable investments are those that have the potential to fill a real need and contribute to people's well-being — in other words, they make sense. Unstable investments are those that are based on loopholes, do not advance the needs of humanity in any way and smell fishy.

An investment opportunity that takes advantage of the implicit trust between a manufacturer and his distributor would probably not fall under the rubric of *hishtadlus*.

Bitachon has to form the backdrop for all of a Jew's financial decisions. Knowing that our *hishtadlus* is only a smokescreen for the miracle that we call *parnassah* can help us to marshal the self-discipline to see the red flags waving ahead.

6

Employment: Making Work Pay

"A person is obligated to
do his hishtadlus, all the
while remembering that
hishtadlus is not what
actually brings parnassah.
Parnassah comes from
Hashem."

("Back to the Workforce:
A New Dimension of Motherhood")

In this chapter:

❯ How to Write a Good Resume | 167

❯ Back to the Workforce: A New Dimension of Motherhood | 171

❯ The Right Job | 177

❯ Locked Into an Intolerable Job | 182

❯ A Balancing Act | 186

❯ Earning a Raise – Every Day at Work | 198

❯ It's Better to Be Smart Than Right | 205

❯ Working From Home and Making It Work | 208

❯ Riding Out the Freelance Roller Coaster | 216

❯ Finding the Right Vocation | 220

How to Write a Good Resume ❯

I recently saw a classified ad for a job I think I would be good at. Now I need to write a resume, but I have no idea how to do that.

Can you please advise me on how to write a good resume?

Writing a resume is the very first step in the process of job hunting. You should prepare your resume even before you start looking through Help Wanted ads; this allows you to prepare your resume properly, without the pressure of having to submit it immediately.

Your resume, or **CV** (short for *curriculum vitae*), is your introduction to a prospective employer, and it determines what the employer's first impression of you will be. First impressions are often lasting impressions. It is therefore critical that your resume be a positive reflection of you and your abilities. Your resume is your opportunity to sell yourself, so it has to highlight your skills, talents and strengths. A resume is *not* the place for bashfulness or misplaced humility. A resume should include the following elements:

❯ **Contact information:** Name, address, e-mail address and telephone numbers where you are easily reachable. All information should be current.

> **Personal information:** Use your discretion when deciding whether to include personal information and which information to include. Depending on which of the following are relevant (and beneficial) to your job search, you might include marital status, number of children, age, place of birth, Israeli ID number, country of citizenship, date of *aliyah* and so on.

> **Current career objective:** Briefly describe the position you are seeking and the type of company/industry you are looking to be employed by. Also indicate if you are interested in a full-time or part-time position.

> **Professional experience:** Start with your most recent job and work backward, indicating the dates you were at each job. If you are still working, you may omit the name of your current employer; just state the type of enterprise. All previous jobs should state the name of the employer or company. Include more detailed information on the most recent position you held (this is likely to be the most senior). Each skill that you have and job responsibility you performed need only be mentioned once (even if you did the same thing in five different places). *Stress skills and achievements over duties.*

> **Education:** List only your highest degrees and schooling. Also include courses that relate to the type of job you are seeking.

> **Languages:** If you speak more than one language, indicate which is your mother tongue. For other languages, state your level of fluency, i.e., speaking, reading, writing.

> **Computer skills:** Computer programs you are familiar with, network and e-mail proficiency, typing skills.

> **Other interests:** This category is optional.

> **References:** It is usually sufficient to note that references will be supplied upon request. If you think a prospective employer would be impressed by a particular reference you have, then include it, along with a telephone number.

Companies generally spend less than thirty seconds reading your resume when they first receive it. If you want to get the job, you have to make your resume stand out.

Here are some helpful tips for preparing an effective resume:

> Keep your resume clear and concise — no more than two pages long. A one-page resume is the most effective.

> If you wish, you may begin your resume with a "Highlights" section summarizing your qualifications (experience, training, significant accomplishments, outstanding skills and the like) in a few short, bulleted points.

> In the professional experience section of your resume, emphasize your skills, accomplishments and any supervisory responsibilities you have had. Quantify your achievements whenever possible, using action verbs in the past tense — for example, "Increased sales by 15 percent," "Succeeded in saving the company $20,000," "Doubled the number of customers." Don't make prospective employers infer how competent you are — tell them!

> Don't use "I" or any other pronouns in your resume.

> Keep the format of your resume consistent, easy to follow and pleasing to the eye.

> Make your resume look professional. Never, never submit a hand-written resume. If you are going to be e-mailing your resume, make sure you save the file with a name that is intelligible and

professional: "Rochel Berkowitz Secretary Resume," not "rb resume new."

> After writing your resume, read and reread it, carefully checking spelling, punctuation and grammar, and making sure it's clear. Check that all the relevant information is included and that you have not repeated yourself. It is highly advisable to have someone else proofread your resume.

> Each time you apply for a job, tailor your resume to fit that particular position. Emphasize qualifications that relate specifically to the job you are applying for. It helps to reread your resume through the eyes of your prospective employer and ask yourself, "If I were him/her, would I want to hire me based on this resume?"

> It is perfectly acceptable to prepare more than one resume and use different resumes when applying for different types of jobs.

> If you are submitting your resume by mail, fax or e-mail, you should prepare an accompanying **cover letter** that briefly describes your suitability for a specific position. This cover letter is the bridge between your resume (the past) and your possible future (employment by the company you are addressing).

> Those living in Israel should prepare a resume in both Hebrew and English and, unless specified otherwise, submit both.

The above section was prepared in conjunction with Temech, a branch of Agudath Israel of America dedicated to furthering employment in Israel.

Back to the Workforce:
A New Dimension of Motherhood

When I got married twenty-six years ago, I worked as a senior-level computer programmer. When my oldest son was born, however, I quit my job to become a full-time mommy. Now, my son is married, and my other children are all in school or yeshivah.

My husband made a respectable living all the years from his business, but now that we have started marrying off children, our expenses have mounted considerably. What's more, the current economic crisis has dealt a blow to my husband's business, and money is very short these days. My husband is urging me to go out and get a job, since I have plenty of time on my hands.

I know that I really should look for a job to help my husband support the family, but there are so many reasons why it's not practical. For one thing, I'm not qualified for any job. I've forgotten most of what I knew about computers — I need help from my kids just to operate our home computer — and anyway, what I knew about computers then is obsolete.

In addition, after spending so many years as a homemaker, my brain is fried, and I have absolutely no interest in sitting in front of a computer. I have no other skills to speak of, so any job I could get would be a low-skilled, low-paid job —

like a cashier or janitor. Frankly, I'd rather be unemployed.

I also want to be there for my younger kids when they leave for school in the morning and come home in the afternoon. And I want to be available during school vacations and bein hazemanim when the older kids come home. I don't want to give up on being a mother now that I can finally enjoy both nachas and a good night's sleep.

I'm nervous about going to work for other reasons, too. I'm plagued with self-doubt, and I don't have the confidence to send out a resume — what resume? — and sit through job interviews. In today's economic climate, I don't see how it's possible for me to get a job. How can I compete with younger, more skilled people who have been in the workforce for years? Even if I do get a job, how do I know that I'll be good at it? I'm a middle-aged Bubby, not a fresh-faced teenager who's allowed to make mistakes.

Is it realistic for me to go out to work at my stage in life? And what kind of job could I possibly get?

You have spent the last two-plus decades doing what a Jewish woman is supposed to do — running a home and raising a family — and it's clear that you have your priorities straight in putting your family ahead of your career. Now, however, you are at a different stage in life, when your family needs you less at home, and your husband needs your help to pay the bills.

It is commendable that you still want to be available for your family, and we appreciate your desire to enjoy some richly deserved *nachas*. The question is what Hashem wants from you at this point — is your *avodas Hashem* to be home full-time with your family, or is it to supplement the family income? If you are unsure, we encourage you to consult *daas Torah*.

Daas Torah may very likely tell you that your place right now is in the workforce. In that case, we assure you that working and being there for your family are not mutually exclusive. It might take some juggling, but many women manage to do it, and we are sure that you can, too. Working might even give you a sense of satisfaction and fulfillment that will help you become an even better wife and mother.

Once you are secure in the knowledge that going out to work is the right thing for you now, concern about the current crisis should not prevent you from pursuing employment. As we mentioned in our discussion of *bitachon*, a person is obligated to do his *hishtadlus*, all the while remembering that *hishtadlus* is not what actually brings *parnassah*. *Parnassah* comes from Hashem, and for Him there is no crisis. If your *hishtadlus* is to go out to work, you have to do everything in your power to make that happen, crisis or no crisis, and you can leave the rest up to Hashem.

It's true that landing a job in today's economic climate is difficult. But landing a job involves some degree of difficulty in any economic climate. No matter how open the job market is, you always have to be willing to promote yourself despite the discomfort involved and you need to be proactive in your pursuit of the job you want. (This is true even after you find a job, since Mesila believes that people should continually strive to upgrade their abilities and increase their earning potential.)

We encourage you to look for a job that will not interfere significantly with your family responsibilities, but we also urge you to be realistic about what your family responsibilities are at this point. Nothing will happen to your teenagers if you are not there with them every moment of their vacation. And it's okay for school-age kids to have a bit more responsibility in the house because Mom works.

Our feeling is that what is really preventing you from going out to work is fear. You are afraid of change, afraid of rejection and afraid of failure. These fears are very understandable, but they are also very debilitating.

If you try, there's a chance you might fail, but if you don't try, you're guaranteed to fail! So instead of focusing on all the reasons why you can't succeed in the workforce, focus on all the reasons why you can succeed, *be'ezras Hashem*.

Reason number one why you can succeed is because you are responsible only for effort, not for outcome. So, as long as you do your *hishtadlus* to the best of your ability, you have a 100% chance of success in fulfilling your obligation to the *Ribbono shel Olam* and to your family. Besides that crucial consideration, there are many other reasons why you can succeed.

You say your computer skills are obsolete. But if you once worked as a senior programmer, it shouldn't be terribly difficult for you to brush up on your skills and bring your knowledge up to date. If you do some research about the current market, you might even discover that there are jobs out there for programmers who know how to work with mainframes, punch cards and COBOL.

You also say that you are not interested in computers anymore and that your brain is fried. How do you know that, if you haven't worked at a computer in over two decades? It is quite possible that if you were to give computers another try, you would find that you are still good at it and that you still enjoy it.

It is possible that the field of computers is not for you anymore. But that does not mean that you're not qualified for anything. If you have managed to run a home and raise a family for twenty-something years, we're sure that on the way you picked up a number of marketable skills — communication, arbitration, early childhood education, teaching, psychology, social work, human resource management, nutrition, cuisine, budget planning, health, nursing, law, finance, interior design and stand-up comedy, just to name a few.

In addition to these skills, you have other valuable attributes that young people lack. You are mature, you have life experience and you are at a settled stage of life. Employers don't have to worry that you will move, take maternity leave or be home for a week with a child who has chicken pox.

The first and most important step in making the transition to the workforce is preparing yourself psychologically. Because returning to the workforce after an extended hiatus can be daunting, we advise you to build up your confidence by talking to the type of friends and family members who will give you encouragement. Discussing your job hunt with people also gives you the opportunity to tap into their creative resources and gain valuable insights and ideas from them.

Part of the process of preparing yourself to join the workforce is deciding on the type of job that you want. *Chovos Halevavos* says every person has a propensity toward one particular vocation, and that is the vocation he should pursue as a means of earning his livelihood (*Shaar Habitachon*, chapter 3).

To apply this advice to your situation, think of what you are good at and what you enjoy doing, and try to envision yourself doing that for a living. If you enjoy talking to people, for instance, you can project that skill into a job as a teacher, a salesperson or a social worker. The position you envision for yourself may involve some sort of training, but the need for training should not deter you from pursuing the job that is right for you.

Once you have decided what you'd like to do and have acquired any necessary training, you can start to look actively for a job. In your case, the technical aspects of finding a job — writing a resume, networking, applying for jobs, going to interviews and following up on job leads — will probably be far less challenging than deciding what it is you want to do and mustering the confidence, ambition and enthusiasm to carry through with that decision.

The Right Job ❯

I have a master's degree in special education, and I taught full-time for twelve years in a school for learning-disabled boys. At some point, I started feeling burned out. I decided to begin working as a salesman for an insurance company. It quickly became obvious that I was not cut out to be a salesman; I sold very little and did not enjoy the work.

I would like to get back into special education, but I'm reluctant to return to teaching in a school. In the past, I tutored learning-disabled kids privately, and it gave me tremendous fulfillment. Now I would like to become a full-time private tutor for boys with learning difficulties. Do you think this is something I could earn a living from?

It is definitely possible to earn a living from private tutoring, especially for someone with your credentials. But that can only happen once you have firmly established your reputation and have built up a full roster of clients.

At this point, you cannot afford to sit around and wait for clients to come to you. To ensure that you have enough money to live on now, we recommend that you look for at least a part-time position working in a school, either mainstream or special-ed. This does not have to be in a classroom setting; it could be in a resource room, with small groups of students or individual students.

Although working in a school might not pay as well per hour as private tutoring, it does guarantee you a steady income. Moreover, it will enhance your image and your marketability. It will be easier for you to attract private students if you are a full-fledged teacher than if you are merely a freelance tutor.

Being employed by a school gives you credibility as a professional. It could also potentially be a springboard for establishing yourself as a private tutor, if you can convince the school's principal, teachers or resource room staff to recommend you to students who need tutoring.

Once you have landed a steady job, you are in a good position to begin marketing yourself as a private special-ed teacher. (Use of language is significant here; if you feel that the word "tutor" carries a less professional connotation than "private teacher," do not use it to describe yourself.)

To establish yourself in the field, you need to *know your market.*

The first step in marketing yourself is defining who your potential clients are. When defining your target market, you should differentiate between users of your services (children) and the people who recommend you (teachers, principals, parents of former students, and others who might pass your name along). Your marketing efforts should focus on people who are in a position to recommend you to the parents of the children you wish to work with.

> Make a list of all the people who could potentially refer clients to you.

> Contact those people directly and ask that they recommend you as a qualified tutor to parents of boys who require extra help.

Focus first on those who are located near you. If necessary, you can call people outside your area later on.

➤ Mention that you would be willing to work with students at school, in their homes or in yours.

➤ Schedule face-to-face meetings with the school principals and resource room supervisors on your list. Once they have met with you, they will feel more comfortable recommending you. During these meetings, you can present your credentials, highlight your areas of specialization and explain what type of students you are qualified to work with.

➤ Put together a professional portfolio to bring to these meetings. This should include your resume, thank-you letters from former students or their parents, letters of recommendation and samples of educational materials you have created or worked on.

➤ Leave some business cards behind at the end of your meetings.

➤ Follow up on meetings with principals and superintendents by periodically visiting or calling. This will ensure that you remain fresh in their minds.

Market positioning is the second step of your marketing efforts. It involves branding yourself and ensuring that your name becomes synonymous with professionalism and success. Public relations, or PR, is a crucial element of this positioning.

➤ To generate PR, you can prepare an article, or a series of articles, on special education and submit the articles to local publications at no charge. At the end of the articles, be sure to include your telephone number and invite people to contact you. Having an article published under your name boosts your professional image, enhances your portfolio, gets your name out there and advertises your services.

> ❯ Do some low-cost advertising, such as placing small ads in community circulars. These ads should highlight your professional experience, areas of expertise and past successes.

> ❯ Another way to position yourself is by writing a book, workbook or teacher's manual on a subject related to your field. This book could generate both PR and income for you.

Make your product the best. The secret to successful marketing is having a good product to sell. Your professional expertise as a special-ed teacher is your product — so make sure it is the very best possible product. And then, be your own advocate.

> ❯ Put together a mental list of reasons why people should hire you to teach their children — and be prepared to share these reasons with anyone you encounter on a professional level.

> ❯ You can also ask friends, relatives, neighbors and parents of former students to pass on your name to anyone whose son might need private tutoring. Networking and word-of-mouth are the least expensive forms of advertising, but they're also often the most effective.

> ❯ Keep up to date. Be familiar with the latest educational methodology. Upgrade your skills. Attending professional development seminars.

> ❯ Inspire yourself. Focus on the inherent value of your work and the impact you can potentially have on your students' lives. If you are convinced that you are indeed a dedicated, talented and professional teacher, others will believe you.

> ❯ Be a professional. When working with private students, begin on time; do not answer telephone calls during a lesson; make your students feel important.

The first few students will probably be the most difficult to find. Once you establish yourself as a successful tutor, however, you will likely find that clients will start flocking to you.

As the demand for your services increases, you can gradually raise your prices. Hopefully, you will eventually reach the point where you are so swamped with work that you will be able to give up your regular teaching job and focus on what you enjoy: working one-on-one with private students.

Locked Into an Intolerable Job ❯

> I have been working in IT (information technology) for about ten years. I do it to support my family, and I have had more than enough in this field of employment.
>
> I would be only too happy to consider something else, but because my experience is in IT, it seems unrealistic to expect that I will find a job that pays as much as I am currently earning — which is barely enough to cover my expenses.
>
> Because I am the sole breadwinner, I feel locked into a job that I can no longer tolerate. Can you give me some advice on how to deal with the situation?

We understand your dilemma, and we commend you for your commitment to supporting your family and for your persistence in coping with an unpleasant job situation.

We will offer several coping strategies, but we would like to preface them by urging you to try your best to focus on the positive aspects of your job. Unpleasant as it may be, it is far better than many other jobs out there, and it is certainly far better than no job at all. Given the sorry state of the economy today, anyone who still has a job and is earning an income has a lot to be grateful for.

Whether your job is "tolerable" or "intolerable" is very much dependent on your attitude and expectations. If you expect your job to always be intellectually stimulating, emotionally fulfilling and financially rewarding, chances are that you will be disappointed. Since the time of Adam Harishon, *parnassah* has been a curse, and no vocation is without its stresses and hazards.

Coming to terms with your current job situation will contribute to your overall happiness and wellbeing. It will put you in a much better position to improve your situation, since a person who feels angry or desperate lacks the equanimity necessary to exercise good judgment and make objective, levelheaded decisions.

Once you no longer have the desperate feeling of being locked into an intolerable situation, you can begin to explore new income possibilities while still working at your current job. To do this, you need to develop a viable alternative source of income so that you can eventually move on to a more rewarding job without jeopardizing your family's financial health.

Some people may tell you that there are no jobs available today and there is no point in trying to improve your employment situation right now. That is simply untrue. There are jobs available today, and the fact that they are scarcer than before makes it all the more important for you to be proactive and take the initiative in pursuing them.

Is there another area of IT that interests you more than the area you currently work in? If so, is there any way for you to upgrade your skills so you are qualified for a job you would enjoy more? Alternatively, can you pursue training in an entirely different field during evening or weekend hours? Do you have a hobby you can use to generate income and eventually turn into a full-time job?

When planning your eventual career switch, you need to believe in yourself and in your G-d-given abilities. Build up your confidence and ambition. You also need to think creatively, focusing on opportunities rather than limitations.

The bad news is that it is difficult to think creatively when you are under financial stress. When people experience financial problems, their creative faculties tend to shut down, preventing them from finding a way out of their predicament. But the good news is that there's a very simple way to circumvent this problem: Ask other people for ideas.

People who are not in your situation have two advantages over you. First, they are not experiencing your stress, so they have free access to their creative faculties. And second, they can consider your options objectively and unemotionally and spot opportunities that you missed because you were too absorbed and emotionally involved in your situation.

Asking people for advice has the added benefit that you get them thinking of job openings that may be appropriate for you. This is called networking, and studies show that up to 70% of jobs are found through networking. A word of caution — don't ask people point blank if they have a job for you; it puts them in an uncomfortable position. Instead, talk about yourself and your situation, and ask for their opinion and advice.

If you feel uncomfortable discussing your situation with others, it might help you to know that people love being asked for advice and will probably be more than happy to offer their ideas of how you could use your skills to generate income. You are under no obligation to follow their advice, but you also should not dismiss it as unrealistic before seriously considering whether it could work.

Don't let the word "unrealistic" get in the way of your aspirations and prevent you from pursuing the opportunities you dream of. Anything can be realistic if you have the will and the drive to make it work.

Along with exploring new income possibilities, you should work on saving money for a fund that will tide you over during the period after you leave your job, when your income will likely be reduced. Since you say you are barely covering your expenses as it is, you will need to increase your income or reduce your expenditures in order to save money for this fund.

Is there anything you can do to increase your income while working at your current job? For instance, is there a possibility that your wife could supplement the family income, even temporarily?

It might be a good idea for you to use Mesila's budget questionnaires to reach an awareness of where your money is going and use that information as a basis for trimming your expenses. If you are able to reduce your expenditures temporarily, you might be in a better position to leave your job and move to a different job that you find more enjoyable, even if it pays less. It is up to you and your wife to decide whether it is practical and worthwhile for you to implement short-term sacrifices as a step toward achieving the long-term rewards of financial stability and job satisfaction.

A Balancing Act ❯

I work as a saleslady in a gift shop to help support my family (my husband is in kollel). My employer treats me very well, and the job is one I enjoy — I'm a people person, and I love talking to the customers and to my coworkers.

I have two issues with my job, however: the pay is very low, and the work I do is not the most intellectually stimulating. I am a bright, capable person, and I am sure there are other things I could do that would allow me to earn more and put my brain and talents to better use.

I feel torn between my family responsibilities, my loyalty to my employer and my own ambitions, and I am also unsure of how I would go about finding a better-paying job. What do you recommend?

It sounds as though you are struggling with three distinct dilemmas. One is how to balance your work with your family responsibilities, the second is how to find work that will bring you the maximum financial benefit and personal satisfaction, and the third is whether to pursue your own interests at the expense of your employer's interests. Although these dilemmas are closely interrelated, exploring them one by one will give you the clarity to make empowered decisions.

Dilemma No. 1: The Challenge of the Working Akeres Habayis

Ideally, every Jewish woman should be home with her family, since *"Kol kevudah bas melech penimah,* The place of the princess is in the home." However, many women today have taken upon themselves the admirable responsibility of helping to support their families and, in many cases, enabling their husbands to learn Torah. In addition, many women today are not comfortable being homemakers exclusively, and they need some other occupation that will keep them stimulated.

These considerations notwithstanding, your primary role is still that of an *akeres habayis,* a homemaker. Therefore, it behooves you to use your time at work in a way that will bring the most benefit to your family and will allow you to be the best *akeres habayis* you can be.

Since you are working to bring the most benefit to your family, you have a responsibility to ensure that you are maximizing — and continually increasing — your earning potential. And since your going out to work is meant to enhance your role as an *akeres habayis,* you have to make sure that the type of work you are doing is harmonious with that role. That means your work cannot override your family responsibilities or compromise your position as a *bas melech.*

Often, these two goals — earning the maximum amount of money and remaining true to your role as an *akeres habayis* — conflict with one another. There are many vocations that would allow you to maximize your earning potential but would be in conflict with your family responsibilities, either in terms of time or in terms of *hashkafah.* On the other hand, the type of jobs that would complement your role as an *akeres habayis* are often part-time, low-skilled and poorly paying.

Your challenge, and the challenge of every working Jewish woman, is to strike the delicate balance between these often conflicting goals. Precisely where that balance should be struck is a highly individual decision, and one that should be made in consultation with *daas Torah*. But it is a balance that can be struck successfully, in a way that will allow you to support your family to the best of your ability without compromising your family responsibilities or your *hashkafos*.

Dilemma No. 2: What to Do

Once you understand where the balance between work and family should be struck, you will be in a position to consider your employment options and think of ways to use your talents and capabilities to the maximum.

We will offer some practical strategies for increasing your income and your level of work satisfaction. Obviously, these strategies have to be implemented within the parameters of what you, your husband and your Rav consider acceptable work conditions.

Employee vs. Self-Employed

In general, there are two ways to earn income: by working for someone else or by being self-employed. The typical advantages of working for someone else are that you draw a steady salary, you are entitled to employee benefits and you work fixed, predictable hours. The drawbacks are that your opportunities for earning are more limited, you must answer to an employer, and you are tied down to a fixed work schedule.

The advantages of being self-employed are that your opportunities for profit are much greater, you do not have a boss on top of you, and you set your own hours and work schedule. The drawbacks are that your income fluctuates, you do not receive benefits and you are not guaranteed to earn anything; you may even sustain losses. Furthermore, your work is your headache exclusively, and you can never really walk away from it.

People tend to categorize themselves either as an employee or as a self-employed individual. In truth, however, the two do not have to be mutually exclusive, especially in today's economic climate. Having a job should not prevent you from doing other things in a self-employed capacity, and being self-employed should not deter you from looking for a steady job. It is important that you not box yourself into a description such as "saleslady" or "employee," because doing so will limit your perception of the options available to you.

Opportunities for Advancement — Right Under Your Nose

When people dream of increasing their earnings or job satisfaction, they instinctively think about working elsewhere. While there are times when people do have to leave their jobs and embark on a new career, in many cases the opportunities for career advancement are right under their noses. When considering your employment options, therefore, the first option you should contemplate is how to move ahead in your current job.

Perhaps your employer would be willing to give you a raise or promote you to a more senior position, such as store manager. Perhaps you can offer to take on additional responsibilities, such as inventory management, planning marketing strategy or opening an additional store location. These responsibilities would likely be better paying and more intellectually stimulating as well.

Taking on these responsibilities may require you to upgrade your skills, possibly by pursuing professional training, but this might be a worthwhile investment for both you and your employer.

Supplementing Your Income on the Side

Besides advancing yourself in your current job, you can supplement your income in many different ways that do not conflict with your job. There are twenty-four hours in a day and six workdays in a week that could potentially be filled with productive, income-generating activity, in addition to your work as a saleslady.

Every person has been endowed by Hashem with talents, skills or knowledge that can be used to generate income, and we are sure that it is possible for you to earn money by tapping into your unique capabilities and strengths.

There are endless possibilities for earning income on the side. Depending on what you are good at, and what services are needed in your community, you could take up private tutoring, cake decorating, telemarketing, freelance writing, hair or wig styling, babysitting or e-commerce. You could also give lessons in any field you are proficient in: art, music, sewing, swimming or dance, to name a few.

As you build yourself up in other types of employment, you can consider whether to reduce the number of hours you work as a saleslady.

Deciding What to Do

When deciding what type of work to do, there are three types of questions to ask yourself:

1. What am I good at? In what area am I skilled or knowledge-able? What do I enjoy doing?

2. What goods or services are missing in my community? What can I provide that no one else is currently providing?

3. What goods or services are popular in my community?

Notice that questions two and three are polar opposites. That is because Hashem has many different ways for people to be successful.

A person can be successful because he fills a particular need that no one else is filling, or he can succeed because he provides something that is in significant demand, even if there are many other people providing similar services. The key is to tap into a demand — existing or latent — and carve yourself a niche by filling that demand in a way that is uniquely yours.

People are generally more motivated and successful when they enjoy and are good at what they do, so it is important to choose an occupation that is suited to your personality and strengths. If you are not sure what you would be good at, you can ask other people for ideas. Professional career counseling can be helpful as well.

Dilemma No. 3: The Employer-Employee Relationship

Your relationship with your employer is primarily a professional one, not a personal one. What is the difference between a personal relationship and a professional relationship?

A personal relationship is one that is based on blood, friendship or ideological conviction. The hallmark of a personal relation-ship — whether it is with a family member, a friend or any Jew — is a willingness to give unconditionally, without focusing on what you are receiving in return.

A professional relationship, on the other hand, is based on mutual benefit. An employer hires an employee because he needs the employee's services, and the employee provides the employer with his services because he wishes to earn a living. A store offers promotions to its customers because it wants their business, and the customers buy in the store because they require the merchandise and services that the store provides.

In a relationship based on mutual benefit, there are no freebies. If a store is offering a promotion or giving something away free of charge, it is hoping that the promotion will ultimately result in increased profits. If an employer gives perks to his employees — such as staff parties or gifts — he is hoping to boost their morale and strengthen their commitment to the company. And an employee who demonstrates outstanding performance is hoping to advance himself and his career prospects.

A professional relationship is somewhat conditional: "I will provide you with what you need if you provide me with what I need." This attitude would be very wrong if it were to exist between spouses, relatives, friends or neighbors. But it is perfectly acceptable — and necessary — between people whose relationship is purely professional and business-oriented.

There are times when a personal relationship might conflict with a professional one — such as when doing work for a family member or when negotiating a business deal with a friend. In these cases, extreme caution must be exercised to ensure that the desire for mutual benefit does not compromise the unconditional giving that characterizes the overall relationship.

In general, however, the distinctions between personal and professional relationships are quite clear. There is work and there is home. There is business and there is family. That is what is meant by the expression, "You don't mix business with pleasure."

Even in a professional relationship, a person has to be a *mentch* and carry out all his *bein adam lechaveiro* obligations. But he is not required to give of himself beyond the point where his efforts are recognized, appreciated and fairly compensated. And he is not required to continue to give of himself if he is not receiving the benefit he deserves in return.

The Limits of Professional Loyalty

In the professional world, loyalty is earned, not blind. If you have loyalty to your employer, it has to be because you are benefiting from your association with her. The better she treats you, and the more generously she compensates you, the more of your loyalty she will earn.

Because your employer provides you with employment and income, you owe her both *hakaras hatov* and professional loyalty. But because your relationship is a professional one, there is a limit to how far your gratitude and loyalty should extend.

Loyalty to your employer requires you to go beyond the call of duty at times, whether that means putting in extra time, helping her out in a pinch or doing things that are not exactly within your job description. It might also require you to turn down work offers that are slightly better than your current position.

But loyalty to your employer does not require you to pass up opportunities for significant financial gain or for advancing your own professional abilities. If there is a serious conflict between your interests and the employer's interests, your interests have to take precedence.

Many women are stuck in dead-end jobs simply because they can't bear to "hurt" the boss by leaving, or because they are too shy to request their fair market value. These women are putting their employers' interests ahead of their own interests and the interests of their families. In doing so, they are actually undermining their whole reason for going out to work!

As a loyal employee, you should do your best to reconcile your interests with those of your employer. That means that you should not run off to another job unless you have a very good reason to do so. It also means that if you do decide to take a different job, you should not leave your employer in the lurch — you should give her ample notice and you should do your best to fill the void that will be left behind you, by helping to find and train a suitable replacement.

Being a loyal employee is not only good *middos*, it is also good business practice. It never pays to burn your bridges behind you, because you never know when you will need a favor from an old employer, and you never know when your old employer will be asked for a reference for you. For all you know, you might end up working for her again one day.

Know What You Are Entitled To

Because you are working for pay, you have to periodically evaluate whether you are being compensated fairly. Keep up to date on what the market value is for the work you are performing. If you feel that a raise is justified, do not be embarrassed to broach the subject with your employer, professionally and confidently. But be aware that if your request for a raise is unfair or unjustified, it can backfire and strain your relationship with your employer.

You should also be aware of your rights as an employee and ensure that you are receiving all the benefits you are entitled to. Are you being paid at least minimum wage? Are you receiving paid vacation and sick leave, and health and pension benefits? If not, it may be time to have a talk with your employer or to seriously consider your other options.

Making the Separation Between Work and Money

The fact that you are working for money does not mean you should be thinking about money at all times when you work. On the contrary — focusing on money causes people to perform their work less professionally and with less passion.

When you work, you should focus on doing your work as well as possible in order to help the people who are benefiting from your efforts.

To illustrate: The doctor who wants to heal people will be a better doctor than the doctor who only wants to earn money, and the saleslady who wants to help people find the right gift will be a better saleslady than the saleslady who only wants to put in her hours so that she can take home her paycheck. Furthermore, the doctor who only wants to make money will ultimately be less successful, and will therefore earn less, than the doctor who is committed to healing. And the saleslady who only wants to take home her paycheck will sell fewer gifts, and receive fewer commissions, than the saleslady who appreciates the value of her work and is committed to satisfying her customers.

In order for any type of work or business venture to succeed, there has to be an altruistic motive masking the profit motive. An altruistic motive can be a desire to help people, a desire to make the world a better place or a desire to sanctify Hashem's Name. From a business perspective, the less obvious it is that you are after someone's money, the more likely you are to earn money, because if people sense that you are altruistically motivated, they will feel more comfortable hiring you or giving you their business.

All employers like to think that their employees are in it for more than the money, and they find it distasteful when an employee is clearly motivated only by mercenary considerations. Similarly, customers prefer to give their business to stores, individuals or companies that seem genuinely interested in helping them.

Focus on the Spiritual Value of Your Work

Being altruistically motivated is important from a Torah perspective as well. Every type of work has value and is a form of *chessed*. The *baalei mussar* urge us to focus on the inherent *chessed* in the work we perform — even if we are paid for it. The following is a free translation of a selection from the teachings of Rav Simcha Zissel, the Alter of Kelm:

"It is a mistake to think that a store owner who makes a living through buying and selling all day is not engaged in *chessed*. A person is unclothed, barefoot, hungry and thirsty, and a store owner provides him with clothing, shoes, food and drink — can there be a greater *chessed* than that? And if you argue that he is taking money for his services, is it wrong for him to support his family in this way?

"However, a person can erase all of this achievement with one silly thought, if he thinks that he is doing everything for his own benefit. If he is a baker, for instance, he should think, 'My main goal in baking bread is that a Jew should have what do eat. But because I and my family need to eat as well, I have to earn money from baking bread — otherwise, I will not be able to bake tomorrow and help people again.'" (*Daas Chochmah U'Mussar* 1:56)

Chazal tell us that Chanoch was a shoemaker by profession and with every stitch he made, he achieved unification with his Creator. Rav Yisrael Salanter explains that Chanoch's mind was not in the heavenly realms while he worked, for that would have interfered with his work. Rather, with every stitch Chanoch made in a shoe, he thought about how to make the shoe as fine and strong as possible, so that the person wearing it would enjoy it. This commitment to helping others, says Rav Dessler, earned him the Torah's description, "And Chanoch walked with Hashem."

Focusing on the inherent value of the work you do will improve the quality of your work, boost your value as an employee and increase the amount of satisfaction and fulfillment you derive from your work. It will also enhance your relationship with your employer, because, as we said, all employers like to think that their employees are in it for more than the money.

We hope these guidelines will give you the clarity of thought necessary to make empowered decisions as to how to balance your ambition with your family responsibilities and your loyalty to your employer.

Earning a Raise — Every Day at Work ❯

I've worked for three years as an administrative secretary for a company that is doing very well. I think that I am a responsible, dedicated and capable worker, and my boss is definitely pleased with my work.

My starting salary at this job was very reasonable, but by now I think it should be higher. My boss has never offered me a raise, however, and I'm uncomfortable broaching the subject with her. Do you have any advice on how I can get a raise?

After working three years for a company, you may very well be entitled to a raise. Generally, it is considered acceptable for employees to ask for a raise of 5%-7% once a year, although that certainly does not mean you will get that every year.

There are several reasons why asking for a yearly raise is justified.

One, inflation pushes the cost of living up continually, and your salary should go up continually to reflect that.

Two, you become more and more valuable to your company the longer you work for them, and you should be paid more for the additional experience you bring to the job each year.

Three, if your job description has broadened to include new responsibilities, if your skills have improved or if your performance has exceeded expectations, then you are now worth more as an employee than you were when you were hired, and you should be compensated accordingly.

To get a raise, you need to do two things: earn the raise, and ask for it. Asking for a raise is not something you will do very often, but earning a raise is something you should be doing during every moment that you are at work.

As an employee, you actually have two jobs. One is, of course, your actual job. The other is to convince your employer that you are worth more to her than you are currently being paid. Your employer has to believe that your salary is money well spent, and you therefore have to prove to her that your value as an employee more than justifies the cost to the company.

To do that, you need to continually increase your value as an employee. How do you do this?

By taking the initiative to acquire new skills. By showing willingness to assume additional responsibilities. By pinch-hitting for your colleagues and filling in gaps. By going the extra mile when necessary and making yourself available when you are needed. And by demonstrating, through action and attitude, that you care about the company.

If you learn new skills, you can command a higher salary because you bring added value to the company. It is therefore to your benefit and to your company's benefit for you to upgrade your abilities and become a better employee.

Before investing time and money in this, however, you might want to check with your boss if she is interested in your improving your skills in this way, because, if so, the company might be willing to fund all or part of a training course.

Throughout the year, you have opportunities to accumulate the brownie points that will ultimately result in a "yes" when you ask your boss for a raise. Every time you go beyond the call of duty, every time the quality of your work goes up a notch, and every time you demonstrate your commitment to your work, you effectively show your boss that you are worth more than you were before.

Earning raises is an integral part of being an employee. In fact, Mesila believes that all employees have an obligation to constantly work toward earning a higher salary.

Why? Because you owe it to yourself as a person to continually improve at anything you do, and because you owe it to your family to increase your earning power and achieve — or maintain — financial stability.

Once you have made yourself deserving of a raise, you need to construct a strategy to get that raise. Do not expect your boss to offer you a raise. If you want the raise, you are going to have to ask for it. No one likes to ask for a raise — especially women. But if you do not ask, the answer will almost always be no.

With the right timing and preparation, you will feel less fear and more confidence in making your request. And if you approach your boss the right way, you will earn more respect in her eyes, and you will not lose anything by asking.

The opposite is also true, however. Asking the boss for a raise the wrong way can be very damaging. Bosses do not like to be asked for raises — it puts them on the spot, it forces them to consider whether they can afford it, and it makes them focus on your short-comings and think of all the reasons why the raise is unjustified.

Since asking for a raise is bound to cause some friction between you and your boss, you need to do everything you can to minimize the damage and maximize your chances of success.

Once you have made yourself deserving of a higher salary than you are currently earning, it is time to think about how to broach the subject with the boss. Here are some practical strategies for getting a raise:

1. **Know what is fair and reasonable.** You will need to look your boss in the eye and tell her exactly how much you would like to get paid. But first you have to be sure that the salary you are asking for is reasonable.

You should therefore do some research to find out the going rate for the type of work you do. Consult with friends and acquaintances in your area who have jobs similar to yours, or ask people in management positions how much they pay employees who do the work you do.

2. **Schedule a meeting.** Don't approach your boss without warning. Schedule a meeting with her at a time that is not too busy or stressful for either of you, and inform her that the purpose of the meeting is to discuss your contract. This way, she will not be caught off-guard when you present your request.

3. **Timing.** The best time to ask for a raise is when the company is doing well and the boss is in a good mood. It is also wise to ask for a raise at a time when your boss is particularly pleased with your performance.

4. **Make the boss feel good.** Think of the things you like about your job, your boss, and your company, and communicate to your boss how much you enjoy your work and why you appreciate being part of the company. Just make sure that you really mean what you are

saying — no one likes to feel that they are being flattered, but everyone appreciates a sincere compliment.

5. **Show proof of your value.** Come to the meeting armed with confirmation of your value to the company. Write up a summary of your key accomplishments over the past year, highlighting instances in which you went beyond the call of duty. Whenever possible, provide facts and figures.

In addition, prepare an outline of your current responsibilities — don't assume that your boss is aware of all the things you do — along with a description of how your job has evolved over time and how you have become more valuable to the company since you were hired. You might also want to include a list of future goals you intend to achieve on behalf of the company. Only ask for a raise if you are convinced that you deserve it — if you have any doubts, so will your boss.

6. **Keep the discussion impersonal.** Your pay raise is based on your contribution to the company, not on your personal financial situation. If your rent has gone up, if you just had a baby or if you have a wedding to pay for, it has nothing to do with your requested raise and should not be brought up in the discussion.

You are not asking your boss for a favor or appealing to her for *chessed* — you are asking for your fair market value. You should only ask for a raise if you feel you have earned it — not because you need it.

7. **Adopt the right tone.** You need to speak to your boss in a way that is respectful, assertive and sincere — not arrogant, demanding or confrontational, and not apologetic, hesitant or pleading.

If your boss turns down your request for a raise, keep your tone professional and businesslike, and do not become upset or emotional.

8.   **Talk the boss' language.** The boss is concerned primarily with the company's bottom line, and the language she understands best is the language of profit. If you can show how you are making the company more profitable, you can show that you are entitled to a greater share of those profits.

9.   **Use win-win tactics.** You and your boss are not adversaries — you are two parties trying to reach a mutually satisfying arrangement. Show consideration for the boss' preferences and limitations. Give her the feeling that you are flexible and willing to come toward her.

10.   **Aim for the high end.** You want to get a raise that will satisfy you, and your boss wants to think that she got a good deal. Does that mean that you should ask for more than you deserve? No. You should ask for the maximum amount that is fair and justifiable, but you should also decide on the minimum you would be happy with.

11.   **Be prepared for any outcome.** Consider all the ways your boss might react to your request. Decide ahead of time how you would respond to these possible reactions.

What will you tell the boss if she says that the company cannot afford to pay you more? How will you respond if she agrees to the raise, but tells you that you should not ask for a raise again for the next three years? What will you do if she offers you less than you hoped for?

You don't have to answer your boss on the spot — it is perfectly fine to tell her that you need time to think things over — but being prepared for any outcome will help you to remain calm and avoid becoming flustered.

12.   **Consider negotiating for perks.** If your boss is reluctant to raise your salary, you can suggest non-cash alternatives: more flexible hours, extra vacation days, additional employee benefits and the like.

13. **Avoid ultimatums.** Do not threaten to quit if your request is not met. Employers want workers who like their jobs and want to stay with the company. If you threaten to leave, you might be shown to the door. Even if you do stay, your threat may strain your relationship.

14. **Express your thanks.** If you are granted a raise, make sure to show your gratitude. And even if you are not granted a raise, a "thank you" is still in order.

Tell your boss that you understand her position, that you appreciate her honesty and that you are grateful that she took the time to meet with you. Then ask her why your request was refused, and what you can do to earn a raise in the future. Her answers will help you develop a strategy for further negotiations.

If your request is turned down, don't think you have wasted your time. You have succeeded in making your boss aware of what a great job you are doing, and you have planted the idea of a raise in her mind.

Most raises are not won after a single conversation; it often takes an ongoing effort.

It's Better to Be Smart Than Right ❯

I am employed by a chessed organization that does wonderful work. Overall, I am happy at my job, but recently, a frustrating situation has arisen.

My contract came up for renegotiation, and I wished to make several changes to it. My employer told me that he was too busy to discuss the contract, but he did agree that I could begin to bill according to the changes I wished to implement and that we would sort things out later.

After billing according to the new contract for six months, my employer finally told me that he was ready to discuss the contract. To my surprise, he gave me a hard time with many of the changes I had asked for.

Six months ago, I would have been willing to be flexible on several of the items. Now, however, I have already billed for six out of the twelve months of the contract, and I feel that it is unfair of my employer to expect me to recalculate all my previous invoices and credit him with the difference. My earnings for the last six months have already been spent.

When I told this to my employer, he disagreed with me vehemently, accusing me of being inflexible. I think he is the one who is being unreasonable.

Who is right?

Having heard only your side of the story, we cannot even attempt to determine who is right. In our view, however, the question of who is right is irrelevant.

According to *halachah*, you might not have any claim whatsoever against your employer. As long as you did not sign a new contract, you were employed under the terms of the old contract. Your employer's verbal agreement that you could bill temporarily according to a new arrangement does not necessarily constitute a binding agreement.

When your employer told you he was too busy to discuss the terms of your new contract with you, he may well have meant that he did not agree to the terms you requested but he was not interested in arguing with you over it at that time.

You, however, read his words as a tacit agreement to the new terms, which may not have been his intention at all. Had you made an effort to clarify the matter at any time since, you might have saved yourself a lot of frustration.

In any dispute, it's better to be smart than to be right. The ranks of the unemployed are full of people who were right.

We advise you to forget about who is right and who is wrong and try to find a compromise that will satisfy both you and your employer. Do not turn this into a matter of principle. It's not your place to punish your employer, even if he was wrong. It will only backfire on you. You should come to the negotiating table ready to recalculate your invoices and credit your employer, if necessary.

But the money is spent, you say. True. But maintaining a healthy relationship with your employer is worth more than the money you are arguing over, however much it might be.

Employees often need favors from their employers. You might need to take off unexpectedly once in a while, you might come late to work here and there, and you might make mistakes in your work. If you have shown flexibility to your employer in the past, he is far more likely to overlook these things.

There is another reason why it's worth keeping your employer happy. Few people stay at a job forever. When it comes time to look for your next job, you need to know that your current employer will have good things to say about you. Future employers will not want to hire you if they hear that you are stubborn and inflexible. No short-term gain justifies the risk of earning that kind of a reputation.

We are not suggesting that you cave in to all your employer's demands. Negotiation is a healthy process, and it's important for both sides to feel that they got a good deal in the end.

You know your employer, and you can undoubtedly figure out which clauses in your contract he really has a problem with and which he would be willing to live with. If you show him that you are willing to give in on the things that are most important to him, you can ask him to give in on what's most important to you.

Difficult as it may be for you to recalculate your previous invoices, you would not want to have money in your possession that was not earned fairly. This is especially so because you work for a *chessed* organization and your salary is paid with *tzedakah* money.

Remember, Hashem has all the money in the world, and He is the only One Who provides *parnassah*. If you are meant to have that money, then Hashem will find a way to return it to you.

Working From Home — And Making It Work! ❯

I have worked as a graphic artist at a small company for a number of years, and now I am thinking of doing graphics on a freelance basis from home. I think this would give me increased flexibility, and I also think I can make more money working on my own than at a salaried job. I have had quite a few people express interest in sending me work.

My question is: How do I work from home in a way that I do not get disturbed — by neighbors, children, relatives and others? And how do I keep myself disciplined enough to actually do my work when there are a million things begging to be done all around me?

Working at home has numerous advantages over working in an office. It gives you greater flexibility, eliminates travel time and allows you to be more available to your family. It also saves you a significant amount of money on transportation, wardrobe costs and rental of office space. In addition, working at home can result in significant tax savings, since many home office expenses can be claimed as deductions from your income.

But there are also drawbacks to working at home. For one thing, there are many distractions in a home office, such as personal phone calls, domestic tasks that need to be attended to and interruptions by family members and visitors.

It can be very tempting to throw in a load of laundry, make a quick phone call, prepare lunch or host company when working at home. It is also difficult to juggle home and work responsibilities when all of those responsibilities revolve around the same geographic location.

In an office, there is a clear demarcation of when the workday is meant to end. Home-based workers have a harder time ending their day; they are always near their work, and there is more of a temptation to "just finish up" or take work-related phone calls at all times of the day.

Another drawback of working at home is the inherent lack of social interaction and the resulting feeling of isolation. Office environments can be conducive to team spirit and healthy competition, but these motivating factors are absent when you work alone, at home. In addition, not getting out of the house to go to work means that you do not get away from any stress or frustration you experience — at home or at work.

To avoid these drawbacks and reap the rewards of working at home, you need to create a home office environment that is conducive to success. To do this, you have to treat your work-from-home as a regular office job. An essential requirement to effectively work from home is the establishment of boundaries for both your time and your space.

As in most areas of personal finance and business, being disciplined is one of the primary keys to success. Here are some helpful guidelines:

Establish set times for work. Create a realistic work schedule, and make sure that you take this schedule seriously. Make sure to start and end work at the same time every day. Without a clearly defined work schedule, the distinction between home and work can be blurred, with your work time turning into family time and family time into work time. You want to avoid the feeling that you are always at work. To do this, you need to have fixed work hours.

Notify your family members, friends, relatives and neighbors of your work hours, and close the door to your office and turn on the answering machine during these hours. If you respect your work time, others will, too.

By the same token, you need to respect your personal and family life, so that others will, as well. Just because you are working from home, you do not always have to be available for work. Resist the temptation to work late simply because you are working from home, and avoid the urge to answer work-related phone calls during family time.

Although it is important to avoid interruptions, it is also important to schedule break times. Take breaks that will help your productivity without distracting you from your work responsibilities.

Once you have created a work schedule that suits your needs, you can enjoy the benefits of the flexibility that working at home provides. You need to have enough discipline to stick to your schedule most of the time, but because working at home is not as rigid as working in an office, you can occasionally adjust your schedule to the demands of work or family.

The key is to ensure that this flexibility works to your advantage, rather than hampering your work or disturbing your personal life.

Keep in mind when working from home that, unlike a salaried position, if the work does not get done, you do not get paid. This reminder should help you to stay on track and fight the temptation to take a "quick break" to clean the kitchen or fold the laundry.

For people who "telecommute" for an employer from home, it is important to remember that using work time for personal needs is essentially stealing from the company. Workers who get paid by the hour must be scrupulous in recording their time, or work out an acceptable arrangement with their employer whereby breaks are allowed or work time is approximated.

Create your own office space. Set aside a specific part of the house for your work, and keep this office space clean, neat and organized. Having a separate room that you can call your office is an advantage, but if you do not have a spare room, you can designate any area within a room to serve the purpose.

Having your own "corporate headquarters" creates a physical and mental separation between your work and your home life. It also helps others in the house realize when you are "at work." Your family members will quickly learn that when you are sitting in your office, you are working and are not to be disturbed.

Designation of office space is also important for taxation purposes, since costs associated with the portion of your house that is set aside as workspace can be deducted from taxes.

Your office space and equipment — especially computer equip -ment — should be completely off-limits to children.

Have a company name. Instead of calling yourself, "Rivka Cohen, Graphic Artist" or "Chaim Stern's Van Rental," create a company name for yourself. Put your company name on your e-mail address and signature, and on your stationery, invoices and other materials.

This will boost your credibility and professionalism, which home-based workers often lack. Doing so will also lead to greater self-respect and personal pride in your work, which in turn will increase the respect you receive from others.

Open a separate bank account. Keeping a separate bank account for all work transactions will help you to distinguish between personal and business finances and maintain control over what is happening in each.

If your work and home accounts are separate, you will be able to create budgets for both and make informed financial decisions. You may also find it easier to file your taxes if your work transactions are completely separate from your personal transactions.

Get household help if you need it. Many women start home businesses believing it will allow them to save money on babysitting and household help. But brace yourself, because that may not be the case at all.

Some people can work at home with babies or young children around; others can't. Some people can tackle housework and family responsibilities while working at home; others can't. It could be your temperament, or it could be the nature of your work.

Working at home doesn't mean you have to be a superwoman. Know your limitations, and get babysitters and domestic help when you need it.

Set goals. Prepare a daily list of tasks to attend to. To avoid boredom and burnout, split up different tasks throughout the day so you can exercise different mental "muscles."

You might also want to establish an "MIT" (Most Important Task) to keep you focused and make sure that you get to the item on your to-do list that is most important.

Besides your daily goals, know your long-term goals, and assess periodically whether your daily work reflects those goals.

Invest in professional supplies and equipment. Working at home does not give you license to be sloppy or unprofessional. Set up your space so that it contains all of the necessary equipment, and don't cut corners. Prepare respectable-looking letterheads, fax cover sheets, e-mail templates and invoices, and make sure all your correspondence is conducted on professional-looking stationery.

Buy yourself an up-to-date, working computer, and equip it with the right programs. Investing in professional hardware, software and supplies will give you the tools to produce quality work in an efficient and timely manner.

Your clients will feel the difference, too: if your computer is always crashing, your e-mail is often down or your programs are outdated, they'll lose patience. While your start-up costs may be higher, buying superior products should save you money, with fewer repairs in the long run.

Once you have invested in professional-grade equipment, make sure that you maintain it properly. Beware of the common habit of snacking at the computer or keeping drinks close by. Should coffee spill on your keyboard, you're the one who'll have to pay for the costly repairs.

Make yourself feel like working. Even though you do not have to leave the house for work, it is important that you look respectable and conduct yourself as though you were working in an office. Taking the time to get dressed in a manner suitable for work will make you feel more professional and behave more professionally.

Remember that your clients can sense whether you are a professional working out of a home-based office or a housewife dabbling on the computer.

Your work environment should also be conducive to getting the job done. Working from home has enough distractions; a cluttered workspace should not be one of them. Whether you set aside half an hour a week or five minutes at the start or end of your day, make sure you allocate time to organize your documents, invoices, receipts, supplies and so on.

Facilitate communication. Because you are working remotely, make sure that there are multiple ways for people to contact you — by telephone, cellular, fax, e-mail, etc. — and see to it that you can be easily reached during your work hours.

You should have a separate telephone line and a separate e-mail account for work. Your work telephone should be off-limits to anyone but you, and it should never be answered by children.

Get out. To avoid the feeling of isolation, try to arrange for some of your work to be done outside the home — by scheduling meetings out of the house, for example, or by participating in professional seminars or conferences.

Upgrade your skills. Working alone at home can make your skills rusty. Be sure to keep on top of the latest advances in your field and set aside time to continually upgrade your skills.

Track your performance. As a home-based worker, you need to keep track of your own hours and expenses. Keeping careful records of all work-related income and expenses will make it easier to file tax returns when the time comes. It will also enable you to evaluate your performance.

In addition, we have found that the awareness that comes from writing down hours leads people to work additional hours.

Occasionally, take the time to ask yourself questions. Am I working too few, or too many, hours? How much am I earning? How much am I spending on work-related expenses? Am I disciplined enough in my work? The answers to these questions should help you to plan your work in the future.

*Please note that any tax advice contained in this section is for purely informational purposes. Mesila is not responsible for tax-related content and encourages you to seek guidance from a certified accountant or tax adviser.

Riding Out the Free-lance Roller Coaster ❱

I work as a freelance writer for a popular publication and feel that I am well-suited for this work and perform quite well at it. It also has the great advantage of working from home.

Working as a freelancer has several drawbacks, however. The first is that I do not receive a steady income; it all depends on how much I work. Sometimes there is a short respite in assignments, which leaves a dent in my monthly salary; other times, such as in Tishrei or Nisan, when a significant chunk of the month is Yom Yov, there is a very marked decline in my salary for that month.

Since that is the nature of my work, I have come to terms with this "roller coaster," but I am curious whether Mesila would encourage me to look for a different job with a steady income, even though it would probably pay considerably less per hour.

Like every job, yours has its advantages and disadvantages. You have a job that you enjoy, you are good at and that offers you the luxury of working at home. However, it does not provide you with a steady income, which can be very unsettling.

From the time of Adam Harishon, *parnassah* was meant to be difficult, and the fact that you experience difficulties with your work situation does not mean you are doing anything wrong. In fact, the *Chovos Halevavos* says that if someone works in an industry that experiences a downturn, he should continue to work in that industry.

While this principle may not be applicable to every situation, it does illustrate the need to exhaust every option within your current employment framework before looking elsewhere.

When people meet with work-related challenges, their response is often to seek new employment rather than look for ways to improve their current work situation, which is where the solution usually lies.

In your case, the solution might be quite simple. Instead of giving up your current job, you might try to look for additional freelance work that can supplement your income. Better yet, you might try to find steady part-time work to augment your freelance work. This would allow you to enjoy the benefits of fixed employment — stable income and entitlement to employee benefits — while reaping the rewards of freelance work — better pay and greater flexibility.

The field of writing lends itself very well to the possibility of working at multiple jobs simultaneously. Since you are a freelancer, you can write articles on any topic you want and submit them to other publications, under a pseudonym if necessary. There is also a considerable need for translating services in the Jewish publication world today, so translating might be an option for you, if you are bilingual.

What do you do when there is a respite in assignments? There is no reason why you have to wait for your boss to send you assignments. Mesila's "Guide to Financial Stability" lists being proactive as one of the elements of financial stability. Be proactive!

Lack of assignments should never prevent you from writing. There is so much that can be written! True stories, fiction, humor, stories for children, poetry, biographical articles, inspirational articles, how-to articles, even recipes.

(This suggestion is actually relevant to anyone who is looking to increase his or her income. There has been an explosion in the Jewish literary world recently, and there are, *baruch Hashem*, quite a number of publications today that are eager, and sometimes desperate, for articles to fill their pages. The trouble is that most people do not have confidence in their writing skills and are afraid to submit, or even write, an article for publication. We encourage people to overcome this fear and begin committing their ideas to paper and submitting them for publication.)

In the writing field, as in many other fields, rejections are inevitable. If an article of yours is rejected, do not be discouraged. Reread it, make improvements if necessary and send it elsewhere! Even if your article is never published, you will have benefited from the exercise of writing. It never hurts to improve your writing skills, and the best way to improve is by practicing.

In addition to submitting material to publications, do some networking. Notify any writers and editors you know that you are available for writing assignments. Offer to send them samples of your work, and ask them to recommend you for jobs that they decide to pass up.

The adage, "It's not what you know, it's who you know," is particularly applicable to writers. For this reason, it is generally a good idea to write under your own name, rather than use a pseudonym. This way, people in the writing world will start recognizing your name and your abilities.

Once you have won the recognition and respect of senior editors and high-profile writers, you are in an excellent position to receive any overflow work they might have. But you have to earn this recognition and respect.

How do you do that? First, by making sure that every piece you write is something you can take pride in. Second, by having your writing appear in print consistently. Third, by capitalizing on every opportunity — and creating opportunities — to be in contact with successful writers and editors.

To ride out the Tishrei and Nisan dry spells, we recommend that you work with annual income figures rather monthly income figures. Estimate your income for the whole year — taking into account busy and slow seasons — and calculate the monthly average. Your spending should be commensurate with that monthly average.

This advice applies to people who perform any type of freelance work or have seasonal employment. It also applies to most businesses, because almost every business has busy seasons and slow seasons.

Finding the Right Vocation ❯

I have several friends who are Mesila counselors, but I have refrained from consulting with them because I do not want to expose myself and my situation. I therefore appreciate the opportunity to ask for advice this way.

My story actually begins ten years ago. After learning in kollel for five years and tutoring students privately, I decided to learn a vocation and begin pursuing a livelihood. I underwent some vocational testing to determine what fields were suited to me, and it was recommended that I try either special education or bookkeeping. My tests also showed that I was suited to office work, not sales.

At the time, I was quite pressured for money. I was offered an opportunity to sell life-insurance policies, and an insurance agent invested his time training me and even paid for me to take a course. I stuck with it for about a year and a half and managed to sell a few policies. Finally, I realized that I was not cut out to be a salesman, and I gave up.

I then began to study special education. I didn't apply myself to my studies, however, and I didn't review the material, so I soon gave up on that option.

After special education didn't work out, I registered for a bookkeeping course. Here I felt that I had finally found the vocation that was right for me. Unfortunately, however, I was absent here and there from the classes, and I only achieved scores of 70% on my examinations. Although this was a passing grade, I did not feel comfortable enough to enter the field. I continued studying to become a tax adviser, but again, I didn't review the material, so I gave it up.

During the last three years, I have been trying to learn a profession, without any results. Baruch Hashem, I was offered a job as a rebbi in a prestigious cheder, and the principal and the parents are very happy with me. The problem is, I am only earning NIS 5,500 ($1,300) a month at the job, which is barely enough for me to live on.

This is the situation I am in right now. I hope that you will be able to help me to decide how to proceed. On the one hand, I feel that the best thing for me would be office work, and I wish I would feel confident enough in my bookkeeping and tax-advice ability to look for work in that field. Or maybe I should go back to study bookkeeping again.

Alternatively, maybe because I was not successful in my studies in that area, I should put all that behind me and find work in a different field, maybe real estate?

It is truly a shame that your embarrassment over your financial predicament has prevented you from seeking help. Just as you would not be ashamed to go to a doctor if you had an earache, you should not be embarrassed to consult with a competent adviser if you are suffering financially.

If you have friends who are Mesila counselors, then you most certainly have no reason to fear exposure. Mesila counselors are professionals who operate with the utmost discretion and sensitivity. They are trained to view people independently of their financial problems.

You do not provide any details about the financial crisis you are experiencing, so we do not have any knowledge of your overall situation. If you provide us with more information about your situation, we can offer you a more comprehensive response.

Before we address your question, we would like to emphasize that Mesila never advises people to pursue vocational training or to leave *kollel* or *chinuch* positions. Once our clients have made these decisions — hopefully in consultation with *daas Torah* — we help them to implement those decisions in the most productive way possible.

Since you are already working, it is clear your only uncertainty is what field to pursue. If you felt that you had found your place in the field of bookkeeping, then we would tend to believe that that is probably your best option.

Clearly, you made a serious mistake by not applying yourself to your studies. On the positive side, however, we commend you for your reluctance to enter a field without first mastering it. Before you take a job, it is important that you feel confident in your ability to carry out your duties properly.

We therefore recommend that you take another course in bookkeeping — but this time, make sure to attend all the classes, review the material and do as well as you can on the examinations.

At the same time, we advise you to keep your job as a *rebbi*, since this provides you with a stable income for now.

You should know that there are organizations and government programs that provide financial assistance to people in your situation. You should consider applying for a subsidy to cover the cost of your studies or for a stipend to help you support your family for the duration of your studies.

If you live near a Mesila branch, we suggest that you apply for Mesila's counseling services. Having a Mesila counselor will help you get your financial problems under control, which will enable you to concentrate better on your bookkeeping studies. Your Mesila counselor will also help motivate you to see the course through until its successful conclusion and can eventually help you find work as a bookkeeper.

Once you become a certified bookkeeper, we recommend that you begin doing bookkeeping work on the side, in addition to your job as a *rebbi*. This will enable you to gain experience and confidence without the pressure of having to support your family as a bookkeeper.

Later, you can decide whether to stick with bookkeeping on a part-time basis, or to leave your job as a *rebbi* and take up bookkeeping full-time. We also advise you to continually upgrade your skills and abilities, possibly becoming a certified accountant or tax adviser at some point.

Please remember that there is nothing shameful about being a Mesila client. In fact, many of our clients — in both our Family and Business Divisions — are financially successful individuals who appreciate the opportunity to receive objective, expert assistance managing their finances.

**For more on work and employment,
see also:**

"Paid Late, Again" Chapter 4
"The Tuition Conundrum" Chapter 4

7

Beginning a Business

"One of the keys to
success in business is the
ability to pinpoint your
strengths and
weaknesses — and
seek help with your
weaknesses."

("Advertising Your New Business")

In this chapter:

❯ Am I an Entrepreneur? Part I | 227

❯ Am I an Entrepreneur? Part II | 231

❯ Starting an Import Business | 235

❯ Advertising Your New Business | 239

❯ A New Invention: From Idea to Reality | 244

❯ Aliyah Issues | 249

Am I an Entrepreneur? ❯

Part I

Photography has been a hobby of mine since I was a teenager. Several years ago, I took a professional photography course, and since then, many people have asked me to take portraits of their children.

Until now, I have not charged for my work, but I have always dreamed of operating my own portrait studio. I already own most of the necessary equipment, and I even have an extra room in my basement set aside for this purpose. The problem is that I have absolutely no business experience.

Before I consider opening a professional portrait studio, I want to make sure I am cut out to be my own boss. How do I know whether I have what it takes to succeed in business?

Your prospective portrait studio already has four of the elements necessary for success. First, you have training and expertise. This gives you a significant edge over the many amateurs trying to market themselves as professionals.

Second, you obviously enjoy photography. Running any business involves a lot of frustration — and unless you really love your field, you can burn out very quickly.

Third, your business will require relatively little financing, since you do not need to invest in photographic equipment or a studio. Starting up in your basement is a very wise move, as it will dramatically reduce your operating costs. You can always choose to move to a different location later on.

Fourth, and most important, is the fact that you are asking for advice. This indicates that you understand the need for professional guidance.

The latest statistics from the U.S. Small Business Administration show that two-thirds of new businesses survive at least two years and 44% survive at least four years. (The previous, long-held belief was that 50% of businesses fail in the first year and 95% fail within five years.)

In other words, one out of every two businesses closes within four years. While these statistics can be discouraging, they're meant to help you understand that success in business depends on your willingness to do whatever it takes to make the business work.

Before you decide to open your own portrait studio — or any other business — you need to evaluate whether you possess the personality traits of a successful entrepreneur.

Ask yourself the following questions:

> Am I an ambitious, self-motivated person? (It takes a great deal of discipline, motivation and drive to be your own boss.)

> Am I willing to take calculated risks?

> Can I handle the many technicalities involved in running a business? (To operate a successful business, you need not only vision and imagination, but attention to detail as well.)

> Am I flexible enough to constantly adapt my business to changing market conditions, keep up with technological advances and continually refresh my professional abilities?

❯ Do I have the persistence necessary to steer my business venture through relentless adversity? (The stress of getting a business off the ground and keeping it operational often takes a toll on people's physical and emotional health. It can also adversely affect their family lives.)

❯ Can I get along with difficult people — a demanding client, for instance?

❯ Am I good with numbers? (Running a business involves plenty of number crunching.)

❯ Do I possess good planning and organizational skills?

❯ Am I optimistic?

If you answered "yes" to most of the above questions, you have the makings of a good potential business owner.

Once you have established that your personality is suited to entrepreneurship, the next step is to learn the basic principles of opening and operating a business. Even if you are indeed "cut out for it," you cannot hope to succeed in business without knowing the basic rules of the playing field. You can familiarize yourself with these conventions by taking a business course, or by speaking to business consultants, lawyers and accountants.

Before you open your portrait studio, you should hire a professional business consultant who has experience working with small start-up businesses. Your business consultant will help you carry out market research, assist you in the creation of a strategic business plan, advise you on how to get your business off the ground and provide ongoing guidance once your business is operational.

Mesila offers professional consultations to people in Israel who wish to open a new business or enhance the profitability of their existing business. One of the primary objectives of these consultations is to help people understand what opening and operating a business entails.

Not surprisingly, we encounter many aspiring business owners who believe that having a good idea is the main requirement for success in business. Our job is to show them that a good business idea is like a seed; it might have potential, but it can flourish only if it is carefully cultivated.

Success in any endeavor depends, of course, on *siyatta diShmaya*. Why some businesses succeed and others fail is essentially a function of *ratzon Hashem*. Nevertheless, the fact that the outcome is in Hashem's Hands does not absolve us from having to invest the necessary effort in any enterprise we choose for ourselves.

In summary, for your portrait studio to have a chance at success, you need to have photographic talent, entrepreneurial spirit, business proficiency, a good professional business consultant and sheer determination. With these in place, you can then *daven* for the *siyatta diShmaya* that will ultimately determine the outcome of your venture.

Am I an Entrepreneur? ❯

Part II

I was taken aback by the way you answered the woman who wished to set up a basement portrait studio. You wanted to know if she had what it takes to succeed. You gave a daunting list of required personality traits, then advised her to take a business course, hire a professional consultant, do market research and create a business plan. Any aspiring entrepreneur would have been discouraged by this advice.

Why couldn't you have simply told her to start small and see how it goes? If the studio is successful in bringing in some side income, then she could start dreaming of entrepreneurship.

Had I read your column twenty years ago, when I was thinking of starting my business, I would have been very discouraged. Yes, I made mistakes along the way, but, baruch Hashem, my business has survived quite nicely — without market research, without a business plan and without professional business consultants.

Mesila welcomes questions and feedback, and we appreciate the opportunity to further clarify our position on opening a small business.

The questioner you refer to indicated clearly that she wished to open a business and specifically asked how to determine whether she was cut out for it. We therefore responded by describing the necessary ingredients for successful entrepreneurship.

The list of personality traits we provided was not meant to be daunting. It was meant to show aspiring entrepreneurs what is involved in opening and running a business. This way, they can make informed decisions about whether to make the attempt.

As you pointed out, we did not recommend that the questioner simply begin small and charge people for portraits, to see what happens. This is because we do not believe that there is such a thing as an income-producing hobby. Once you begin to charge people money for a service you provide, you irrevocably cross the line from hobby to business. And once you are in any business, no matter how small, there are risks.

What kind of risks does a small, home-based portrait studio engender? Portraits cost money to develop and print. Photographic equipment is fragile; it needs to be maintained, repaired and upgraded frequently. Even if no money is invested in advertising or corporate identity, there are other sales and marketing tools that may need to be created or purchased, like receipt books, computer hardware and software, stationery, business cards and envelopes.

An accountant will almost certainly have to be hired. And there is always the question of what the person could be doing during the time she devotes to the portrait studio. If she would be working at another job, the lost income would also be a risk factor.

Regardless of how small the operation is, protocols will need to be established for hours of operation, inquiries, receipts, speed of delivery, setting up and canceling appointments, price setting and satisfaction guarantees.

When the questioner took portraits for a hobby, client satisfaction was not a very significant consideration. No one, for example, would have expected a refund if they were disappointed with the way their portraits turned out or with the amount of time it took for their portraits to be ready.

However, clients' expectations will invariably be much higher when they are required to pay for their portraits. The level of professionalism, quality and service will come under close scrutiny.

If a portrait studio is charging people money, it is, in effect, competing with larger portrait studios — including department stores. It is pointless to charge people money for portraits unless you have something to offer that other portrait studios do not. This is called a niche, or an edge, and it can be anything from originality of poses to personalized attention. (Low prices can also be a niche; however, it is unlikely that a small, home-based portrait studio can offer better prices than Sears or Wal-Mart specials.)

Finding a niche requires market research and the help of a business consultant. This does not mean that the portrait studio has to be "grandiose"; it just means that it has to follow the rules of business.

Advising someone to jump into a business venture of any size and "see how it goes" is, in Mesila's view, very bad advice. The fact that some people do succeed in business without market research, a business plan or a business consultant is no justification for encouraging a person to go it alone and be unprepared.

We would also like to point out several things:

1. You opened your business twenty years ago — when terms like "e-commerce," "offshore" and "outsourcing" were not very popular. The business environment today is incomparable to what it was two decades ago. Today the cards are stacked much more heavily against aspiring business owners than they were then.

2. You write that you did make some mistakes. These mistakes probably cost you quite a bit of money and heartache. Instead of learning the hard way, as you did, why should an aspiring business owner not learn from professionals — before making the mistakes?

3. Just because you succeeded does not mean others will. As we pointed out previously, statistically, most small businesses fail within a few years, usually leaving their owners with debts and other headaches.

Mesila encourages people to find ways to turn their business dreams into reality. Our objective is not to discourage people from opening businesses, but to take steps to increase their chances of success.

Starting an Import Business ❯

> I live in Israel, and I have a cousin in the United States who manufactures a low-cost, high-quality line of leather accessories. These accessories are sold in major department-store chains across the United States and Europe.
>
> I work as a saleslady in a store that sells similar accessories, and I think there would be a demand here in Israel for my cousin's line. My cousin is willing to give me exclusive rights to distribute his products in Israel, but only on condition that I guarantee him a minimum order of thousands of pieces.
>
> I have a small basement apartment that I could use as a warehouse to store the goods, and I would like to begin importing them and offering them to stores. How do I start?

We congratulate you on your enterprising attitude and on your willingness to start a large-scale import operation from scratch.

Opening an operation such as the one you describe has many logistical elements, such as building a brand, making agreements with store owners and/or distributors, making land and sea shipping arrangements, coordinating legal and taxation issues and arranging suitable storage facilities.

The first thing you need to do is check the tariff code of the items you wish to import and obtain some important information. What is the country of origin? Can goods legally be imported from that country to Israel? Does that country have a free-trade agreement with Israel? What kind of taxes or tariffs will you be charged?

Once you have this information, you can start working on a business plan that will detail how your import business will operate, how it will be financed, what your true costs will be after shipping and duties, and what profits you expect to earn. Your business plan should also include a description of your market edge — i.e., what differentiates you from your competitors.

Before implementing your business plan, you need to perform some market research. The Israeli market is tiny compared to the U.S. and European markets, and you need to find out if the existing demand is indeed sufficient to warrant opening the type of import operation you describe.

As part of your market research, you should visit stores in different cities, see what's on the shelves, and talk to customers, distributors and store managers. All of the information you gather should be written down.

Before visiting stores, develop a list of questions, such as: Are there customers for this new line of products? What similar products are available, and how much is their retail cost? What type of store sells these products? How many of these products are typically sold? Would store managers be willing to incorporate your line into their merchandise?

Once you have mapped out the market and collected all this information, you need to organize it in a well-structured report, which you can then share with your cousin's company in the United States.

At that stage, you might want to consider traveling to your cousin's

U.S. headquarters to learn the business and observe from up close how the operation works. A good salesperson has to know his merchandise inside out and be able to answer questions from potential buyers without hesitation.

You can ask your cousin and his staff to show you how they market their product in the United States and Europe. This will teach you how they managed to build a successful model. In addition, find out who their salespeople and representatives are. Talk to these people, hear how they attracted department store chains and other wholesale clients, find out how they do their pricing, and learn from them how to begin your own business.

We would advise you to enlist the help of your cousin's company and Israeli distributors in building a price list. You should also obtain a price quote from a freight forwarder to determine what your shipping costs will be.

From your question, it appears that you have an advantage over your competitors in the existing market because of the high quality and relatively low wholesale cost of your products. Remember, however, that low wholesale cost does not necessarily translate into low retail costs after the import process is finished, because every middleman involved needs to turn a profit.

Once you have performed your market research, completed your business plan and built your price list, you can enter negotiations with distributors and department store chains in Israel.

At this point, we would not advise you to take on the entire responsibility for dealing with the merchandise. Owning a basement apartment does not automatically qualify you to manage a warehouse. Managing a warehouse is a job in and of itself, and it requires a substantial investment of time and money. You also need to develop systems for trucking, loading, unloading, storage, inventory control, security, insurance and more. In Mesila's view, you would be better off setting up a system wherein most of the logistics are handled by the retailers you will be dealing with.

For your purposes, there are two major types of retailers: department-store chains and individual stores. Selling to department store chains seems like an attractive option for you, because there is a possibility that the financing costs and storage arrangements will be seen to by the chains, and if so, you might not have to assume much risk.

Selling to individual stores is much more difficult, however, since it requires you to make all of the technical arrangements. We therefore advise you not to work directly with stores but to work through a distributor.

Find an existing distributor and come to an agreement that he will assume the burden of financing and the business risk initially. The distributor may be willing to assume the risk if he likes the product, because he is merely adding another line of products to his catalogue and the risk to him is therefore not that high.

If you were to assume the risk yourself, however, you would have to set up all the infrastructure necessary for successful distribution. That infrastructure is complex and is difficult to build from scratch. Later, when your operation becomes more established, you can consider assuming those risks yourself.

Before you do any of this, however, make sure that you have a legally binding contract with your cousin protecting your rights as an exclusive agent to Israel. Otherwise, the distributor can easily cut you out and begin dealing directly with your cousin's company.

Since we are not familiar with all the details of your prospective business, the recommendations we have offered here are merely suggestions. We strongly advise you to meet with a professional business consultant before implementing any of these recommendations.

Advertising Your New Business ❯

I have been working for close to a decade in a very success-ful business that buys antique items from the public and resells them to dealers. For years, I did most of the buying and selling, while my boss and his other employees handled the running of the business. I recently decided to leave the business and go out on my own, since I feel that I know the business inside out.

I know that the first thing I need to do to get my new busi-ness off the ground is advertise, and so I hired an advertising agency to help me. They created some nice ads, but I have no idea whether the ads will work, and I am hesitant about investing so much money in something so intangible. How can I know whether the ads will bring me business?

We would like to preface our answer by pointing out that going from being an employee to being an entrepreneur is a very perilous route — especially when you are going into direct competition with your former employer.

When you worked for your former boss, he and others took care of things like cash flow, financing, inventory control, accounting and the like, leaving you free to focus on what you did best: buying and selling antiques. But as important as buying and selling is, it is only one aspect of the overall business. As a business owner, you will be responsible for all aspects of running the business — including many in which you have no experience.

Before starting your own business, you need to acknowledge that, like every businessperson, you have strengths and weaknesses. One of the keys to success in business is the ability to pinpoint your strengths and weaknesses — and seek help with your weaknesses.

Because you are going into head-to-head competition with your former boss, your new business is a high-risk venture. Even if you think there is enough business to go around, people will need to have a very good reason to bring their merchandise to you, rather than to your former boss. Advertising alone will not convince people to do this.

To your credit, you acknowledge that advertising is a weak point for you. But you also seem to think that advertising is the first thing you need to do to get your business off the ground. When opening a business, advertising should actually be the last thing you do.

First, you need to build a business plan, create a budget, develop a marketing strategy and take care of all the technical details of setting up your business. Your experience in buying and selling antiques will probably not take you very far in any of these areas.

Because your question is specifically related to advertising, we will focus on guiding you through the process of creating successful advertisements. Please keep in mind, however, that advertising is only one small aspect of opening and running a business.

Before you can even think about advertising, you need to create a solid marketing strategy and establish your marketing position. The success of your new business will depend largely on the strength of your marketing efforts, so it would be a good idea for you to hire a professional business consultant who specializes in marketing and advertising.

Your consultant can help you identify your niche, position your business vis-à-vis the competition, develop a good marketing strategy and formulate the message you want to convey to your potential customers.

Then, you and your consultant can build a reasonable advertising budget, establish advertising objectives (e.g., increasing sales, enhancing customer awareness), and decide on a method of gauging the success of your advertising campaigns.

At that point, you will be ready to contact an advertising agency. Your consultant should be able to recommend a good advertising agency, and might even be able to negotiate better prices for you.

Getting back to your question, it is understandably hard for you to evaluate the effectiveness of the advertisements your agency has designed. You are not a marketing/advertising professional, and the professionals at the advertising agency will obviously be biased in favor of the ads they themselves have created.

Based on the information you have provided, it sounds as though you are relying on your advertising agency to develop both your advertisements and your marketing strategy. This is a mistake that many small- and medium-sized businesses make, typically due to the lack of a professional marketing manager.

To advertise effectively, you need both a strong message and a good vehicle. Advertising agencies know how to create the vehicle to deliver your message, but they are not usually qualified to decide what your market-positioning strategy should be.

Large advertising agencies try to address this problematic issue by employing a strategist — a marketing specialist who, for an additional fee, builds a marketing concept for the client. This marketing concept is forwarded to the agency's creative team, which then builds an advertisement to act as the vehicle for that concept.

Even if your advertising agency does have a strategist on board, it would be wiser to retain the services of an independent business consultant who can help you with all aspects of your business.

Another point to consider when working with an advertising agency: the agency's fee is a percentage of your advertising budget, which means that the larger your advertising budget, the higher the agency's profits. Your objective, however, is to keep your advertising budget as low as possible. This creates a potential conflict of interest.

A good way to avoid this potential conflict of interest is to create a marketing strategy and concept with your business consultant before approaching an advertising agency, and then you can work closely with your business consultant vis-à-vis the advertising agency. The consultant will look out for your interests, guiding you through the process of turning your marketing concept into a compelling advertisement.

To summarize, working with a professional business consultant will significantly lower your business risks. Your consultant will help you:

1. Create a business plan and operating budget.
2. Identify your customer base and niche (market segmentation).
3. Distinguish yourself from the competition (market positioning).
4. Develop a marketing strategy and concept.
5. Build an advertising budget.
6. Define your advertising objectives.
7. Work with your advertising agency to ensure optimal results.
8. Evaluate the success of your advertising campaigns.

9. Periodically adjust your marketing strategy to reflect changing market conditions.

Although consultants generally do charge a lot, the money you invest in a consultant should save you money in the long run — and often, in the short run as well.

A New Invention:
From Idea to Reality ❯

I have an idea for a simple invention that I think people would find both useful and beneficial. I do not wish to divulge too many details about the invention, for obvious reasons, but I will say that it is a small foam device designed to ease a common form of physical strain.

I met with managers of two different department stores to find out if they would be interested in offering my invention for sale, but neither one seemed very enthusiastic about the idea. Nevertheless, I think it is a good idea, and I am sure that once they see it and use it themselves they would be willing to market it in their stores.

I spoke to experts in the foam industry, and they told me that, locally, it would cost about $2,500 to create the mold necessary to begin production of my invention and another $5,000 to produce a thousand of these items. Manufacturing in China would be much cheaper, but I would have to produce far more than a thousand items at a time.

Currently, I work at a low-paying job that barely supports my family. I am hopeful that my invention will change this, but right now I don't have the money to pay for an initial run. To begin producing my invention, I will need to borrow money.

Having no experience in manufacturing or marketing, I am not sure how to proceed. Can Mesila advise me what my next steps should be?

We are intrigued by your mysterious invention, and we applaud your initiative in looking for a way to manufacture and market it. We also commend you for doing some serious research into how to begin producing your invention, for finding out from department store managers if they would be willing to sell it, and for your persistence in the face of their unenthusiastic response.

The majority of good ideas for inventions never reach the market, mostly because the people who think of these ideas tend to be creative and imaginative rather than business-minded and down-to-earth.

In addition, ideas for inventions — even the most useful inventions, like the telephone, photocopier and radio — are often greeted at first with apathy.

Like these famous inventions, your invention might very well prove to be useful and popular. On the other hand, it might not. Because there is no way to know at this point which way your invention will go, we advise you to continue to look for a way to turn your invention into reality, but in a way that minimizes risk.

If you had some start-up capital of your own, you could perhaps afford to invest some money into trying out your idea. Without this start-up capital, however, you have to be extremely wary about investing borrowed money into an idea that might not get off the ground.

At this point, we would advise you to look for a professional business consultant who can guide you through the steps of turning your idea into reality. Together, you can create a business plan detailing who your potential market is, the size of your potential market, and the costs of manufacturing and marketing.

Your consultant may recommend that you present your business plan to venture capital (VC) funds or investors who can potentially finance the start-up costs of producing your invention.

Before you can finance the production of your invention, you need to calculate what the real costs are. You already know roughly how much production costs would be, but you also need to take into account non-production related costs.

Your invention will need an attractive form of packaging, which requires design and production of its own. You also need marketing tools such as a catchy name for your product and some form of promotional advertising to introduce your invention to people and convince them that it is really something necessary. And, of course, before marketing your invention you will need to protect your rights to it by taking out the necessary patents.

All of these things cost money. In fact, the peripheral costs of marketing your invention might easily eclipse the costs of producing a trial run of the invention.

Moreover, handling all the tasks involved in taking your invention from concept to reality can be very time-consuming, and that might come at the expense of your job. We strongly caution you against slacking off at your job at this point; as low-paying as it might be, right now it represents your entire livelihood, and you absolutely cannot afford to risk that.

It is important for you to realize that your idea cannot possibly come to fruition with you working on it alone. While it costs money to hire a business consultant and prepare a professional business plan, this expense pales in comparison to the cost of manufacturing and marketing a brand-new invention. It is far better to spend money on a consultant than to go ahead by yourself and possibly make very expensive mistakes along the way.

To reduce your costs and your risks, we recommend that you start with a small market trial of your invention. This market trial should be a crucial element of your business plan.

Rather than producing a thousand or more, try to find a way to produce fifty or a hundred. Consult with experts in the foam industry to find out whether you can do this without investing in a specialized mold. Mass production in China should be out of the question at this early stage.

Once you have a few samples of your product, look for creative, low-cost ways to market them. You can try selling them at street fairs; you can find a place to set up a small vendor's stand; you can ask stores to put a few of them on display; or you can post signs advertising your invention and sell it from your home. See if people are interested in buying the item, and ask them if they have any ideas for improving it.

During the market trial, you should sell your invention at the price that you are planning to charge when you begin mass-producing the product. This may be lower than your initial cost price, and you should therefore be prepared to take a loss on the market trial. Later, you can find ways to reduce your costs (such as by manufacturing larger quantities or manufacturing in China), and create a reasonable profit margin for yourself.

To determine what price to ask for your product, you should speak to distributors and retailers to find out how much they would sell such an item for. You should also ask potential customers how much they would be willing to pay for such an item. When speaking to people, pay attention to their reactions to the product. Do they seem enthusiastic about it?

You can also ask people if they would be interested in buying the product, and if they can think of any added features or improvements that would make them more interested in buying the product. Their verbal responses and body language can give you valuable cues that can help you gauge the demand for the product.

Your business consultant may also want to put together a focus group to help you gauge the demand for your product and fine-tune it before you begin to manufacture it.

The responses to any questions you ask people about your product should be written down. Later, you can review these responses and use them to estimate the demand for your product and decide on a price that is neither too expensive nor too cheap.

If your market trial shows promising results, you can begin approaching store managers once again — this time, equipped with samples of your product, the results of your market trial, and the confidence that you have a product that not only can sell but has already sold.

If your trial is not successful, then you have lost very little. You can still try to improve the idea, fine-tune the business plan, and introduce it to other potential entrepreneurs.

Do not be discouraged by failure or lack of enthusiasm; if you think you have a good idea, keep on looking for ways to bring it to fruition. At the same time, however, do not risk your family's financial stability by pouring significant amounts of money into an idea that has not yet proven itself.

Aliyah Issues ❯

We made aliyah from the United States with our five children several months ago and are still looking to establish ourselves financially in Israel.

I am an engineer and my wife is a medical technician. She is looking for a job in her field, but I am thinking about going into business. I have worked as an engineer for the past twenty years and I feel it's time for a change. I also don't think I know Hebrew well enough to work as an engineer in Israel.

We have rented out our home in the States and we are renting an apartment in Israel. Now we are thinking of selling our U.S. home to buy something here, so we can feel more settled.

Before I go into business or sell my house, I would like to know what Mesila has to say about these two courses of action.

While we would not categorically rule out either possibility, our recommendation is that you postpone these weighty decisions to a later date, when you are indeed more settled in Israel.

As new immigrants, you and your children have to get used to a new language, an unfamiliar culture and a different standard of living. You also have to make new friends, get to know your neighbors, learn how to navigate your surroundings, and help your children adapt to their new environment and a different educational system.

There is so much change taking place in your lives right now that we do not think it is a good idea to introduce any more change. In Mesila's view, both you and your wife should start seeking work in your respective fields. Even if you had some savings to tide you over at the start, worrying about *parnassah* can hamper one's ability to make levelheaded decisions, and it is therefore important for you to begin earning a steady income as soon as possible.

You say your Hebrew is not good enough to work in engineering, a field in which you have decades of experience. Why, then, do you think your Hebrew will be good enough to become an entrepreneur, an area in which you do not have expertise?

If you are serious about earning a living in Israel, whether as an engineer or as an entrepreneur, it is critical that you attend an *ulpan* to upgrade your knowledge of Hebrew. Knowing the language well will increase your chances of landing a good job, give you greater confidence at work and, in general, ease the acclimatization process.

Many people who move to Israel make the mistake of thinking that "everyone knows English nowadays" and that they will be able to manage without much Hebrew. But that is rarely the case in the work world. Even if you are in a field where fluent English is an advantage, most everyday work conversations, meetings and reports are in Hebrew. Job seekers who stumble over their Hebrew during telephone calls and interviews are far less likely to land the jobs they want.

You need not put your job hunt on hold while attending *ulpan*; even if prospective employers are concerned about your ability to speak Hebrew, they will probably be satisfied when you tell them that you are in the process of studying it.

Once you have established your income and established yourself in Israel, you can re-evaluate going into business.

There are a number of reasons why we think it is unwise for you to go into business at this point:

1. Any new business venture carries the risk of failure. You are too new in the country to experience business disappointment or failure.

2. Before entering the business world, you need to assess whether you are cut out to be an entrepreneur. If, indeed, you possess the qualities of successful entrepreneurs — ambition, vision, self-discipline, flexibility, persistence, optimism, good communication and negotiation skills, and so on — then you can begin to study the market, learn the rules of business and develop the skills necessary for entrepreneurship. This is a process that takes time.

3. The Israeli business environment is unforgiving, to say the least. To survive in the battlefield of Israeli business, you need to be a warrior, and it is very difficult to be a warrior on foreign territory.

With regard to buying a new home, we encourage you to delay purchasing a home in Israel for a few years. Because your home in the United States is rented out and is earning income, you have no reason to rush on selling it. First get used to life in Israel and be sure you are able to make it here.

The reality is that many "Anglo" *olim* return to their countries of origin within a few years of making *aliyah*. We are not trying to discourage you about the prospects for your future in Israel, but we are cautioning you not to make hasty decisions that you may regret.

Until you are firmly settled in the country — financially and emotionally — it makes sense to keep your options open.

We wish you a *yishuv tov*.

For more on starting a business, see also:
"The Right Job" Chapter 6

8

Managing a Business

"Many businesses fail because their owners view the business as their own property and the business money as their own money.
It's not."

("Business vs. Family Finance")

In this chapter:

❯ Business vs. Family Finances | 255

❯ Doing Business on the Books | 264

Business vs. Family Finances ❯

Several years ago, I borrowed money to buy a van and opened a private car service. Baruch Hashem, my car service has become quite popular, and I am very busy.

For several years, I struggled to pay back the loan I took for the van. Now that I have finished repaying the loan, I was hoping I would not have to struggle anymore, but that does not seem to be the case.

I very often find myself strapped for cash, and never manage to put anything aside for savings. I have a few friends who also drive for a living, and they seem to be managing nicely. None of them is getting rich as a driver, but they all agree that if you are transporting people full-time, you should be able to earn a decent living. I have compared my prices with those of other drivers who are doing well, and my rates seem to be average, perhaps even a bit on the higher end.

People usually pay me in cash, and I use that cash to pay for my expenses. If I am charging relatively high prices and am busy all day, shouldn't I be making a good living? Why am I always struggling to make ends meet?

You say you are working full-time and charging relatively high prices, but you give no indication of approximately how much you earn or spend in an average day, week, month or year. To evaluate your situation accurately, we would need to review your revenues, your work-related costs and your family's expenditures. We suspect, however, that these figures are almost as unknown to you as they are to us.

People usually pay you in cash, you say, and you use that cash to pay for your expenses. Which expenses are you referring to? Gas? Food? Rent?

Based on the information you provide, it would appear that there is no separation between your business and personal finances. You are operating only one account, an amalgamation of your car service revenues, vehicular costs and personal expenses.

When you go to the dentist, you pay with the money you earned that morning from transporting a family to the country. When you drive passengers to the airport, you pay for gas and tolls with the money you were supposed to give your wife for groceries. When you have a particularly good day, and you come home with a bulging wallet, you treat your family to supper at a restaurant.

We don't know if any of the above scenarios actually happens to you. These are just typical examples of what might be going on with your finances.

With no clear demarcation between business and personal finances, you have no way of knowing how much of your income is going back into the business and how much is going to support your family. If you worked at a salaried job and earned a regular paycheck, you would know exactly how much your income is and how much you can spend without going into debt. In your line of work, however, it is not so simple to know how much you are earning. Your income fluctuates on a daily basis, and you have no paycheck against which to balance your expenditures.

To take control of your finances, you have to begin managing your business finances and personal finances separately. This separation is critical for successful management of any business, even a no-frills business like a private car service.

A business needs to be viewed as a completely separate entity and treated as such. Even though you own the business, you cannot take money out of it at will. Many businesses fail because their owners view the business as their own property and the business money as their own money. It's not.

The business is a separate account, from which money can be withdrawn only under specific conditions and at predetermined times. Taking money out of a business at whim is actually a form of stealing: stealing from your creditors, stealing from your suppliers and stealing from your employees. Even if you do not have any creditors, suppliers or employees, taking money from the business at whim is still a form of stealing: It robs you of any awareness of what is going on in the business and hampers your ability to make informed decisions.

Siphoning money from the business to the family before putting money back into the business is a recipe for killing the business. At Mesila, we often explain this concept to clients with an analogy: If you want a cow to produce milk, you need to feed it. Many people starve the cow that is their business and their livelihood, milking it continually without giving anything back.

Business owners have to remember that business-related expenses always take precedence over personal expenses. Business expenses are priorities because they are the fodder that feeds the cow that gives the milk. If you feed your children before feeding the cow, eventually there won't be any more milk with which to feed the children. If feeding your children is your priority, as indeed it should be, then you have to make sure that your cow (or your van, as the case may be) is well fed.

To get your finances in order, the first thing you need to do is open an account for your business. This "account" can simply be a second wallet, although we recommend that it be an actual bank account, since it is easier to keep track of bank transactions than of the money that goes in and out of a wallet.

From now on, your business and family accounts should be run as two completely separate entities. Having two separate accounts will help you maintain control of what is happening in each and will also give you the discipline to keep the two apart from one another.

Once you have separated your business and family finances, how do you make sure both are being managed correctly? By keeping accurate records of every transaction you make, both at work and at home. Having these records will give you a clear picture of exactly what is happening with your finances, but there are other reasons why it is important for you to keep records.

There are two fundamental — and somewhat conflicting — ingredients to financial success in any field. The first ingredient is passion for what you do, and the second ingredient is the desire to earn financial compensation. If a person does his work only because he wants to make money, he probably will not do very good work and he probably will not make too much money. On the other hand, if a person does his work because he deems it enjoyable, important or beneficial, and is not driven by the urge to earn money, he might do very good work, but he will probably not earn much money in the process.

As a driver, you need to enjoy and value your work — independent of the money it brings you. But you also need to maintain a strong awareness of the fact that you are working to make money. Many people pursue their livelihood on autopilot, doing the same thing day after day without ever assessing the financial benefit it brings them, evaluating their options for increasing that benefit or taking proactive measures to improve their financial standing.

Keeping records of your transactions will force you to connect to the numbers aspect of your business, which will help you run your business proactively. Additionally, keeping track of your income and expenses will empower you to make informed financial decisions in both your business and family finances and create a budget plan that will help you maintain financial stability.

You say you are constantly struggling to make ends meet, despite earning what you consider to be a respectable livelihood. This type of financial chaos is the inevitable result of poor record-keeping. Without accurate records of what is coming in and what is going out, you cannot possibly know what is really happening with your finances. Even if you manage to stay out of debt, you have no way of ensuring that you are financially prepared for eventualities such as the need to replace your vehicle, your washing machine or your children's clothing.

From now on, no money should ever enter or leave either of your accounts without being recorded in a notebook, daily planner or computerized spreadsheet. (Don't use scraps of paper; they tend to disappear.)

Before you transfer money from your business account into your personal account, you need to develop an organized system of calculating your gross and net income.

Calculating gross income is simple — it's just a matter of adding up all of the money that goes into your business account. But calculating net income (i.e., take-home profit) is a bit more complex.

Before you can calculate your take-home profit, you need to deduct all of your business expenses. To do this:

a) Calculate your average monthly and yearly business expenses, including:

- fluctuating expenses (such as gas, tolls, repairs and taxes)

- fixed expenses (such as vehicle financing, depreciation, insurance and accounting)

b) Multiply monthly expenses by twelve.

c) Add annual expenses to that figure to arrive at an estimated yearly expense total.

d) *A word of caution:* In your industry, it is very difficult to predict your expenses accurately. If this is the first time you are making this calculation, pad your estimated yearly business expenses by 10%-15%, to allow for fluctuation and unexpected costs. In subsequent years, your estimate will probably be more accurate, so padding it by 5% should be sufficient.

e) To calculate the cost of depreciation, we advise you to ask an accountant what the official government figures for vehicular depreciation are (i.e., the amount the government allows you to deduct from your taxes to cover depreciation). You might think these figures are very conservative, but they are based on professional analysis and are probably more accurate than any figures you can come up with on your own. As your vehicle ages, it will cost more to maintain, so be sure to consider that in your expense budget.

f) At the end of every year, it is important that you compare your actual recorded expenses to your estimated expenses to see whether your business expense budget was accurate.

Once you have an idea of how much money needs to be set aside every year for business expenses, you can calculate what your take-home profits are. In your type of business, it is difficult to predict how much you will earn in any given period.

Because your profits depend on how much you drive, the method we recommend for profit calculation is dividing your yearly expenses by the number of kilometers (or miles) you drive every year. The figure you obtain is your cost per kilometer. This is what you do with that figure:

a) At the end of every week, or every month, check how many kilometers you drove.

b) Multiply the number of kilometers by your cost per kilometer, and set aside that amount of money to cover the expenses that correspond to the amount of kilometers you accumulated.

c) What is left in your business account is your take-home profits, which you can now transfer to your family account.

During busy seasons, you might find yourself with a lot of money left over in your wallet after deducting for business expenses, while during slow seasons, you might have very little left over. The key to maintaining financial stability is to be disciplined. During busy times, put away money for slow times.

Your family budget should be built at the same time that you build your business budget. Track your family's expenditures (fixed and fluctuating, monthly and yearly) to determine how much money you need to live on. Then compare your family's expenditures to the average profits yielded by your car service. This will allow you to determine whether your lifestyle actually reflects your income.

Mesila has created a set of budget questionnaires to help people build family budgets easily and efficiently. (The appendix contains samples of these budget questionnaires.)

If your income and expenditures are not balanced, you will need to find alternative ways of generating income or make lifestyle adjustments to reduce your expenditures. One straightforward way to generate additional income is by notching your prices up slightly and seeing what happens. If you are still busy, then you lost nothing; if you see you are losing customers, you can always go back to your original prices.

In any event, you should have an answer prepared for customers who ask you why you charge more than some other drivers. Is there any added service you provide that other drivers do not? Is there something that differentiates your car service from others?

To reduce expenditures, we suggest that you look for creative ways to lower your repair and maintenance costs. This might mean learning to do basic maintenance and repairs yourself or finding a cheap, but competent, mechanic. It might also mean using generic, rather than brand-name, parts.

In addition, it is critical to exercise caution when lending or renting out your van. When you give your van to other drivers, you have no control over the way those drivers use (or abuse) it, and the wear and tear your van absorbs might very well outweigh any potential gains.

We also recommend that you meet with a professional business consultant and build a cash flow plan. Your plan should take into account your vehicle financing, maintenance, repair and depreciation costs and other business expenses, as well as your personal living expenses. The plan should also determine how often you should expect to replace your van and how much money needs to be set aside every year to cover that purchase. Generally, it does not pay to wait until your van breaks down completely before replacing it. Three years is usually a reasonable estimate for the lifespan of a car-service van.

There is no such thing as a no-risk business. Carefully research any industry or business before jumping into it. Learn the risks, find out how to minimize them, get professional advice — and only then decide whether or not it is for you.

Doing Business on the Books ❯

I run a women's clothing store from my basement, and the store's finances are a mess. The store is not an official business, and all the income is "off the books." I try to keep handwritten records of all the transactions, but it's almost impossible to keep track of every sale, purchase and return.

A bookkeeper friend advised me to get a vendor's permit, issue proper receipts, hire an accountant and start reporting the store's income to the authorities. She said that once my business is set up "on the books," it will be easier for me to ensure that all transactions are properly documented and recorded.

If I have to report my income, however, most of my profits will go to taxes. I also don't have the time or the know-how to handle all the technicalities and paperwork involved.

Do you think I should become "official," with all the expense and hassle that entails?

Yes! We agree with your bookkeeper friend fully.

First of all, running a business "off the books" is illegal and has halachic implications that are beyond the scope of this column. But even from a purely business-related standpoint, running a business "off the books" is extremely objectionable.

For one thing, if you are eventually caught — and there is no way to guarantee that you will not be caught — you will be presented with a bill that will wipe out whatever profits you made by trying to outsmart the authorities.

Even if you are never caught, however, you are doing yourself a great disservice by running your business "off the books."

Because you are not an official business, you have to restrict your business activities to ensure that you stay out of sight of the authorities. You have to keep your advertising efforts very low-key, you must exercise caution when dealing with your suppliers, and you need to trust that the people coming to your store will not report you. Moreover, you are actually stifling the potential growth of your business.

If you were to get a vendor's permit, you would have the option of moving your business out of your basement into a retail location with higher visibility, increased foot traffic and greater respectability. Without the permit, you are stuck in your house — and that may not be the optimal location for your store.

There's an old saying: "A business that is run under the table cannot grow higher than the table." Until you register your store with the authorities, it will never be able to compete with "real" stores. Yes, "real" stores have to pay taxes, but they are free to do whatever they think will maximize their profits without having to look over their shoulders.

But there is another important reason why it is in your interests to run your business "on the books." It is virtually impossible to keep accurate business records if you do not maintain financial transparency vis-à-vis the authorities. And for a business owner, accurate record keeping is not optional; it is a fundamental part of running a business.

If you do not keep good records, how can you know what your take-home profits are? For that matter, how can you know that your business is making money at all?

In today's competitive business environment, profit margins are usually very tight. You can only know what your true profit margins are by keeping accurate records. And you can only make informed decisions about your business if you know what your profit margins are.

Accurate financial records can also alert you to potential red lights, such as a worker stealing or a problem with your pricing. Financial records tell the story of what is going on in the business; without them, you are operating blindly.

If you are trying to stay out of view, accurate record keeping is difficult indeed. As long as you have to cover your tracks, you cannot take the chance that someone might discover your records, and you certainly cannot avail yourself of the professional tools available to help business owners track their revenues, costs and profits.

Record keeping for a contemporary business is too complex a task to be tackled with pen and paper alone. But if your business is "off the books," what other system can you use? You certainly would not want to keep computerized records, for fear of being caught.

Running a business legally automatically gives you a framework in which to set up an efficient record-keeping system. The need to report all your transactions forces you to run your business in a disciplined, professional manner and eliminates the need for hand-written records scrawled on scraps of paper in codes you once devised but no longer understand.

You are concerned that most of your profits will disappear when you begin to pay tax. How do you know that? Did you speak to a competent accountant before arriving at that conclusion? If not, we suggest that you do so. You might be pleasantly surprised to discover that many creative — and legal — accounting solutions exist to help small business owners reduce their tax burden.

If, indeed, all of your profits would disappear if you were to pay tax, then your profit margins are probably too small to justify your store's existence in the first place. In Mesila's view, a business that can only remain profitable by dodging the taxman is not a viable business.

You also say you do not have the time or know-how to handle the technicalities and paperwork of running an official business. We therefore recommend that you hire a good accountant or book-keeper who can help you with the technicalities and paperwork.

You are not saving yourself paperwork by staying off the books — instead, you are letting your business drown in a sea of haphazard, poorly recorded transactions.

Even if you were to decide, for your own reasons, to continue running your business "off the books," you would still have to go through the hassle of calculating your profits. Otherwise, you have no way of knowing how much money your business is earning — or losing.

9

The Blessing of Financial Independence

"Money is not
necessarily
the solution to financial
problems."

("Can I Take Tzedakah
on a One-Time Basis?")

In this chapter:

❯ Financial Independence:
  A Function of Mindset, Not Money | 271

❯ Can I Take Tzedakah on a One-Time Basis? | 276

❯ A Goal for All Families | 280

Financial Independence:
A Function of Mindset, Not Money ❯

My net annual income is about $80,000. With six children, all of whom are in school or playgroup, my annual expenses are about $100,000. We live very modestly, and the only major "luxuries" we allow ourselves are summer camps for the children (which we feel is necessary for various reasons) and a second car (which is also necessary because we live in a suburban area).

In order to cover my shortfall, I need an additional $20,000 a year. There is nothing left to cut from our budget, and it is not feasible for either my wife or I to increase our income significantly, especially in the current economic climate. I am loathe to accept community support, but I fear that I will have to do that. Do you see any other alternatives for me?

We are impressed with your desire to remain financially independent and not accept community support, despite your ongoing struggle to cover your expenses.

You understand, surely, that there are no instant solutions to complex financial challenges, nor is there any one piece of advice that can magically dispel your dilemma.

We do have an answer to your question, but we have to warn you that our answer is hard-hitting. Since you have asked the question, however, we will tell you the answer, in the hope that you will not take umbrage or feel that we are passing judgment on you. The fact that we don't know you should make it easier for you to realize that we are talking about people in general terms, not about you specifically.

Now, for our answer:

If financial independence were important enough to you, you would find a way to manage with $80,000.

It's a tough pill to swallow, we realize. But it's the truth — and there are two reasons why we know that it's the truth.

Reason number one: There are other families the same size as yours who do manage to live on $80,000 a year or less — so it is possible, theoretically, for you to manage on your income.

You may be thinking, "Those families are different." And you are right — they are different; every family is different. But that doesn't mean that you can't learn from them. Sure, you can find reasons why they can manage and you can't — but if you are genuinely interested in living within your means, you'll take an honest look at families like yours who do manage and imitate some of the lifestyle choices that allow them to preserve their financial independence. Imitating the lifestyle choices of these families may involve a different kind of house, car, menu or education, but it does not mean that you need to compromise your *hashkafos* or values.

Reason number two: Parkinson's Law states that work expands to fill the time, and the same is true of money. Expenses rise to meet income, because when funds are available, they find a destination. And when people's income rises, their needs rise, too — but their needs usually rise more than their income.

Let's say you did manage somehow to increase your income to $100,000. What would happen? Would you find that all your financial problems would be solved?

We doubt it. What would probably happen is that your expenses would rise to match and exceed your income. We project that if you were earning $100,000, your expenses would rise to $125,000. All told, you would be worse off than you are now — now, you only need an extra $20,000, not $25,000.

Let's take this a step further and project what would happen if you would be earning only $60,000 now. Would you still need $100,000 to live on? Probably not. If you were earning $60,000, our guess is that you would say that you need less than the $80,000 you are currently earning.

Please do not take offense. We do not know you at all, and we are not accusing you of being a bad or irresponsible person. All we are saying is that there is a tendency for people to need just slightly more than they have. People whose income is $25,000 will typically need $30,000; people whose income is $50,000 will typically need $60,000; and people whose income is $150,000 will typically need $180,000.

The arithmetic is imprecise, but the principle is accurate. It might be a consolation to you to know that this principle applies to the majority of people — the numbers might be different, but the problem is the same. For proof of this principle, you don't have to look further than the current credit crisis, which is a direct result of people thinking that they had more money than they actually did.

Why do people think this way? Because they don't work with precise calculations; they work with estimates. Just the fact that people give round figures when stating their income and expenses is proof that the figures they are giving are not exact. And when estimating, the natural tendency is to err on the side that is more convenient.

When people calculate their income and expenses, it is more convenient for them to overestimate their income (because then they have more money to spend) and to underestimate their expenses (because then they do not have to restrict their spending as much). See the chapter on budgeting for more on this topic.

If you are not managing now, it is far from certain that you would be able to manage if you had $20,000 more. Our experience is that the same people who can't live on $80,000 also can't live on $100,000, or on $200,000. What matters is not how much money people have; what matters is the way they manage their money — do they habitually need more than they have, or do they make it their business to manage with what they have?

Since we do not know the details of your situation or lifestyle, we cannot challenge your assertions that there is nothing left to cut from your budget and that it is not feasible for you to increase your income significantly. Besides, you are the best judge of what your needs are, and we therefore would not question any of your lifestyle choices even if we knew what they were.

All we can say is, rarely have we encountered a family that could not reduce its expenditures or increase its income at least somewhat. In the quest for financial independence, every drop counts, especially considering that the alternatives — borrowing money or accepting charity — are highly unappealing, from both a practical perspective and a Torah standpoint.

Many people in situations similar to yours feel they are victims of circumstance. "What can I do?" they reason. "I have only X amount of money, and I can't manage on that amount." Are they wrong? No. It's true that they have only X amount of money, and it's true that they can't manage. But if they would truly value financial independence, they would find a way to manage.

We believe that it is possible for you to be financially independent. What is not possible is for you to maintain your current lifestyle and be financially independent. Given the choice between your lifestyle and financial independence, which do you choose?

If your lifestyle is nonnegotiable, then you will have to sacrifice your financial independence in order to accommodate your lifestyle. But if your financial independence is nonnegotiable, then you will have to modify your lifestyle in order to preserve your financial independence. The latter choice might be very difficult at first, but in the long term, it will improve your quality of life, for "A person desires one measure of that which is his more than nine measures of that which belongs to his fellow" (*Bava Metzia* 38a).

It also helps to remember that in any financial situation you could possibly be in, there would always be things that you would not be able to have. Since the line of financial restraint will inevitably have to be drawn somewhere, you might as well draw it inside financially independent territory.

The first and most important step in achieving financial independence is taking a long, hard look at your scale of priorities and asking yourself where on that scale financial independence belongs. The only person who can answer that question is you — and the only person you have to answer to is yourself.

Can I Take Tzedakah on a One-Time Basis? ❯

I work as a sofer, and I earn a modest income that is usually enough to cover my family's needs on a month-by-month basis. I have never earned much money, but I also never thought of myself as "poor."

Several months ago, I injured my wrist, and I was sidelined from work for about a month. During that period, I had no choice but to borrow money from a gemach and from a couple of friends in order to get by. Now, I am, baruch Hashem, able to work again, but I am left with a considerable amount of debt that I do not see how I can repay. A local tzedakah organization is aware of my financial plight, and they offered me a one-time grant to pay off my debts and put me back on my feet.

To me, taking tzedakah is anathema, and I would like to avoid it at all costs. But I honestly don't really see any option at this point. Is there anything Mesila can do for me?

You are to be commended for your reluctance to take *tzedakah* money. Jews have always gone to great lengths to avoid taking alms and for good reason.

The *Gemara* says a person's world is dark for him when he depends on others for sustenance, and that his life is not a life (*Beitzah* 32b). Obviously, taking *tzedakah* money is something the Torah views as a last resort, and something that should be avoided if at all possible.

Lehavdil, in the world of economics, evidence abounds that welfare programs actually increase dependency and perpetuate poverty. When people get money for doing nothing, they invariably lose some of their motivation to work. This is a psychological reality that is difficult to overcome.

In over a decade of working with families experiencing financial difficulties — and these, by the way, are not limited to "poor" families — Mesila has found that money is not necessarily the solution to financial problems. Financial problems are usually the result of lack of knowledge and poor financial management skills.

The fact that some *tzedakah* organizations today are beginning to offer Mesila-style counseling services is an indication that more and more people are coming to realize this truth.

In your case specifically, taking *tzedakah* on a one-time basis might cover your shortfall for the time being. But it will not prevent a similar crisis from recurring in the future. It also establishes a dangerous precedent. Once you cross that line, it will become far more difficult for you to refrain from accepting *tzedakah* again.

Let's face it: Living from month to month leaves you little financial breathing room, and you could easily land in debt again in the future. This is not a pessimistic view of your situation; it is a realistic assessment.

If there is a Mesila branch in your community, we encourage you to apply for our counseling services. Mesila can help you develop a budget that will allow you to cover your living expenses, pay off your debts (slowly, if necessary), and save money for unforeseen expenses or "rainy day" situations such as an injured wrist. (Mesila includes unforeseen expenses in the category of foreseeable expenses. Smart budgeting always takes rainy days into account.)

A Mesila counselor can also help you find ways to increase your income and decrease your expenditures. This will give you the financial breathing room that will allow you to ride out minor financial crises that may arise in the future.

The *Gemara* observes, "*Ein chavush matir atzmo mibeis ha'asurim,* A prisoner cannot release himself from prison" (*Brachos* 5b). When people are in the midst of difficult situations, they often are powerless to extricate themselves from their predicaments.

This principle is extremely applicable to people going through financial difficulties. Even if you are a financially responsible person, you might find it extremely beneficial to have a resourceful, experienced and objective Mesila counselor tackling your financial issues together with you.

Before applying to Mesila, however, be aware that our counseling services are far-reaching and very thorough. Helping a family achieve financial stability is not something that can be accomplished overnight. It takes months, and sometimes years, of counseling before the family becomes fully self-sufficient.

If there is no Mesila branch in your area, then we would recommend that you take the *tzedakah* offered to you, but that you try to view it as a loan, not as a handout. You can then slowly save up money to repay the "loan."

When you save up enough money, you can make a donation to the organization that gave you the money. In this way, you can avoid the stigma of taking *tzedakah*.

If your local *tzedakah* organization offers any type of counseling, we strongly encourage you to accept it. These counseling services may not be as comprehensive or as structured as Mesila's, but they are certainly helpful nonetheless.

The *Mishnah* says that if a person needs *tzedakah* but refrains from taking it, he will eventually be able to support others with his own money (*Pei'ah* 8:9). Although this *mishnah* does not apply to some-one who is unable to survive without taking *tzedakah*, we believe that in your case it probably does apply.

If you can find a way out to avoid taking *tzedakah*, you will reap the benefits of remaining financially independent both in this world and the next.

A Goal for All Families ❯

I am an almanah with several children, most of whom are in their teens.

When my husband was niftar he left a small life-insurance policy, invested in mutual funds, and I have spent nearly half of it. I feel that the remaining life-insurance money should be left to grow and help the children when the time comes for them to marry.

I bring in a small income from a secretarial job, and I also receive government benefits. My income and government benefits are not quite enough for me to live off of, but the members of the community where I live are very kind to me, giving me large cash gifts several times a year, usually before Yom Tov. Baruch Hashem, we have all that we need and much, much more.

The problem is that it is very hard for me to budget this way. I don't know when I will receive money or how much it will be. I have a feeling that I am spending too much and that my children are getting accustomed to a lifestyle standard that they (and I) will not be able to maintain when they have their own families.

When I discuss concerns with Rebbetzins, gvirim and even friends, they all reply by saying, "Don't worry, you and your *kids have suffered enough; of course you need this much household help. You should be happy, your kids should be happy; it's okay to treat yourself once in awhile."*

My food bill seems astronomical, but I don't know how to keep it down, and I have no idea how it compares to other people's. When I try to discuss this with the people who help me, they tell me not to worry, that my family should have good food and that if I need anything more, I should just ask. So I accumulate large credit card bills and pay them off with a line of credit at the bank, which gets partially paid off by a "gift" at some point and so on. It's hard for me to budget or make financial decisions regarding what and what not to spend when I don't know how much I'll be getting and when.

Is there anything I can do to make my financial situation more stable? I dream of being financially independent, but I am not sure if it is a realistic goal.

We are deeply impressed by your aspiration to reach financial independence, despite the many challenges of single parenthood. In the section about the dangers of accepting *tzedakah*, we write that people who take *tzedakah* often lose their motivation to be financially independent. You seem to be an exception to this rule.

You brought up a number of points in your letter, and we will address them as six distinct issues. We ask, however, that you view all of the following advice merely as suggestions that might theoretically be appropriate for someone in a situation similar to yours. Before deciding whether to implement the suggestions below, we urge you to discuss them with *daas Torah* and not to make the decisions on your own.

1) We agree with you that it is a good idea to leave your insurance money to grow. This is in keeping with advice from the *midrash* quoted by Rashi — "A person is not permitted to sell his field, except when under the pressure of poverty" (*Vayikra* 25:25).

Even when a person does sell his field, the *midrash* continues, he should not sell all of it, since it is *derech eretz* for a person to leave a part of his field for himself.

In other words, an asset — especially one that generates income — should not be sold, except under extenuating circumstances.

This is not something you should decide on your own, however. We recommend that you discuss this issue with a Rav to find out (a) whether it is permissible for you to put aside this money while accepting money from others and (b) if you are required to inform some or all of the people who give you money that you have this life-insurance policy (if they are not already aware of this).

2) Living off credit cards and bank loans is problematic, for several reasons. One, owing money is a form of bondage (see *Mishlei* 22:7), and a very stressful form of bondage, at that. Two, you have to pay interest, which, when avoidable, is essentially money in the garbage. And three, it is difficult to limit your expenditures when you are living off an almost endless line of credit.

It is therefore crucial that you begin living off money that you have, not money that you anticipate having.

To reverse the cycle of debt that you are in, you have to (a) pay off your current debts and (b) make a firm decision not to take loans in the future. We understand that this will be very difficult for you, because it will require you to change long-ingrained habits, but the benefits of living debt-free definitely justify the effort.

To become debt-free, you need to find a way to save up enough money to live without having to borrow. We can suggest two possible methods for you to do this:

Method No. 1: Cut back on your expenditures until you manage to save enough money to pay off your debts and cover your living expenses.

This is not something you can expect to accomplish over a short period of time. Rather, each time you receive a gift, you can try to put aside a portion of it, say 25%, in a separate bank account. It might take a year or two, but you will eventually save up enough money to start living from your own cash reserves, rather than borrowing money against unpredictable future gifts.

Method No. 2: Request a grant that will allow you to repay your debts and cover your living expenses until the next gift arrives. (From what you describe, there seem to be people who would be willing to help you in this way, especially if you explain to them that a one-time grant will allow you to become financially stable.)

By the time this grant is used up, you will hopefully have received the next gift, which will then tide you over for the next period.

Becoming debt-free does not require you to make permanent reductions in your standard of living. What it does require you to do is to procure extra money — either by reducing your expenditures temporarily or by obtaining a one-time grant — so that you can pay off your debt and begin living in the black, not in the red.

Once you have begun living debt-free (which we think is a very realistic and very necessary goal), it would be advisable for you to close your line of credit and exchange your credit cards for a debit card, which only allows you to spend money that you already have.

To continue living debt-free, you should divide each pre-Yom Tov gift into six monthly portions (or four, or three, depending on how often you receive these gifts) as soon as it arrives, to ensure that the money will last until the next gift. This means that you will have to work with a fairly consistent expenditures budget and not spend more than your predetermined allotment in any given month.

Obviously, there will be times that you will have no choice but to exceed your expenditures budget. When this happens, don't give up. Accept it as a fact of life, and don't let it discourage you from continuing to stick to your budget.

3) With regard to your dream of becoming financially independent: If being financially independent is very important to you, we believe it is attainable. "In the way a person wishes to go, he is led," *Chazal* say.

Once you have begun to live without debt, you can look for ways to trim your own extras from your budget. When it comes to the children's extras, however, you have to be much more careful.

Before deciding to make your children feel the pinch, you should consult with the *mechanchim* of each of your children and discuss whether it would be harmful to them to reduce some of their extras. If the *mechanchim* are of the opinion that your children would be able to handle a moderate reduction in their standard of living, you can then convene a family meeting to discuss ways to cut down your expenditures. As you say, it is worthwhile for your children to learn good financial habits at this stage in their lives — provided that you and their *mechanchim* feel that they are emotionally prepared to cope with some fiscal restraint.

The key here is to avoid extreme measures — both with yourself and your children. From what you describe, it appears as though you are living on a generous budget. There is a happy medium between penny-pinching and extravagance. Cutting back on your expenditures does not mean that you have to live tightfistedly.

If you do decide to trim the extras from your budget, make sure that you provide yourself and your children with meaningful substitutes so that you do not feel deprived. Exchange the fleeting pleasure of a shopping spree for the lasting pleasure of going to a weekly *shiur*, or replace the experience of dining out with the experience of hosting guests for Shabbos.

Instead of offering your daughter a new game or a new skirt as a reward, offer her a learning *seder* with Mommy — in *shemiras halashon*, *Pirkei Avos*, *hilchos Shabbos* or even Rabbi Zelig Pliskin's book on happiness. She might be horrified by the idea at first, but chances are you will both find the shared *seder* deeply rewarding.

4) If you decide to implement any of the above suggestions, we encourage you to do so gradually. Sudden, radical lifestyle changes are very stressful, and they rarely last. Do not sacrifice your family's happiness on the altar of instant financial independence.

Instead, make financial independence a long-term goal, and continually implement small, sustainable changes to help you reach that goal. In this way, you can maintain a healthy atmosphere in your home while finding satisfaction in the knowledge that you are working to become financially independent.

Keep in mind, as well, that financial independence is not an all-or-nothing proposition, and partial financial independence is also a goal worth striving for. Every tiny step you take toward weaning your family off outside support is a monumental achievement that shows you are succeeding in your quest.

10

Peace and (Financial) Harmony

"In Lashon Hakodesh, the same shoresh is used for 'fighting' (milchamah, lilchom) and for 'bread' (lechem)… which suggests that money is at the root of almost all conflict."

("Tackling Financial Problems – as a Team")

In this chapter:

❭ In Pursuit of Financial Harmony | 289

❭ Tackling Financial Problems — as a Team | 295

In Pursuit of Financial Harmony ❯

I read your advice on how widows and orphans can work toward financial independence. I had my husband read it, too, and he saw his childhood right away.

My husband grew up as an orphan from a young age in a close community renowned for its tremendous chessed. From the time that there was no father running the house, whether or not there was money was irrelevant. Food, clothing and household items were purchased and trips were taken based on whether they were deemed "necessary," rather than if they were affordable. As you know, the word "necessary" can be a relative term and is open to misinterpretation.

Until today, my husband has a hard time differentiating need from want and curbing his spending due to budgetary restrictions. Children from wealthy homes have exactly the same problem, except for one difference — they come from wealthy homes where the need for budgetary restrictions is not so pronounced.

It took years of struggle and an impossible financial situation with absolutely nowhere to turn except for shamefacedly asking for tzedakah before my husband finally understood that he needs to make some changes. My reading him Mesila articles aloud from time to time helped, too.

Perhaps you can devote an article to discussing situations like mine, in which the husband — who rightfully wants to be the decision maker in financial matters, since he is the one with the responsibility of breadwinner — does not have sound financial understanding, and the wife is better with money. How can I preserve shalom bayis and guide my husband on a more stable financial path?

Thank you for your feedback and for your important question. It is gratifying to hear that our advice is helpful and that we are bringing about change in people's financial attitudes and habits.

Money management plays a pivotal role in *shalom bayis,* and we welcome the opportunity to explore this very relevant topic. We will begin by outlining fundamental attitudes and habits that have to be in place in order to keep money from becoming a source of tension or strife in the home. Then we will go on to answer your question of how a financially savvy wife can guide her husband along the path to financial stability without damaging their *shalom bayis.*

Among most couples, there is usually one person who is better at financial management and will naturally gravitate toward handling most of the family's financial transactions, such as banking, bill-paying, bookkeeping and the like. The division of a married couple's financial tasks can be done in any number of ways, and it is up to every couple to find the arrangement that works best for them.

Regardless of the way a couple divides the financial management duties, however, it is critical that both husband and wife be aware of what is going on with their finances and involved in financial decisions.

As a rule, financial information should never be concealed from a spouse. Whether the goal is to avoid criticism over a purchase — "I don't want my husband to be upset that I spent so much money" — or to protect a spouse from financial worries — "I don't want my wife to know how little money we have in the bank" — keeping secrets erodes the trust that forms the foundation of a healthy relationship. (Every rule has exceptions, and in certain less-than-ideal situations it may be necessary for one spouse to conceal financial information from the other. We recommend that a Rav or competent marriage counselor be consulted in these situations.)

Lack of awareness on the part of one spouse is very often the reason for, or at least a contributing factor in, unhealthy financial behavior. This lack of awareness can happen either because the person is not involved in the family finances — intentionally or unintentionally — or because the person chooses to ignore financial realities.

Ignoring financial realities does not make someone a terrible person. In fact, it's something we all do at times. When we feel that we absolutely need something, we are quick to reassure ourselves that we can afford it, whether or not that is the case. We are quick to justify our own expenditures — which we consider necessary and important — and just as quick to condemn our spouse's expenditures, whose necessity and importance we don't always appreciate.

Even if we do not relate to or understand our spouse's spending habits, we have to resist the urge to jump to the conclusion that he or she is wasteful or a spendthrift. Instead, we need to work on improving communication and learning to understand and respect the other person's needs and desires.

Just as it is important that both spouses be aware of what is going on with the family finances and involved in the decision-making process, it is also important that each spouse have a certain measure of autonomy when it comes to spending decisions. People feel stifled and controlled when they have to give a reckoning to their spouse for every penny they spend or obtain permission for every minor purchase.

Both husband and wife should have the freedom to spend a certain amount of money, within reasonable limits, without having to inform or consult with the other. Each couple can decide for themselves what constitutes "reasonable limits," taking into consideration their budget, their lifestyle and their personalities. In some families, there is an official "*shalom bayis* fund" for this purpose. In other families, there is an unspoken understanding that it's fine for husband and wife to spend small amounts of money at their discretion. Which method is better? Whatever works for you.

Beyond these small amounts of money, however, both spouses have to be aware of, and agreeable to, the way their money is managed. This means that even if only one spouse is actually managing the money, the other still has to be involved in the decision-making process.

A spouse who has a serious problem with money — such as compulsive overspending, a gambling addiction or extreme miserli -ness — may need to be excluded completely from financial decisions and management. (In these situations, as well, a Rav or counselor should be consulted.) But if a spouse simply has poor financial management skills, or tends to spend money in a way that is incongruous with the family's financial abilities, we recommend that he or she still be involved in the family's finances.

It is inevitable that spouses will have differences of opinion with regard to how money should be spent. But if the lines of communication are open, they should be able to express their feelings and preferences and have those feelings and preferences understood and respected. In an atmosphere of understanding and respect, it should be possible to reach financial decisions that are mutually acceptable.

Now let's get back to your question. If your husband has expressed an interest in being involved in financial matters, he will likely be hurt if you attempt to exclude him. Instead, we recommend that you find a way to make sure he is involved in the finances and still ensure that the finances are managed correctly.

You write that your husband wants to be the decision maker and that you are better with money. This does not have to be a contradiction. It is possible that your husband will be satisfied with an arrangement wherein you discuss financial issues with him and reach mutually acceptable decisions, and then you go on to oversee the implementation of those decisions yourself by deciding when to buy, where to buy, how to pay and so on. For example, your husband will likely not object to your being the one balancing the checkbook, as long as he has a say in the checks that are being written.

When discussing financial matters with your husband, try to keep the discussion calm, unemotional and impersonal. Don't give instructions, and don't insist that things be handled a certain way. When the financial facts are presented clearly, in a nonthreatening, nonconfrontational way, chances are that your husband will be able to recognize what exactly the problems are and even suggest possible solutions.

There are two steps to changing a bad financial habit: The first is to recognize that it exists, and the second is to find ways to overcome it. If it is your husband who has the bad habit of overspending, he has to be the one to recognize the habit, and he has to decide how to overcome it. If you are the one who recognizes his bad habit, and you are the one offering suggestions for overcoming it, you will likely trigger a defense mechanism that will cause your husband to deny, defend or counterattack.

How can you help your husband recognize and overcome his habit of overspending? By talking about yourself and your concerns, not about him and his financial ineptitude. Describe the situation and how it affects you, without painting him as the terrible ogre who has wrought disaster upon the family finances. Tears and emotional outbursts will not be effective, since they preclude the rational dialogue that is the basis of healthy communication.

When you present the situation to your husband as your problem, not as his, he is far more likely to acknowledge that he has a bad habit that needs to be addressed. Once he is aware of the habit, allow him to suggest ways to work on it. You can offer your ideas, as well, but only in the context of a two-way discussion — dialogue, not diatribe.

You can also continue to read Mesila publications to your husband, or provide him with other educational material on the subject of financial management, but only as long as he is interested and wants to listen.

At the same time, we encourage you to demonstrate to your husband in as many ways as possible that you look up to him and respect his abilities as the breadwinner. It is important for a man to feel that he is succeeding in his financial responsibilities, and if you can find a way to give him that feeling, he may not object to being less involved in day-to-day money management.

There will always be ups and downs, but if you are working as a team, you will be able to weather the difficult moments much more easily.

Tackling Financial Problems — as a Team ❯

I am married with two children, ages 4 and 2, and my husband is a full-time kollel student. Our only income, besides the small stipend my husband gets from his kollel, is the money my husband makes selling esrogim before Sukkos and baking matzos before Pesach.

I am willing to work and I have experience in office management, but my husband is insistent that I be home when the children come home from playgroup at 1 p.m., which basically makes it impossible for me to find a job. Because we have so little income, we often have to borrow money. We are in quite a bit of debt, but I don't know exactly how much we owe, and I don't think my husband does, either.

The financial pressure is unbearable and is causing a lot of tension. For example, when my sister-in-law recently got married, I wanted to buy, or at least rent, a gown to wear to the wedding. I thought that it was a reasonable request, but my husband said it was out of the question. This did not do good things for the atmosphere in our home, to say the least.

My main financial goal right now is to be able to buy an apartment so that my family will have a normal place to live. We used to live in a rented apartment, but we had to move *out of our last apartment and we could not find anything else that was reasonably priced. We then moved into my in-laws' tiny basement apartment.*

My husband promised that it would only be for a month, but it has turned into six months already, and there is no end in sight. I am miserable living like this.

I would like to enlist outside help — by applying to Mesila, perhaps — but my husband is not interested at all. When I suggested that we apply to Mesila, he said that Mesila has very strict rules and that if we become Mesila clients we will not be allowed to have a car or even buy ourselves yogurt. I am therefore turning to you for help in this forum. Do you have any suggestions for me?

From the way you describe your situation, it appears that you have two problems. The first is money, and the second is that you and your husband do not see eye to eye with regard to the first problem. Of the two problems, the second is probably the more significant. That is because it is almost impossible to solve a money problem — or any other problem — if husband and wife disagree over how to tackle it.

You may find it reassuring to know that it is common for financial problems to cause friction in the home. In *Lashon Hakodesh*, the same *shoresh* is used for "fighting" (*milchamah, lilchom*) and for "bread" (*lechem*) — i.e., economic sustenance — which suggests that money is at the root of almost all conflict.

You are interested in seeking help, which indicates that you recognize the need for outside intervention. This takes great courage on your part, and we commend you for that courage and for your pragmatism, as well.

It is very natural and understandable that your husband does not want to seek outside help and have other people tell him how to handle his personal finances. For the head of a household, it can be extremely demeaning to have someone else involved in this domain.

Your husband might be relieved to learn that Mesila does not have any rules about cars or yogurt. We leave it to our clients to decide if they want to have their car and not eat yogurt, or sell their car and eat yogurt, or earn enough to have their car and eat their yogurt, too.

Mesila does not dictate to anyone how to spend their money, nor do we get involved in people's personal lifestyle decisions. What we do do is help people reach a clear awareness of what is going on with their finances — exactly how much income they have, exactly how much they are spending and exactly how much they owe. Once this awareness is reached, we encourage our clients to come up with their own ideas and make their own decisions as to how to go about improving the situation. We then help them to find ways to implement those decisions and turn their ideas into reality. While Mesila counselors might suggest possible solutions, they will never impose these solutions on a family.

You write that your main financial goal is to have a home of your own. While this is indeed a worthwhile goal, it is possible that your main financial goal right now should be to get out of debt.

Debt is an insidious enemy, one that silently grows until it engulfs a person's entire life.

Eventually, *gemachim*, banks and other creditors will start demanding their money back, and they may take aggressive steps against you. Worse, a person who borrows money knowing that he is unable to repay it is called a *rasha* — and you certainly would not want to be in that category.

The first step in getting out of debt is becoming aware of exactly how much you owe and to whom. Then you can work on developing a debt recovery plan. It is difficult to do this alone, however, especially when you are under stress. We therefore recommend that you find a qualified counselor — in Mesila or elsewhere — who can help you take an objective look at your situation, establish financial goals and develop a plan for paying off your debts and achieving your financial goals. But before you can enlist outside help, you and your husband have to synchronize the way you view your finances and become active partners in your journey to financial stability.

It will take careful thinking on your part to decide how to present this information to your husband. If you present it in a way that he perceives as badgering or confrontational, it will make him even less inclined to apply to Mesila. But if you use your *binah yeseirah*, your woman's intuition, to figure out how to speak to him in a way that shows that you respect him as the head of the household, you may succeed in motivating him to seek help.

For more on money and marriage,
see also:

"In Defense of Budgeting" Chapter 2

11

Our Financial Future: Children and Money

"When children absorb
a value system in which
spiritual achievements
are paramount, they
are far less likely to feel
deprived, even if their
friends have more than
they do."

("Children's Needs and Wants")

In this chapter:

❯ Preparing Children for a Lifetime of Financial Responsibility | 301

❯ Children's Needs and Wants | 305

❯ Should Kids Pay Their Own Way? | 309

❯ $600 Designer Glasses: A Shortsighted Proposition? | 315

❯ Giving Children the Gift of Financial Independence | 321

Preparing Children for a Lifetime of Financial Responsibility ❯

My 10-year-old daughter recently earned about $200 by help-ing in a day camp. To her, it seems like a fortune. She now wishes to use that money to buy herself extra junk food and things she claims all her friends have.

It kills me to see her squandering her money, but she says she is the one who earned it, so she has the right to decide how to spend it. My wife and I are unsure how to respond. What do you think?

The *Midrash* says that when Hashem told Moshe to collect the *mach-atzis hashekel*, He showed him a *matbei'ah shel eish*, a fiery coin. The *matbei'ah shel eish* can perhaps be understood as a metaphor for money in general: both fire and money are necessary for survival, but both can be enormously destructive when uncontrolled.

Just as young children should not be allowed to play with fire, they should not be given free rein in handling money. Money is not a toy. It is a potent, intoxicating and dangerous substance whose use needs to be supervised and controlled.

"I worked for the money," your daughter says indignantly, "so it's mine."

Well, she's not quite right. According to *halachah*, a minor does not have the power to make a *kinyan*. Therefore, a girl under the age of 12, or a boy under the age of 13, cannot take possession of any object or money.

If *halachah* bars minors from taking possession of money, this is an indication that it is not good for children to be independently wealthy. No matter how bright they are, they do not possess the emotional maturity to make the correct decisions with regard to money. They should therefore not be allowed to taste the heady feeling of financial autonomy, nor should they be burdened with the weighty responsibility of managing their own finances.

If your 10-year-old daughter has earned money, it technically belongs to you, not to her. To your daughter, however, your taking control of her hard-earned wages may seem utterly unfair, so you will have to be very careful to present it to her in a way she can swallow.

Only a few generations ago, it was common for children to work to supplement their parents' income. In many Third World countries, this is still the case: Children are expected to contribute to the family's livelihood, and they hand their earnings over to their parents as a matter of course.

In Western society, however, it would be unthinkable to expect children to give their money to their parents. While this attitude is not the Jewish one, we and our children have unfortunately absorbed this approach from popular culture, and it is not easily eradicated.

We therefore do not recommend that you seize your daughter's money and use it to buy groceries. While it may halachically be permissible to do so, *halachah* also dictates that we use *seichel* in educating our children. Appropriating your daughter's money will undoubtedly infuriate her, and it is therefore a highly inadvisable course of action.

Instead of exercising your halachic right to your daughter's money by appropriating it, you should express to her, gently and lovingly, that the money must be spent at your discretion. At the same time, communicate to her that you have a great deal of respect for her and her efforts, and that it is your parental duty to help her use the money she earned in the way that will be the most rewarding and productive.

Your daughter's newfound wealth puts you in the position to teach her crucial values and attitudes toward money. Teach her about *maaser kesafim*, about *tzedakah* and about respecting other people's money. Teach her that money is important — not as an end, but as a means.

Teach her the value of saving money, the value of planning how to use money, and the value of establishing priorities when spending money. Teach her that having money is a responsibility, but that having money does not make anyone a better person. And teach her that money, her own or other people's, should not be the topic of idle conversation.

You cannot impart these attitudes and values to your daughter by lecturing to her in a vacuum. But you can teach her these attitudes and values by involving her in the decisions that will be made with regard to her money.

Suggest positive ways she can use her money, and give her the opportunity to share her own ideas. Explain to her the various options for safeguarding money — bank accounts, *gemach* deposits or the old-fashioned coin bank — and decide with her how much should be put aside for savings and where the money will be kept. Show her that you respect her input, but make sure that she understands that the final decisions regarding her money must meet with your approval.

Ideally, the time to discuss with children how to use their money is before they start earning it. This way, parents can explain ahead of time what will be done with the money, before any misunderstandings arise. Preparing a child in advance of a potentially challenging situation is always easier than trying to deal with the situation after it has occurred.

Teaching good financial habits should be part of the *chinuch* we give our children. By demonstrating to our children the importance of handling money properly, we give them the foundation for a lifetime of financial responsibility and stability.

Children's Needs and Wants ❯

I am living within a budget that allows me to manage, but does not allow for major luxuries. Our apartment is functional, not beautiful; my clothes are from a gemach and so are the baby's. I can afford tutors for my children, though, and I make sure that my son's private rebbi is paid properly.

I tell my children about needs and wants, and I attend to all of the former and a little of the latter. I teach the older ones to earn their own money for luxuries, and they babysit and deliver newsletters. But my children are ashamed of this attitude. For example, "everyone" in my 13-year-old daughter's class has a digital camera — and she doesn't.

Should I change my philosophy due to my children's embarrassment? Am I giving them good chinuch or just being stingy?

It is clear that you have your spending priorities straight. The question, however, is whether your children are being impacted negatively by the spending priorities you have established.

Children and teenagers need to have the security of knowing that their parents will provide for all of their needs. You obviously understand that, since you say you attend to all of your children's needs and some of their wants. But how are you determining what your children's needs and wants are? Often, the barometer of a child's needs is not necessarily what parents consider needs, but what the child's social environment has established as needs.

Needs are very subjective. In every community, there are different standards as to what children "need." Children, especially teenagers, crave fitting in with their peers. If all or most of your child's peers have a particular item, then your child might have a *need* for that item as well, even if you don't consider it at all necessary.

Obviously, you do not have to allow your children to be swept along with every fad, especially those that are not in keeping with your values. But if a child has a legitimate need, it is preferable to find a way to supply that need rather than tell the child, "We can't afford it." If money is tight, then parents have to use some creativity in finding inexpensive, alternative ways to provide for their children's needs — for example, learning to sew clothes, or buying clothes at thrift shops.

It is not a good idea to make children earn money to pay for things they really need — even if the need is a subjective one. It is, however, legitimate to suggest that older children pay for, or at least chip in for, things they *want*.

With regard to the specific example you gave of "everyone" in your 13-year-old daughter's class having a digital camera, you have to do your research. Find out if "everyone" really means *everyone*. If, indeed, everyone (or just about everyone) in your daughter's class has such a camera, then it is a need, and you should find a way to get it for her. If "everyone" means 20-30% of the class, however, then it is a want, not a need.

That is where *chinuch* comes in: You, as a parent, have to decide if this situation calls for teaching your daughter budgetary restraint, allowing her to use her own money, or indulging her.

How, you may ask, do we expect you to continue paying your children's tuition and private *rebbe'im* if you have to supply your children with cameras and other whims? The answer is that as you become more tuned in to your children's individual needs, you will find that is possible to save money in ways you never thought of. In the process of identifying needs, you will discover that some of the things you thought were "needs" were not really needs at all. You will understand, for instance, that the child who needs the digital camera really has no need for the new school supplies you were planning to buy her, while her older sister needs a new wardrobe more than she needs the vitamin supplements you insist she take.

If your children are expressing dissatisfaction and shame with the way you are providing for them, that is a warning sign that you might be depriving them of some of their needs. Deprivation is not *chinuch*; it actually teaches children to crave material possessions, accomplishing exactly the opposite of what *chinuch* is supposed to achieve. The way to be *mechanech* children not to ascribe importance to material acquisition is by ensuring that material possessions do not become a focus, by virtue of either their presence or their absence. The less you turn money and possessions into issues, the more you will prepare your children for a life that emphasizes *ruchniyus*.

We at Mesila are staunch proponents of controlled consumption and *histapkus bemu'at*, yet we strongly encourage families to create an atmosphere where money and frugality are not center stage.

Words like "expensive" and "afford" should be used sparingly around children (and, for the sake of *shalom bayis*, between spouses, as well). Similarly, *histapkus bemu'at* and *mesirus nefesh* for Torah are concepts that are not meant to be talked about, but practiced — happily.

By fostering an atmosphere of appreciation for Torah, *mitzvos* and *Yiddishkeit* in your home, you can subtly redirect your children's interests away from the many material enticements the world has to offer, and, in that way, prevent many "needs" from arising.

When children absorb a value system in which spiritual achievements are paramount, they are far less likely to feel deprived, even if their friends have more than they do. As important as it is to supply children's material needs, it is even more important to provide them with things money cannot buy: attention, love, discipline, security and *mesorah*.

If, despite your best efforts, you find that you simply do not have the means to supply all of your children's material needs, you should take comfort in the knowledge that you can supply your children with the things they need most.

Finding the right balance between exercising fiscal restraint and providing adequately for children can be challenging. For every family, the balance is different — and within every family, the balance shifts as the family dynamics change. As in all aspects of parenting, we need to seek guidance and *daven* for the *siyatta diShmaya* that will help us meet our children's needs in the best possible way.

The above section was prepared in consultation with expert mechanchim.

Should Kids Pay Their Own Way? ❯

Advice for parents who are forced to make drastic cuts in their family budgets

I lost my job several months ago, and I am having a hard time finding a new position. In the meantime, we have had to make drastic cuts in our family's standard of living.

These cuts have significantly affected my children — especially the teenagers — and I worry that I am not providing them with the things they need and are used to having.

Should I encourage my teenage children to work and use their own money to pay for the things they need? In general, how much should I involve them in our financial situation?

The first thing you and your children need to know is that you are not alone. Today's economic crisis has affected almost every family and has made it difficult or impossible for many parents to provide their children with many of the extras — and even some of the basics — they are used to giving them. While this situation is painful for the children, and even more painful for the parents, there are ways to minimize the pain and still provide for your children adequately.

Children's Most Basic Need

In our quest to provide our children with the things they need, or think they need, we often overlook the fact that one of the most basic needs every child has is the need for security. Security for a child means feeling that my parents are able to take care of me and provide me with everything I need. But it also means knowing that my parents have firm limits, and that they are able to say "no" when necessary.

Understanding how and when to say "no" is an important part of *chinuch*. At times, we say "no" to a child's request because we feel that the item he desires is not in his best interest. At other times, we say "no" because we simply cannot afford to provide the child with the item he has requested. In either case, our challenge as parents is to say "no" in a way that will promote feelings of security, not deprivation.

Security is unrelated to financial bracket. Children of rich parents do not necessarily feel more secure than children of poor parents, because security is a byproduct of good *chinuch* and emotional health — not of money. Although it may seem to be more difficult to give a child a feeling of security when there is not enough money to give him what he wants, it is in some ways even more difficult for wealthy parents to decide where to draw the line and to say "no" — even though money is no object.

It should be a comfort to you to know that your children do not have to lose their feeling of security just because you are struggling financially. And you do not have to spend more on them than you can afford in order to give them a feeling of security.

Security on a Shoestring Budget

How do you foster feelings of security on a shoestring budget? First, by creating a happy, relaxed home environment and projecting the feeling that you are satisfied — genuinely — with what you have, even if it is less than you are accustomed to. Second, by seeing to it that your children's physical, emotional and spiritual needs are somehow being met. And third, by ensuring that your children fit in with their peer group and are not noticeably disadvantaged.

Although money does play an important role in meeting your children's needs and enabling them to fit in with their peer group, it is possible to achieve these goals even with limited financial resources. Needs do not necessarily have to have a price tag; they can often be met creatively, in ways that cost little or nothing.

For instance, love and attention are free, and in most situations, they are a far better alternative to prizes, toys and treats. Entertainment and recreation do not have to cost very much — a family picnic or an outing to a local park can provide more fun and memories than an expensive vacation or hotel stay. Food, clothing and housing have a broad range of what is considered normal. As long as your children meet the minimum standard that is acceptable in your society and their peer group, you are doing fine.

Should the Kids Pay?

Ideally, if you can afford to pay for the things your children need, then you should be the one to pay. When children see that their parents are willing and happy to buy them what they need, it contributes to their feeling of security. It also reinforces the children's feeling of dependence on their parents, which bolsters parental control and authority. As children mature, their dependence on you, and your authority over them, should naturally decrease, until the point that they are ready to begin building their own homes and take responsibility for their own lives and finances.

But as long as a child is dependent on you, the fact that he has his own money — whether he received it as a gift or worked for it — is not a reason for him to have to support himself, even partially. If he has his own money, he can save it or use it to pay for extras, not for his basic needs. Even if he tells you that he wants to use his own money to pay for the things he needs, you should still offer to pay — if you can.

If, however, you cannot afford to pay for your children's needs, then you should encourage them to pay for those needs on their own, even if that means that they have to go out and earn their own money. In this way, you show your children that you want to give them what they need, and that if you could give it to them, you would. The knowledge that you care about them and truly wish to provide for them goes a long way in building a child's sense of security, even if you are not actually fulfilling those needs yourself.

Children feel much more deprived when they sense that their parents do not understand or respect their needs than when they realize that their parents want to provide for them but are simply unable to. If you can show your children that you understand their needs and that you are willing to help them do whatever they can to ensure that those needs are met, then it is far less likely that they will suffer the pain or bear the scars of deprivation.

To illustrate, let us take the example of two teenagers, Chani and Rivky, who need new winter coats. Chani's parents tell her, "Sorry, we can't afford to buy you a new coat. You'll have to manage with what you have."

Rivky's parents tell her, "Times are tough, and we don't have money to spend on a new coat. But if you want to go out and babysit so that you'll have your own money to spend, we'll be happy to help you find babysitting jobs, and we'll manage without your help in the house for a while so that you can work to pay for a coat that you'll feel good in."

Even if Rivky does not end up buying herself a new coat, chances are that she will feel far less resentful and deprived than Chani, who will likely feel that her parents just don't understand how embarrassing it is to be seen in an old, shabby coat that is hopelessly out of style.

The Danger of Guilt

Parents often feel guilty when they cannot afford to buy their child an item he needs, and this might cause them to try to convince the child — and themselves — that he doesn't really need it. They may even express disapproval when the child tries to find alternative means of obtaining the item, since that makes them feel inadequate as parents.

A much healthier approach is simply to express to your children that you wish you could give them what they need, but since you can't, you are willing to help and encourage them to obtain it through other means. This might mean helping them to find ways to earn money, or it might involve some creative thinking on your part to meet their needs in ways that you can afford.

There is no reason to feel guilty about your financial situation, since that has been decreed by Hashem. By accepting your situation, you put yourself in a much better position to help your children, since you no longer have to grapple with your own negative feelings, and you can be open with them about what's happening and brainstorm together to find suitable alternatives.

Involving Children in the Family Finances

Being open with your children about your financial situation and limitations does not mean that the children have to know every detail of what is happening with your finances. In fact, the fewer details they are privy to, the better. Why worry them needlessly with information they cannot fully comprehend or with problems they have no way of solving?

In general, the only time children should be made aware of what is happening with their parents' finances is when there is a change in the family's lifestyle that will affect them directly. For instance, if a child's summer camp or swimming lessons are going to be cancelled for financial reasons, the child deserves a brief explanation of why this is happening. The child should be given enough information so that he can understand and appreciate the need for cutbacks, but only as much information as he can comfortably digest.

Children tend to become very anxious when they see that their parents are suffering financially, and your job is to explain the situation to them in a way that is both truthful and reassuring.

When explaining the situation, show empathy for the difficulty that the children may experience as a result, but do not fall into the trap of pitying them. By pitying the children, you show that you are not fully accepting the situation, and that makes it much more difficult for the children to accept the situation in a healthy way and find ways to cope with it.

If you empathize with the difficulty while focusing on the positive and projecting an attitude of acceptance, you will impart to your children valuable coping strategies for this and other challenges they will face in life.

May you have *hatzlachah* in your job search, and may you have the *siyatta diShmaya* to navigate this challenging time successfully.

*Mesila wishes to thank Rabbi Zecharya Greenwald, principal of Meohr Seminary in Jerusalem, and author of **Parenting with Success**, for his help in preparing this section.*

$600 Designer Glasses: A Shortsighted Proposition? ❯

I live in an affluent community, and although everyone has been affected to some extent by the economic downturn, I have not noticed any marked reduction in people's standard of living. The younger generation certainly does not seem to be feeling the pinch.

Not long ago, my teenage daughter asked me to buy her a pair of designer eyeglass frames priced at $600. When I told her that I thought $600 was outrageous for a pair of glasses, she told me that her friends are wearing glasses that are even more costly. I could not argue with that — her friends have expensive taste and their parents barely restrict their spending.

Although I am not as well-to-do as some of the parents of these girls, I can afford to buy my daughter the glasses she wants. Should I do so?

Times have changed, and the realities of today are completely different from the realities people lived with even a generation ago. Your question is a perfect example of why Mesila is needed today. Forty years ago, or even twenty years ago, this question could not have existed. But today it is an important and relevant one.

Like any *chinuch* question, this one depends on many factors, not all of which are spelled out in your letter. One factor to consider: How many of your daughter's friends are wearing these designer glasses — 20%, 50% or 90%? Another factor to consider: How is your overall relationship with your daughter? If you say no to her, will she be able to accept it without questioning your love and concern for her? And a third factor: Is your daughter going through a difficult time in her life?

If only a few of your daughter's friends are wearing these glasses, if your relationship with her is generally good and if she is not experiencing any particular difficulty right now, then there are a number of reasons why spending $600 on glasses might not be wise.

With $600, you can buy glasses for an entire family, or feed a poor family for several weeks. To spend that kind of money on glasses will either cause the glasses to take on inflated significance, or reduce the value of $600 in your daughter's eyes. Neither of those options represents good *chinuch*.

We are not saying that people who have money should not spend it on themselves. Quite the contrary — if Hashem gave you money, you should appreciate and enjoy the gift He has given you. But even when spending money that you can afford to spend, you should not go overboard and lose all perspective of the value you are acquiring with your money. What value will you acquire by spending $600 on glasses that you would not acquire if you spent $50, $100 or $200? Will your daughter see any better, look any better or be more comfortable in these glasses? We doubt it.

Chances are, the only added value you would be getting is the designer label. If so, why would you pay $600 to provide free advertising for a company in Paris, Milan or New York whose merchandise is grossly overpriced?

Then there is the question of sensitivity to the *tzibbur* — i.e., your daughter's peer group. There is already peer pressure among your daughter's friends to wear designer eyeglasses, as evidenced by your daughter's desire to buy them. If your daughter begins wearing these glasses, it will only reinforce the trend and intensify the peer pressure on those girls whose parents cannot afford to spend $600 on glasses. That may be insensitive, especially at a time when the entire world is experiencing an *eis tzarah*, a time of economic distress.

It is always prudent to avoid conspicuous consumption (see *Biur Halachah, Hilchos Yom Tov* 529:1), but during an *eis tzarah* there is even more reason to avoid it. Flaunting the fact that you are still able to spend money freely might make you vulnerable to *ayin hara* — and this is something that cannot be remedied by tying a red string to your daughter's glasses.

Beyond these considerations, buying your daughter $600 glasses sets a dangerous precedent by introducing her to a level of spending that may be unsustainable. While she might be happy with the glasses now, she may be very unhappy in the future if she has to go back to the kind of glasses worn by the proletariat. And once she sees that it is acceptable to spend $600 on glasses, she will likely want to spend similar amounts of money on other items she wants.

In the not-too-distant future, your daughter will be married, *b'ezras Hashem*, and who knows if her husband will be able to keep up the level of spending you have conditioned her to? For that matter, who knows if you will be able to maintain this level of spending? We are not wishing hardship on anyone, but if there is one lesson to learn from the current economic crisis it is that no one's financial future is certain. Spending so much money on glasses is therefore short-sighted (pardon the pun), and might ultimately be a major disservice to your daughter.

Even if you were a billionaire and you could be reasonably certain that your daughter would always be able to afford $600 glasses, it would still be in your daughter's best interests to experience the disappointment of not getting things she wants. The Steipler Gaon said the reason so many people today are unhappy and depressed is because they never lacked anything when they were growing up, so they never developed coping skills to deal with disappointment. They therefore fall apart when they are confronted with life's inevitable disappointments.

Life's disappointments can be much worse than not getting $600 glasses, and these disappointments often happen in areas of life where money is useless. You would not want your daughter to fall apart if she is not accepted to the seminary of her choice or if she is turned down during the *shidduchim* process, and the best way to prepare her for these possible disappointments is in the training ground of eyeglasses and other minor letdowns.

The higher people's expectations are, the more likely they are to be disappointed when those expectations are not met. There is a danger, therefore, in indulging wants, whether our children's or our own. Each time we say "yes" to a child's want, we reinforce it and turn it into more of a need. Conversely, each time we deny our children something they want, we teach them to want less.

But this is true only of wants, not of needs. Needs, if unmet, only become more intense and lead to feelings of deprivation.

To illustrate: If a person is hungry and does not yield to the urge to eat, he will only become hungrier, because he has a real need for food. But if a person wants chocolate and does not give in to the urge, eventually his desire for chocolate will abate and it will become easier for him to resist the temptation.

Because needs tend to intensify with time and wants tend to abate, a good way to determine whether a child's request represents a need or a want is to see what happens when you say no: Is the child able to forget about the item after a few days, or does she continue asking for it incessantly?

If your daughter needs the glasses — and it is possible that she does — then you should consider getting them for her, because otherwise, she will feel deprived and her craving for the glasses will intensify. But if she only wants the glasses, then her initial disappointment at not getting them will fade quickly, and she will be a stronger, happier person for the experience. Stronger, because she has learned how to handle disappointment, and happier, because her expectations have been lowered and it is therefore easier for her to be content.

It is normal for children — and adults — to want things, especially things that their friends have. Before dismissing your daughter's request as outrageous or frivolous, it is important to understand why she wants the glasses and empathize with her desire. Once you understand why she wants them, you can look together for alternative ways to satisfy the hunger underlying her desire. That hunger may be for attention, for social acceptance, or for a boost to her self-image.

If you sincerely try to understand your daughter's desire for designer glasses, you may be pleasantly surprised to realize that "yes" and "no" are not your only two options. Between $600 glasses and nothing there is plenty of middle ground, plenty of room for flexibility. One possible idea would be for you to buy her something of lasting value — a piece of jewelry, perhaps — instead of spending the money on faddish eyeglasses. Another idea would be for her to shop around and try to find similar eyewear at a more reasonable price. There are many other ways to make both her and you happy — the key is to put yourself into a mindset of consideration, rather than opposition, and chances are that she will follow suit.

If you are in such a mindset, then even if you decide not to buy her the glasses, you will be able to cushion the "no" with understanding, compassion and love so she can accept it without anger or resentment.

In summary, we recommend that you carefully consider the pros and cons of buying your daughter the glasses, evaluate whether her request represents a need or a want, identify the hunger underlying the request, and look for a way to satisfy that hunger without compromising your values or your relationship.

After you consider the general guidelines we have offered, we suggest that you consult with a *chinuch* expert in order to receive specific guidance for your situation.

Giving Children the Gift of Financial Independence ❯

I am a successful businessman, and my family lives on quite a high standard. I had no trouble marrying off my oldest son and daughter, baruch Hashem, but now that they are married, the troubles have started. My married children want to continue living on the same standard as they lived when they were in my house, and they lead lifestyles that are extravagant, at least for young couples. When I was their age, I didn't even own a washing machine! And they don't need a washing machine — they send most of their clothing to the dry cleaners. ...

I give my married kids money all the time, and I even allow them to put many of their purchases on my credit card, but they constantly ask for more.

I think that my son and daughter need to have an outside party supervise their spending habits and teach them how to create and live within a budget.

Does Mesila provide that service? If not, is there anything I can do to teach them to live with what they have? And what can I do to ensure that my younger children do not make the same type of demands of me when they get married?

As we have mentioned in the past, the type of assistance that Mesila provides is not at all effective for people who do not want to be helped. We therefore only help people who turn to us of their own accord.

Since your children have not turned to us for assistance — why should they? — we cannot help them. But since you have turned to us for advice, we may be able to help you.

Supporting married children is noble and commendable, and it is something that Jews throughout the ages have done. But giving creates dependency. The more money or things you give your children, the more they expect to receive, and the less motivated they are to put effort into earning their keep.

In their heads, parents want to know that their grown children are financially independent. In their hearts, however, parents want to feel that their grown children are still dependent on them in some way. This conflict of head and heart leads many parents to give their children as much money as they want — and then grumble about how spoiled and dependent today's generation is.

As parents, our job is to do what is best for our children — and what is best for them is to be dependent only on the *Ribbono shel Olam*, not on us or on any other human being. How can parents encourage their children to become financially independent if they are the ones supporting them? By supporting them in a way that maximizes financial independence. Consider the following two scenarios:

Yaakov and Esther Katz receive $2,000 from their parents every month. That amount is enough for them to live on, but does not allow much room for luxuries. They have to plan carefully to ensure that they have enough money to cover the occasional unexpected expense and to manage during more expensive times such as Yom Tov seasons.

If they ever want to treat themselves to something, like a vacation or something for their apartment, they have to save up for several months. Their parents don't ask them any questions about how they spend their money, and they don't ask their parents for money, even when things are tight.

Aharon and Miriam Cohen put all of their monthly bills on their parents' credit cards, and they pay for other expenses with the cash their parents give them when they visit. Whenever they need money, they just ask their parents. They can treat themselves to extras whenever they want, and their parents always foot the bill — although they do grumble a bit when they don't like the way Aharon and Miriam are spending their money.

Which couple is better off? Is it the Cohens, who can spend whatever they want without worrying about not covering their budget? Or is it the Katzes, who live with a tight budget and would not think of asking their parents for more money?

In Mesila's opinion, the Katzes are far better off than the Cohens. They have a clearly defined budget, so they know exactly how much money they have to spend. They also have the freedom to make their own spending choices. Although they are being supported by their parents, they are the ones responsible for managing their finances, and the money they are spending belongs to them, not to their parents.

The Katzes thus learn the principles of wise financial management, and those principles will stand them in good stead for the rest of their lives. When it becomes necessary for them to manage without their parents, they will probably find a way.

The Cohens, on the other hand, are totally dependent on their parents financially. They have no budgetary limitations, and therefore cannot possibly learn to manage their finances correctly. As free as they are to spend money, they do not really have any money of their own to spend, since they have to either ask their parents for money first, or know that their expenditures will show up on their parents' credit card statements. They always have to worry that their parents will disapprove of their spending choices, whether or not they voice that disapproval.

Although the Katzes have less — less money, fewer possessions and less financial breathing room — they actually have a lot more than the Cohens: more freedom, more independence and greater financial stability. We would venture to say that they are also happier, at least from a financial perspective.

Getting back to your situation, your children are not really responsible for their high level of need, since they were brought up that way. They do not know or care how you lived when you were their age, and you can be sure they have no interest in hearing about it. They only know how they lived in your house, and they are quite happy to continue living that way.

You, however, are disturbed by their spending habits and by their level of dependence on you. But rather than trying to supervise or monitor their spending habits, your goal should be to instill in them the value of financial independence.

We therefore recommend that you begin to give your married children a definite annual or monthly sum of money, and then allow them to make their own spending decisions and live with the consequences of those decisions. Emphasize to them that you don't want them to have to feel dependent on you, and that you are therefore stepping out of their finances. At the same time, make it clear to them that you are there for them, and that they can still turn to you for help in difficult times.

In general, the less involved parents are in their married children's finances, the better it is for everyone. And more valuable than any money you can give your children is the ability to manage their money independently. You can decide whether to give your children money and how much to give them, but once you give it to them, you would be wise not to tell them what to do with it.

You should also talk to your children — both young and old — about the value of financial independence. Explain to them the physical and spiritual benefits of being financially independent. Tell them how great *tzaddikim* — from Avraham Avinu on down — went to lengths in order to remain financially independent. Be very careful, however, not to say anything that could be construed as criticism of your married children or of their lifestyle.

If you want to make sure that your younger children do not make undue demands on you, we would suggest that you convey to them, while they are still living in your house, that you do not have unlimited financial resources. How do you do this? First, by modeling financial restraint and denying yourself some of the things you want. And second, by not giving them everything they want.

No matter how high a standard of living you maintain, there should always be things that you refuse yourself and your children. Otherwise, you create ever-greater levels of need — and the more people need, the more difficult it is for them to manage in times of financial strain.

Children who get everything they want from their parents develop a sense of entitlement — "*ess kumt mir*" — that does not serve them well when they encounter life's inevitable disappointments. Setting boundaries for children and telling them "no" (when warranted) teaches them discipline and self-restraint, two attributes that are indispensable for a happy and successful life. As a leading *mechanech* put it, "Parents have to learn to give the gift of 'no.'"

When a parent says "no" at the appropriate times, in the context of a warm, loving relationship, he plants in his child the seeds of financial independence. A child brought up in this way will limit the demands he makes on his parents and will stop looking to his parents to provide for him as he gets older and becomes able to provide for himself. He is also far more likely to appreciate what his parents give him.

Every situation is different, of course, and what works for one child might not work for another. Parents therefore have to exercise judgment when deciding how best to encourage their children to value financial independence and work toward that goal. What's important is that financial independence be fostered — in your family and in every family.

**For more on children and money,
see also:**

"A Goal for All Families" Chapter 9

12

Integrity
at All Costs

"If a person wishes to
become wealthy, he
should be honest in his
financial dealings."

(Niddah 70b)

In this chapter:

❯ A Message for the Yamim Nora'im | 329

❯ Glatt Kosher Money | 333

❯ Keeping the Shul Afloat | 338

A Message for the Yamim Nora'im ❯

Soon we will be saying *Tefillas Ne'ilah* — the climax of *Yom Kippur*, and, in many ways, the pinnacle of the *Yamim Nora'im*.

At the very end of the *Ne'ilah Shemoneh Esrei*, after an abbreviated *Vidui*, we recite the moving *tefillah* of "*Atah nosein yad laposhim*," in which we describe how Hashem's Hand is outstretched to accept those who do *teshuvah*.

Then the *tefillah* goes on to give the reason why Hashem wants us to do *teshuvah*: *Lemaan nechdal mei'oshek yadeinu* — so that we can avoid *oshek*.

Oshek (literally, oppression) means refusal to pay someone to whom you owe money, whether it is someone who has loaned you money or someone who has provided you with merchandise or services.

Teshuvah is generally viewed as a means of drawing closer to Hashem by cleansing ourselves of the sins that distance us from Him. But in *Ne'ilah*, we don't say that the reason Hashem wants us to do teshuvah is because He wants us to be close to Him. Instead, we say that Hashem taught us to do *teshuvah* "so that we can avoid *oshek*."

Why is this cited as the reason why Hashem wants us to do *teshuvah*?

Apparently, putting an end to *oshek* is the ultimate example of what *teshuvah* is supposed to achieve.

Ne'ilah follows closely on the heels of *Maftir Yonah*, which is the story of Nineveh's *teshuvah*. In certain respects, the *teshuvah* of

Nineveh was the ideal form of *teshuvah* — the people of Nineveh did not merely fast and cry out to Hashem; they returned that which did not belong to them — reversing the *oshek* they had committed.

As *Chazal* tell us, the people of Nineveh went so far as to demolish an entire castle just to return a stolen beam to its owner (*Taanis* 16a). It was this commitment to action — not their sackcloth and tears — that Hashem noted.

We spend much time during the *Yamim Nora'im* reciting supplications for mercy and forgiveness, including *Selichos*, *Vidui* and *Avinu Malkeinu*. But for *teshuvah* to be effective, these supplications must be accompanied by action. And this action is not only in the realm of *bein adam laMakom*.

As a community, we rally at various times to strengthen our *tznius*, our *shemiras halashon* and our Shabbos observance. But what about *oshek*?

Mesila representatives visited Harav Ahron Leib Steinman, *shlita*, to introduce Mesila's work to him and receive his blessing. After hearing about Mesila's efforts to encourage people to budget correctly, Rav Steinman answered, "The idea of teaching people to live with a budget is very important, because a person who lives without a budget [eventually] comes to *gezel*. ...

"How is it possible for a person to live without a budget? A person has to make a budget to know how much he earns and to make sure that he spends accordingly. If a person borrows without knowing how he will repay, but thinks that when the time to repay arrives, he will borrow from a different source to repay the first loan, that is *gezel*. ..."

Rav Steinman went on to quote *Chazal's* principle that one ill-gotten *prutah* wipes out all of a person's money. He emphasized that *gezel* is a primary cause of financial difficulties — not only for the person who actually transgressed the prohibition of gezel, but for anyone who accepts money from that person, as well.

If gezel and oshek are the cause of financial woes, then it must be that honesty and integrity in financial matters are the keys to enjoying the brachah and shefa Hashem wants to give us.

We Yidden are not known to be burglars. But gezel and oshek come in many forms, some of them very subtle:

> Oshek includes refusal to pay even very small sums of money — the price of a telephone call, for instance. ("The chutzpah of that store to charge for a local phone call. I'm not paying!")

> It includes refusal to pay rent, return a deposit or pay back a loan. ("My landlord refused to put in new windows, so I'll just put them in myself and take the price off the rent.")

> And it includes refusal to pay a worker's wages. ("My sheitel macher did a lousy job, so I'm not paying her.")

Mesila does not pasken halachah but does promote financial responsibility. For a Jew, financial responsibility begins with adherence to the many mitzvos and halachos governing money and extends to a commitment to refraining from even the subtlest forms of gezel and oshek.

Beyond what the letter of the law demands, however, there is the spirit of what the Torah wants from us. By definition, a Torah lifestyle has to emphasize spiritual achievements over material acquisition. (This applies to all segments of society – not just kollel families, incidentally.)

On Rosh Hashanah, our income for the entire year will be determined. We need to decide how we plan to use that income and to ensure that our financial habits reflect our priorities and values.

The values that Mesila promotes — controlled consumption, living within a budget, financial independence, careful management of finances to avoid incurring non-payable debts — are all Torah values. Inculcating these values in our lives will help us to find not only the path to financial stability, but the path to *teshuvah sheleimah* as well.

Glatt Kosher
Money ❯

I was under the impression that I am entitled to a certain tax benefit, but my accountant, who is a frum, ehrliche person, recently informed me of a residency requirement that I do not meet, which technically disqualifies me from the benefit.

This residency requirement is an obscure clause in the fine print of the law. The clause is so obscure that I know many honest, upstanding individuals who receive the benefit, even though they do not meet the requirement. When I asked them about it they said they had never even heard of the requirement and their accountants had never mentioned it to them. When I asked other accountants, they said there is no reason why I should not apply for the benefit, since this clause is vague and rarely enforced.

In my case, there is no way I could be caught in violation of the residency requirement, since I could easily show (through utility bills, bank statements, pay stubs and the like) that I meet it. Even if I am thoroughly audited, there is no chance of me being caught or of a chillul Hashem happening as a result of my receiving the benefit.

The amount of money in question is considerable, and my financial situation is not such that I can easily pass up this money. When I asked my Rav whether I should accept the

> benefit, he told me that his Rebbe, who was an adam gadol, refused to pasken questions of this nature, and he takes the same approach.
>
> So now I am in a quandary. On the one hand, I don't want to do anything that is not 100 percent honest, and my accountant feels that my taking the benefit would be unethical. On the other hand, I don't want to be a fool and pass up money that I very badly need, especially since everyone else is taking this money.
>
> If my Rav had told me not to take the money, I would have listened without thinking twice. But he did not tell me that. What do you advise?

"I have rarely seen a *passul esrog*," a well-known Rav once commented, "and I have rarely seen kosher money. But somehow, people always come to ask if their *esrogim* are kosher, and hardly anyone comes to ask if his money is kosher."

We are impressed, therefore, that your first step was to ask a Rav this question. If your Rav didn't want to tell you what to do in your specific situation, then we certainly can't. But we'll try to help you by analyzing his answer and offering some general guidelines for situations like yours.

When a Rav says he does not want to answer a question of this nature, it means that the action in question is not absolutely forbidden, but it may lack an element of *yashrus*, integrity. It may also mean that the Rav is not sufficiently versed in the legalities of the issue to render a *psak*.

In the absence of halachic guidance, let's explore your two options from a practical, non-halachic standpoint.

The first option is to accept the benefit. You now have a windfall. You can do many wonderful things with this money — support Torah learning, give *tzedakah*, buy your wife some new jewelry for Yom Tov, take extra cleaning help before Pesach, fix your leaky boiler, perhaps even spend more time learning yourself.

You can sleep comfortably, because there is no way you will get in trouble with the government. (This, by the way, is what everyone thinks — until they get caught.)

But — and this is a big but — if you feel deep down that you really were not entitled to the money, your conscience might bother you. Despite all the good things you have done with the money, you could well be haunted by the knowledge that it is a bit tainted. And the feeling of having money that is not *glatt kosher* is not a good feeling. Even if the discomfort passes, as it generally does, it does not leave you with the feeling that you are an impeccably honest person. You can't fool yourself.

Having taken the benefit once, you will likely take it again in future years. It will probably not take long before you, like "everyone else," do not think twice about taking this benefit. Eventually, you will tell yourself that it's not questionable at all.

How do we know this? From a *kal vachomer*. "Once a person sins and repeats the sin, it becomes permitted to him," the Talmud teaches (*Yoma* 86b). Eventually, it is said, the person comes to view the sin as a *mitzvah*. If that is true even of an actual sin, it is certainly true of something that cannot definitely be called a sin.

Accepting the benefit therefore has two possible downsides: one, that you might suffer pangs of conscience, and two, that you will probably get used to the idea of taking money to which you may not be entitled. Before going this route, you have to be convinced that you are entitled to the benefit, and make sure you feel comfortable accepting it — not just this year, but in future years as well.

Now let's explore your second option: not taking the benefit. Without the money, you will probably have to struggle significantly. You will not be able to give as much *tzedakah* as you would like or make the type of Yom Tov you would like. You might even have to give up some of your own learning time to replace the money you passed up.

"Did I do something wrong by not taking that money?" you may wonder. "I could have served Hashem so wonderfully with it."

But then you'll tell yourself that you gave up the money because of *yashrus*. The seal of Hashem is *emes*, and Hashem will not have any complaints against you for doing what you felt was the more honest thing to do.

Your livelihood for the year was determined on Rosh Hashanah. During the rest of the year, you are required to engage in *hishtadlus*, effort, as a conduit for that livelihood to reach you. If something is of questionable integrity, it is highly doubtful that it is the type of *hishtadlus* that is required of you.

If the money was meant for you, Hashem will find another way to get it to you. And if the money wasn't meant for you and you do get it, Hashem will find a way to make you lose it. The bottom line is, nobody ever benefited in the long run from compromising on integrity.

If you pass up the benefit because you are committed to *yashrus*, you may lose money, but you will certainly gain in self-respect. And being able to look yourself in the eye and say, "I am honest," is a priceless asset.

Even if "everyone else" does something that lacks integrity, it does not give you license to follow suit. You are living your own life, not anyone else's, and when you come up to Heaven after 120 you will have to account only for your actions, not theirs. Besides, it is possible that their accepting the benefit does not represent a lack of integrity. Perhaps their circumstances are different from yours; perhaps they received different *piskei halachah* from their Rabbanim.

It is also possible that accepting the benefit is not at all unethical and does not represent a lack of *yashrus*. If that is the case, then you should not pass up money to which you are entitled, despite your accountant's misgivings.

In order to determine conclusively whether you are entitled to the benefit, we recommend that you consult with an accountant who has experience with these issues and can advise as to what the law is in your situation. If after consulting with another accountant you are still unsure what is the right thing to do, you should consider posing your question to a different Rav who will be willing to *pasken* for you.

Keeping the Shul Afloat >

I am the gabbai of a shul. Part of my job entails selling aliyos in the shul every Yom Tov.

With Pesach approaching, I would like to bring up the issue of people buying aliyos and not paying for them. Unfortunately, this happens unbelievably often. I just can't understand how a person can have the nerve to bid on an aliyah when he still owes money for his last half-dozen aliyos.

I hesitate to ask people to pay up, since I feel uncomfortable pressuring people for money. Besides, it is hard for me to keep track of all the aliyos that are sold over Yom Tov. I do not always remember who bought which aliyah and for how much.

Since I am the one who pays the shul's bills, I am the one who suffers when the money does not come in. But since I do not get paid to act as gabbai, why should I have to hound people to pay the money they owe the shul?

I would like to hear your suggestions for dealing with this problem.

As the *gabbai* of a shul, you fill a voluntary, and usually thankless, position. Not only do the efforts of a *gabbai* go largely unacknowledged, but a *gabbai* also has the unenviable duty of pursuing people to fulfill their financial commitments to the shul.

People are obligated to pay for their *aliyos* in a timely fashion, and it would be nice if they would remember to pay without having to be prodded. But your job is not to fume over the way people disregard their obligations to the shul.

Your job, as *gabbai*, is to fulfill your obligations to the shul. The fact that you are not compensated for your efforts does not absolve you of these responsibilities. If collecting the money owed to the shul is too time-consuming or stressful for you, you should consider appointing a treasurer to take over that aspect of your duties.

A shul, like any other not-for-profit operation, must be run like a business to survive financially. To succeed, a business needs to have a record-keeping system and a procedure for dealing with clients who don't pay up.

As *gabbai*, you are the manager of the business known as your shul. You therefore need to keep accurate records of all the shul's transactions, including the purchase of *aliyos*. You also need to institute a collections system to ensure that people pay the shul the money they owe.

There are several halachically acceptable methods of recording the sale of *aliyos* on Yom Tov; ask the Rav of your shul which method he prefers. Having accurate records will empower you to be more confident and less apologetic when approaching members of your shul for payment.

A collections procedure for the *aliyos* sold on Yom Tov could include a verbal reminder within a week of Yom Tov, then a written invoice at the end of the month. If you are uncomfortable asking people for money face-to-face, you can mail them written pledge reminders instead.

Having an organized collections system in place will help you to differentiate between two types of delinquent *aliyah* buyers. The first and more prevalent type are the people who sincerely intend to pay for their *aliyos* but are simply forgetful. For these people, one or two reminders are usually enough to get them to fulfill their pledges.

The second type of delinquent *aliyah* buyers are the chronic non-payers, the people who get caught up in the thrill of bidding on *aliyos* but do not make the mental connection between buying *aliyos* and paying for them. No matter how many reminders you give these people, they will always have an excuse for not paying.

Businesses do not supply goods and services to clients who do not pay; neither should shuls. When chronic non-payers "buy" *aliyos*, they are not only causing the shul a financial loss, they are also preventing the *ehrliche* members of the shul from buying *aliyos*. They should therefore be barred from tendering bids for *aliyos* and possibly from other shul privileges as well.

The decision to bar someone from bidding on *aliyos* should be based on clear, consistent criteria — amount of money owed, length of time owed, number of unpaid pledges and so forth. Consult with your Rav to determine these criteria and to decide how to notify chronic non-payers of their exclusion from the future sale of *aliyos*.

It is not pleasant to chase people for money, and it is even less pleasant to deny people the right to bid on *aliyos*. But you are actually doing people a great service by ensuring that they do not default on their commitments to the shul. When a person buys an *aliyah*, he is in effect making a *neder*. Failure to fulfill one's *nedarim* results in grievous consequences — for instance, death of one's wife and children, *chas veshalom*, as discussed in *Shabbos* 32a.

Although your job as *gabbai* might not seem very rewarding, it serves as your entry ticket to the elite class of *oskim b'tzorchei tzibbur*, those who are busy with the needs of the community. And for people in such a category, the reward is enviable indeed.

For more on financial integrity,
see also:

"Doing Business on the Books" Chapter 8

Appendix I:

Mesila's Guide to Financial Stability

"Do not make us need
the gifts of human hands
nor of their loans,
but only of Your Hand."

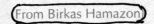
From Birkas Hamazon

In this chapter:

❯ Introduction | 345

❯ Part I: Attitudes and Attributes | 347

❯ Part II: Action | 351

Introduction ›

Mesila's "Guide to Financial Stability" briefly outlines twelve key points – including attitudes, attributes and actions – necessary for achieving financial stability. There is much more to be said about all twelve of the points, so this guide should be viewed only as a basic introduction to these ideas.

The twelve points in this guide are closely interrelated.

Throughout the guide, words and ideas that are linked to a different point appear in boldface, to reinforce the message that the twelve points form a harmonious unit only when all twelve are in place.

What Is Financial Stability?

Financial stability is the ability to handle your financial obligations in a way that contributes positively to other areas of your life. If you are financially stable, then your finances should enhance – not detract from – your health, your relationships, your quality of life, your peace of mind and your service of Hashem.

Financial instability is what happens when finances become a source of anxiety, difficulty, or strife.

Financial stability is not a function of how much money you have. There are millionaires who suffer from terrible financial instability, and there are low-income families who are models of financial stability.

The Two Elements of Financial Stability

Financial stability has two elements: Divine assistance (*siyatta dish-maya*) and effort (*hishtadlus*). Hashem decides how much money you will have and what financial challenges you will face. *You* decide how you will use your money and how you will cope with the challenges you are given.

The way to merit Divine assistance is by praying for it. "What shall a person do in order to become wealthy? ... He should ask for mercy from the One to whom wealth belongs" (*Niddah* 70b). *Tefillah* is necessary for success in every aspect of a Jew's life, and financial management is no exception. Consequently, the twelve points outlined in this guide all need to be accompanied by *tefillah*.

The second element of financial stability – effort – is Mesila's primary focus. In this guide, we will outline the basic attitudes, attributes and actions that are the building blocks of financial stability.

Part I:
Attitudes and Attributes

1. Bitachon: Trust in G-d, the Ultimate Provider

Unlike the other aspects of achieving financial stability, which are related to effort (*hishtadlus*), having *bitachon* actually helps improve your financial situation and is the vehicle for blessing. In his classic ethical work, *Chovos Halevovos*, Rabbeinu Bachye writes that a person who trusts in Hashem will be provided for at all times, as the verse states, "Cast upon Hashem your burden and He will sustain you" (*Tehillim* 55:23).

Someone who has *bitachon* understands that Hashem alone determines what the outcome of his efforts will be, but, nevertheless, he carries out his responsibilities as best as he can because that is what he is obligated to do.

If you have *bitachon*, you also have tranquility and peace of mind. The peace of mind that results from *bitachon* gives you the ability to make wise financial decisions and successfully cope with financial challenges.

The subject of *bitachon* is one that requires lifelong study and effort, for it is not easily mastered. *Bitachon* cannot be pure lip service, nor can it be used as a justification for passivity or irresponsible behavior.

2. The Value of Financial Independence

Every individual is allotted a certain amount of income by G-d, and should aspire to receive that income directly from G-d, and not indirectly via other people. "Do not make us need the gifts of human hands nor of their loans, but only of Your Hand," we say in *Birkas Hamazon*.

Every person has a natural desire to be financially independent, as the Talmud says, "A person desires one measure of that which is his more than nine measures of that which belongs to his fellow" (*Bava Metzia* 38a). This desire should propel you to look for respectable ways of earning a living and motivate you not to accept charity or **loans**.

"In the way that a person wishes to go, he is led," the Talmud teaches (*Makkos* 10b). The first step in becoming financially independent, therefore, is *wanting* to be financially independent.

3. Initiative & Control

To achieve financial stability, you need to believe that you have the power to take control of your finances. You can take the initiative to **increase your income**, and you can create and follow a **budget** that will allow you to live within your means and meet your financial goals.

You are not always in control of your circumstances, but you *are* in control of the way you react to your circumstances. When faced with a challenging situation, you can choose to wallow in self-pity, blame other people, and bemoan your terrible fate. Or you can choose to find solutions and opportunities, think creatively, and take steps to improve your situation, without sinking into despair or paralysis.

Focus on your abilities and gifts, not on your limitations and deficiencies. Set ambitious goals for yourself, and believe that nothing can stop you from reaching those goals. Teach yourself to be proactive, rather than passive, and recognize the potential that Hashem has endowed you with – including the potential to support yourself and your family independently.

4. *Self-Discipline and Persistence*

Self-discipline means doing what you know you need to do, despite whatever difficulty and discomfort might be involved. Once you have come to a decision about what needs to be done, self-discipline will allow you to follow through with your decision. And a healthy measure of persistence will help you to stick to your decisions and not become distracted from your goals. The other points in this guide will help you to reach correct financial decisions, and discipline and persistence will bring those decisions to fruition.

Self-discipline and persistence are necessary in order to reach any worthwhile goals, and financial stability is no exception. To keep your finances – and your life – in order, you and the members of your family need to be able to tell yourselves "no" and tolerate a certain amount of inconvenience in order to stay within your budgetary limits. Having self-discipline will allow you to withstand consumer enticements, avoid overspending, and steer clear of **loans** and other types of "easy money."

5. *Contentment*

"Who is wealthy? He who is content with his lot" (*Avos* 4:1).

Many people mistakenly think that in order to be wealthy, you need to have a lot – a lot of money, a lot of possessions, a lot of property. But the Torah teaches us that if you are content with *your* lot, you are wealthy. Having more just makes you want even more, as the *Midrash* says, "One who has a hundred, wants two hundred" (*Koheles Rabbah* 3:10). A home where the atmosphere is one of contentment is a rich, happy and healthy home.

Discontent is the archenemy of financial stability, for it leads people to want and need more and more and more. But no amount of material acquisition can drive away the feeling of discontent and bring a person lasting happiness. That is because the root of discontent is in the soul, which thirsts for spiritual fulfillment (*Koheles Rabbah* 6:6).

"The soul cannot be filled," King Solomon tells us (*Koheles* 6:7), for it does not accept the currency of the physical world. Money and earthly pleasures are like saltwater to the parched soul; instead of quenching the soul's discontent, they intensify its yearning for the true pleasure of closeness to Hashem.

The understanding that it is not money or possessions that bring happiness can go a long way in helping you exercise financial restraint and **self-discipline**. If you know material acquisitions are but cheap substitutes for true fulfillment, you will find it much easier to stay within your **budget** and keep your finances under **control**.

6. *Integrity*

For a Jew, integrity involves adhering to the many *mitzvos* and *halachos* governing money and abiding by the law of the land. Integrity also requires us to go beyond the letter of the law and do what is right, even when we are not absolutely obligated to do so.

Honesty and integrity bring blessing in all areas, including finances. The Talmud says that if a person wishes to become wealthy, he should be honest in his financial dealings (*Niddah* 70b). Conversely, one who is dishonest in his financial dealings brings misfortune not only upon himself but upon others who receive his money (*Sefer Chassidim* 1075-1076).

Obviously, then, financial stability can only be achieved if your financial dealings are completely free of any trace of theft, fraud or deception. But there is another reason why integrity is necessary for achieving financial stability. If you are careful with other people's money, you will be careful with your own money, as well. When you earn your money honestly, that money is meaningful to you, and you are less likely to fritter it away irresponsibly.

Part II:
Action ❯

7. The Family Budget

a. Awareness

The first and most important step in budgeting is reaching an aware-ness of exactly what is happening with your finances: how much you are earning, how much you spend, what you are spending on, and what your assets and liabilities are. Mesila's experience has shown that the most people are surprised to discover what these numbers are – and just knowing these numbers prompts people to implement changes.

The natural tendency is to avoid confronting financial realities and problems, but burying your head in the sand can only make things worse. If you and your spouse are aware of exactly what your financial situation is, you will be motivated to take **initiative** and do whatever you can to improve it. Awareness on the part of both husband and wife is therefore a large part of the solution to most financial problems.

b. Planning Your Budget

Once you are **aware** of your financial situation, you can develop a budget that reflects your income and your needs. The budget cannot be overly restrictive – if it is, you will not be able to stick to it – and it has to take into account ongoing expenses, one-time future expenses and unforeseen expenses.

Consistently following a realistic, well-planned budget is the foundation of financial stability. Having a budget spurs you to look for ways to **increase your income**, obligates you to limit your spending, and prevents you from purchasing on impulse.

A budget is basically a projection of your income and expenses over the next few years. The first step in developing a budget is tracking your earnings and expenses over a period of time and arriving at an accurate estimate of your yearly income and expenditures. Your next step is to ensure that your budget is balanced – i.e., that your expenditures do not exceed your income. If your budget is not balanced, then you need to find ways to increase your income and/or reduce your expenditures. Next, you need to consider your short- and long-term savings goals. Once you have an accurate picture of your income, your expenditures and your future needs, you can develop a budget that will decide how your money is going to be used.

Your budget is a powerful tool. It will help you prepare for times of financial challenge, it will allow you to withstand financial pressures, and it will give you the security of knowing that your finances are being handled responsibly.

8. Maintaining Order: The Divide-and-Conquer Approach

To maintain control over the family budget, you need to separate living expenses from debt and personal finances from business finances.

Loans cannot be considered income, nor can their repayment be considered a living expense. Debts and living expenses have to be viewed as two distinct financial obligations and managed as two separate accounts. Your salary is meant to cover your living expenses, while debts should be repaid from a surplus carved out of your income.

Similarly, business revenues are not expendable family income. The business and the family are two separate financial entities and must be managed as such. A business has to be treated as a separate account, from which money can be withdrawn only under specific conditions and at predetermined times.

When business and family finances get mixed together, it becomes impossible to handle either of them efficiently. Separating business finances from family finances makes it possible to reach an **awareness** of what is happening in both, make informed decisions, and create accurate **budgets** for the business and the family.

Only when there is a clear demarcation between family finances, business finances and debts can you gain **control** over your financial situation.

9. Income: Finding Ways to Make it Grow

Finding ways to continually increase your income is one of the best things you can do to achieve and maintain financial stability. The more income you have, the more breathing room your **budget** will have and the easier it will be for you to meet your financial obligations.

Your income does not have to be static. You have the ability to increase your income — by taking on additional hours of work, by turning a hobby into a source of income, by learning new skills, and by becoming more professional in your work. If your chosen occupation is Torah study, you can join paying *kollelim* or learn with private students for pay. No matter what your situation, there is always something you can do to increase your income.

Be confident in your abilities and in your earning power. Look for work that you enjoy, since you are more likely to succeed at something you enjoy. When looking for work, be **persistent** and do not allow yourself to become discouraged by rejection. Even if you are unemployed for a period — by choice or by chance — try to maintain a constant presence in the workforce, because it is easier to find work when you are already working. Once you have found work, make yourself increasingly valuable as an employee, and be accommodating and flexible.

It is important to be **content** with your chosen occupation and to recognize the value of your work. Whatever your occupation, you should take pride in it, do it well, and look for ways to make it more financially rewarding.

10. Managing Your Expenditures

To spend wisely, you need to differentiate between needs and wants. No one can have everything they *want* – "A person does not leave this world with half of his desires in his hand" (*Koheles Rabbah* 3:1) – but you must find ways to acquire the things you really need.

The trouble is that wants often masquerade as needs. Taking a good, hard look at your motivations for spending money can help you to distinguish between real needs and needs that have been created by social demands, pressure from family members, or your own emotional state. (Think of all the money people spend to lift their spirits, squelch feelings of inadequacy, or fill an emotional void such as the desire for love or attention.)

It is important to remember that not every need requires you to spend money. Many emotional needs can be fulfilled without spending money, and you can also look for creative ways to meet your physical needs while keeping your expenditures to a minimum. But be realistic about what your needs are, and avoid drastic spending cuts – they rarely last.

Distinguishing between wants and needs will help you to establish spending priorities and ensure that you spend your money on the things that are most important and beneficial to you.

11. Loans: How and When?

Loans are a powerful, but dangerous tool. The decision to take a loan is essentially a decision that your need for money *now* justifies the reduction in future income that will result from having to pay back the loan.

When you borrow money, you are imposing a form of bondage on yourself: "A debtor is a servant to the creditor" (*Mishlei* 22:7). A loan taken unnecessarily is something that "destroys the soul's dignity, and causes shame to yourself and to others" (*Igros Chazon Ish* 2:12).

Before taking a loan, you have to carefully consider what type of loan to take, how much to borrow, and when to take the loan. It is forbidden to borrow if you do not know that you will be able to repay (Rabbeinu Yonah, *Avos* 2:9). When determining how much you can afford to repay in the future, you have to take into account how much of your income you can assign to debt repayment and how much must be left to cover your living expenses.

Many methods of payment are basically hidden loans: credit cards, post-dated checks, installment plans, even your account at the grocery. These convenient methods of payment, as well as the availability of interest-free loans from *gemachim*, can cause you to borrow money without even realizing.

If you wish to achieve financial stability, you need to exercise extreme caution with regard to loans. Do not borrow a penny more than you need, never borrow money to invest in risky investments, and be extremely careful when signing as a guarantor on other people's loans.

12. Savings

Good financial management always includes some form of savings and planning for times of financial challenge in the future. Saving and planning for the future are no contradiction to **bitachon**, and are actually described as a mitzvah (*Responsa Shevet Halevi* 4:1)

Saving is a habit that requires **self-discipline** and **persistence**, but the effort is well worth it. No matter how tight your budget, you should always put aside some money for savings. Instead of using your money for non-essential purchases, put it away in a safe place and save it for the future. Every penny adds up, and if you consistently put aside money, you will eventually succeed in accumulating a respectable amount of savings. Beware, however, of risky or questionable investments that can destroy all of your hard-earned savings.

There are two types of savings – short-term and long-term – and every person needs some of both. Short-term savings are intended to tide you over in the event of temporary lack of income. They are also intended to help you cover large expenses, foreseeable (such as an upcoming bar mitzvah) and unforeseeable (such as an expensive home repair). Long-term savings is the money you will need for times of considerable financial strain, such as marrying off children and old age.

Appendix II:

Budgeting Worksheets

In this chapter:

❯ Transactions Record | 359

❯ Monthly Budget | 360

❯ Annual Budget | 362

❯ Balance Sheet | 364

❯ Cash Flow Plan | 365

Transactions Record

Page #_____ Balance forwarded from previous page _____

No.	Date	Details	Amount		Necessity of Expenditure		
			Income	Expenditure	Vital	Beneficial	Luxury
1							
2							
3							
4							
5							
6							
7							
8							
9							
10							
11							
12							
13							
14							
15							
16							
17							
18							
19							
20							
21							
22							
23							
24							
25							
26							
27							
28							
29							
30							

Total Income | Total Expenditure | New Balance

Total expenditure (by degree of necessity):

Vital ❯ [   ] Beneficial ❯ [   ] Luxury ❯ [   ]

Monthly Budget
(Current/Projected)

A. Monthly Income

Source: Salary/Wages (net)	Amount	Source: Interest/Dividends	Amount	Other Sources	Amount	Other Sources	Amount
Husband		Investment type		Rent			
				Child benefits			
				Unemployment benefits			
Wife				Social Security / Social Insurance			
				Pension/Retirement Fund			

Total Monthly Income

» $

B. Monthly Expenses*

Expense Category	Amount	% of Total Expenditure
1: Housing		
2: Food & Household Items		
3: Bills & Utilities		
4: Education & Children		
5: Transportation		
6: Health & Personal Care		
7: Leisure		
8: Miscellaneous		

Space for Calculations

* See itemized list of expenses on next page.

Total Monthly Expenses

» $

C. Monthly Balance

Total Monthly Income (end of section A)		Total Monthly Expenses (end of section B)			circle	Monthly Balance
$	−	$	=		+ −	» $

Itemized List of Expenses for Section B of Monthly Budget

Item 1: Housing	
Rent	
Mortgage	
Property tax	
Building dues	
Cleaning help	
Outdoor maintenance	
Other	
Total:	

Item 2: Food & Household Items	
Meat & fish	
Fruits & vegetables	
Bread & baked goods	
Packaged foods	
Beverages	
Snack foods	
Restaurant & takeout	
Health food	
Household items	
Paper goods	
Cleaning supplies	
Other	
Total:	

Item 3: Bills & Utilities	
Social Security / Social Insurance	
Telephone	
Cell phone	
Electricity	
Gas / Heating oil	
Water	

Life insurance	
Internet/Cable	
Appliance service contracts	
Bank charges	
Credit card charges	
Interest charges	
Other	
Total:	

Item 4: Education & Children	
School tuition / playgroup	
Daycare	
School transportation	
Babysitting	
Private lessons	
Tutoring	
Baby items	
Pocket money	
Support for single children	
Support for married children	
Other	
Total:	

Item 5: Transportation	
Auto lease	
Gasoline	
Tolls	
Buses	
Taxis	
Carpool	
Other	
Total:	

Item 6: Health & Personal Care	
Health insurance	
Medicines	
Vitamins	
Fitness	
Therapies	
Alternative medicine	
Contact lenses & solutions	
Toiletries & cosmetics	
Health & beauty treatments	
Haircuts	
Other	
Total:	

Item 7: Leisure	
Newspapers & magazines	
Gifts	
Flowers	
Stationery & crafts	
Lottery & raffle tickets	
Entertainment	
Other	
Total:	

Item 8: Miscellaneous	
Tzedakah	
Support for parents	
Savings plan	
Dry cleaning	
Pet expenses	
Other	
Total:	

Annual Budget
(Current/Projected)

D. Periodic Income

Periodic Income	Amount	Comments
Year-end bonus		
Tax refund		
Government benefits		
Charitable assistance		
Gifts		

Reduction of Income	Amount	Comments
Nissan		
Summer		
Tishrei		

Periodic Income		Reduction of Income		Total Periodic Income
$	−	$	=	$

E. Periodic Expenses*

Expense Category	Amount	% of Total Expenditure
1: Housing		
2: Clothing		
3: Education & Children		
4: Transportation		
5: Health & Personal Care		
6: *Yomim Tovim*		
7: Leisure		
8: Miscellaneous		

Space for Calculations

* See itemized list of expenses on next page. Record only those expenses that are not included in your monthly budget.

Total Periodic Expenses
$

F. Periodic Balance

Total Periodic Income (end of section D)		Total Periodic Expenses (end of section E)		circle	Periodic Balance
$	−	$	=	+ −	$

G. Annual Balance

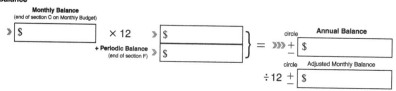

Monthly Balance (end of section C on Monthly Budget)			
$	× 12	$	
	+ Periodic Balance (end of section F)	$	

circle   **Annual Balance**
+ − $

circle   Adjusted Monthly Balance
÷12   + − $

Itemized List of Expenses for Section E of Annual Budget

Item 1: Housing	
Homeowner's insurance	
Heating oil/gas	
Home repairs	
Appliance purchases	
Appliance repairs	
Furniture	
Lighting	
Kitchen supplies	
Pest control	
Other	
Total:	

Item 2: Clothing	
Clothing – parents	
Clothing – children	
Shoes – parents	
Shoes – children	
Jewelry & accessories	
Outerwear	
Head coverings	
Shaitel care	
Other	
Total:	

Item 3: Education & Children	
Enrichment for children	
Courses & shiurim	
School activities & other costs	
School supplies	
Summer camp	
Day camp	
Other	
Total:	

Item 4: Transportation	
Car insurance	
Car inspection & licensing	
Car repair & maintenance	

Emissions testing	
Parking & tickets	
Shipping	
Postage	
Other	
Total:	

Item 5: Health & Personal Care	
Medical expenses	
Medical equipment	
Dental & orthodontic	
Glasses	
Contact lenses	
Other	
Total:	

Item 6: *Yamim Tovim*	
Tishrei:	
Arba minim	
Succah	
Shul seats	
Yom Tov food	
Clothing & shoes	
Chol Hamoed outings	
Other	
Total - Tishrei:	
Purim:	
Mishloach Manot	
Matanot L'evyonim	
Costumes	
Gifts	
Other	
Total – Purim:	
Pesach:	
Matzah	
Yom Tov food – general	
Wine	
Fruits & vegetables	
Meat & fish	

Cleaning help & supplies	
Dishes & utensils	
Clothing & shoes	
Chol Hamoed outings	
Afikoman presents	
Other	
Total – Pesach:	
Shavuos	
Chanukah	
Tu b'Shevat	
Other	
Total - all *Yamim Tovim*:	

Item 7: Leisure	
Vacations	
Summer residence	
Recreation	
Electronics	
Sports & hobbies	
Toys & games	
Music	
Gifts	
Photography	
Simchas & parties	
Other	
Total:	

Item 8: Miscellaneous	
Tzedakah	
Shul dues	
Aliyos	
Seforim & books	
Computer equipment	
Personal article insurance	
Government documentation	
Other	
Total:	

Balance Sheet

A. Assets

	Asset Type	Amount		Asset Type	Amount
Bank Accounts	Checking accounts		**Property (market value)**	Home	
	Savings accounts			Summer residence	
	Certificates of deposit			Other property	
	Cash			Personal valuables	
Securities	Stocks/Shares			Retirement funds - IRA / 401(k) / RRSP (Canada) etc.	
	Bonds			Life insurance (cash surrender value)	
	Mutual funds			Loans owed to you	
	Hedge funds				

Total Assets ▶ $

B. Details of Loans Owed to You

	Borrower	City	State / Province	Phone	Amount owed	A/D*
1						
2						
3						

* A = agreed, D = disputed

C. Liabilities

Debts to Government, Utilities, and Service Providers

	Owed to:	Amount		Owed to:	Amount	Owed to:	Amount	Owed to:	Amount
Government	Social Security / Social Insurance		**Utilities**	Electricity		Bank overdraft		Medical expenses	
	Income tax			Telephone		Post-dated checks		Dental expenses	
	Property tax			Cell phone		Credit card balance		Grocery	
				Gas / Heating oil		Mortgage		Tuition	
				Water		Rent		Student loans	

Total Debts (services) ▶ $

Debts Owed to Banks, Loan Funds and Private Lenders (If space is insufficient, complete the list on a copy of this form.)

	Bank / Lender / Loan fund	City	Phone	Amount	Single payment: Date	Monthly payment: # of payments	Monthly payment: Each payment:	Remainder owed
1								
2								
3								
4								
5								

Total Debts (loans) ▶ $

D. Total Liabilities

Total Debts: Services + Loans		Total Loan Guarantees*		Total Liabilities
$	+	$	= ▶	$

* If you have signed on a guarantor on other people's loans, indicate the total of the guarantees.

E. Net Worth

Total Assets (end of section A)		Total Liabilities (end of section D)		circle	Net Worth
$	—	$	= ▶ ±		$

Cash Flow Plan

A. Projected Annual/Periodic Expenses by Month

In section E of the Annual Budget, you entered totals for each of the eight periodic expense categories listed. Now, calculate what portion of those periodic expense categories can be assigned to specific months and record the amounts below. The portion of the periodic expense categories that is unpredictable should be recorded under "Remainder."

For instance: Most purchases in the clothing category typically take place at the beginning of the winter and summer seasons, so you might assign 40% of your clothing budget to the month of September and 40% to the month of April, and then record the remaining 20% under "Remainder," since you don't know in which month you will incur the remaining clothing expenses.

Month	Projected Expense: Category 1	Projected Expense: Category 2	Projected Expense: Category 3	Projected Expense: Category 4	Projected Expense: Category 5	Projected Expense: Category 6	Projected Expense: Category 7	Projected Expense: Category 8	Total Projected Expenses: All categories
1									
2									
3									
4									
5									
6									
7									
8									
9									
10									
11									
12									
Total									
Remainder									

B. Cash Position by Month

In this table, enter monthly estimates for each of the positive and negative cash flow categories and calculate the monthly balance. If the monthly balance is negative, indicate how you plan to cover the deficit by recording the proposed adjustment source and amount.

Month	Positive cash flow				Negative cash flow							Monthly Balance	Adjustment	
	Projected Monthly Income	Projected Annual/ Periodic Income	Remainder	Other	Projected Monthly Expenses	Projected Annual/ Periodic Expenses (from Table A above)	Savings Plan	Debt Repay-ment	Remainder	Other			Source	Amount

About Mesila

Mesila is a nonprofit organization dedicated to empowering families and businesses to seek, achieve and maintain financial stability. With chapters across Israel, as well as branches in the United States, Canada and England, Mesila is guiding hundreds of families, businesses and students along the path to financial independence, through its counseling and preventative education programs.

Mesila is dedicated to:

- Raising public awareness of the importance of financial stability and independence.
- Promoting the development of attitudes and habits that lead to financial stability.
- Giving business owners the professional tools to manage their businesses correctly.
- Guiding people to create and implement sustainable, long-term solutions to the economic challenges they face.

Mesila Guiding Principles

1. We help people help themselves.
2. We believe in people's ability to change.
3. We do not give up, for we believe that where there is a will, there is a way.
4. We uphold uncompromising standards of integrity, transparency and accountability.
5. We strive for absolute professionalism and give preference to quality over quantity.
6. We help people regardless of affiliation or background.
7. We believe that every person can be helped, provided they are willing.
8. We do not attempt to influence people's ideological beliefs and value systems.
9. We prefer not to lend or give money to help people solve their financial problems.
10. We work to identify and correct all the factors that caused or contributed to financial difficulties.
11. We promote financial management principles and attitudes that are universally relevant, while avoiding specific tips and suggestions.
12. We are committed to continual learning, improvement and growth.